The Search for

Self-Definition in

Russian Literature

EDITED BY

The Search for

E W A M. T H O M P S O N

Self-Definition in

R I C E U N I V E R S I T Y P R E S S

Russian Literature

H O U S T O N , T E X A S

Library of Congress
Cataloging-in-Publication Data

The Search for self-definition in Russian
literature / edited by Ewa M.
Thompson. — 1st ed.
    p.   cm.
Selected papers from a conference
held at Rice University, Sept. 22–23,
1989.
    Includes index.
    ISBN 0-89263-306-9 : $21.95
    1. Nationalism and literature—
Congresses.   2. Russian literature—
History and criticism—Congresses.
3. Soviet literature—History and
criticism—Congresses.   I. Thompson,
Ewa M. (Ewa Majewska), 1937–   .
PG2987.N2S43   1991
891.709'358—dc20   90-53698
                                    CIP

Contents

Foreword

Nationalist ideology is undoubtedly one of the most controversial topics in the Soviet Union today. Indeed, President Mikhail Gorbachev's policy of *glasnost'* has opened a Pandora's box, releasing a flood of Russian nationalism with its unacceptable concomitants of anti-Semitism and xenophobia, and also—perhaps inadvertently—allowing the open expression of nationalism among the constituent states of the Soviet bloc, inside and outside the Union, in a process that has completely transformed Eastern Europe and now threatens the integrity of the Soviet Union itself.

It has, of course, always been a characteristic of Russian literature that the majority of writers should eschew art for art's sake and, indeed, play an active part in the intellectual and ideological development of their country; in our century one has only to think of Solzhenitsyn's apt definition of a writer as a "second government." Thus, literature is a natural medium for the expression of nationalist ideology, and the theme of the roundtable conference from which the present collection of papers arose is one of central importance for our understanding of both Russia and its literature. The contributions that follow vary widely in both theme and approach, although a number of names and topics recur with great frequency; together the papers offer a valuable composite view of nationalist ideology in Russian literature over a period of two centuries.

At the beginning of the modern period Pushkin emerges from Marcus Wheeler's analysis as hardly an ideologist of post-Petrine Russia, but rather as an advocate of balance between patriotism and Europeanism, between monarch and popular will, between public opinion and the influence of such dominant personalities as Napoleon and Byron. His dream (not unlike that of the Soviet president, and equally remote) was of a *pravovoe gosudarstvo*, and his outbursts against, for example, Poland do not reflect a central part of his personality or thinking. The case of Dostoevsky, whose patriotism rapidly declined into nationalism, is more extreme; Louis Allain argues against reading the novels alone but recommends including Dostoevsky's journalistic works, several of which reveal decidedly unpleasant aspects of Russian nationalism. However, nothing that Pushkin or Dostoevsky wrote can begin to compare to the vilification of Poland by Soviet writers in connection with the invasion of Poland on September 17, 1939. In her discussion of this deplorable episode Ewa Thompson successfully reverses conventional wisdom, showing that the heyday of Russian nationalism was during the Soviet-Nazi Pact, whereas later in the war toleration and even encouragement of other nationalities were in evidence.

Stalin, who never lost his foreign accent and could on occasion dismay his entourage by speaking Georgian to Beria and his bodyguards, was also adept at exploiting Russian chauvinism, bigotry, and anti-Semitism for his own purposes. However, his demands for nationalistic populism in literature, as in the other arts, were, according to Yuri Glazov's richly anecdotal chapter, sincere in themselves, since he had poor taste. It is hard to consider the problem of anti-Semitism and Russian literature without the name of Vasilii Grossman immediately coming to mind. Few writers have undergone so great an evolution of views as he, and his conclusion that Stalinism and fascism were of equally low moral status is one of the severest indictments of the Soviet dictator ever made. John Garrard's comprehensive chapter demonstrates Grossman's deeply humanitarian nature and his belief above all in the significance of free individuals during a period when freedom and democracy were no more than remote dreams for a Russia seeking scapegoats for the disasters and miseries of wartime Stalinism. Disturbingly, the anti-Semitic aspect of this search for scapegoats has been revived recently and now appears to flourish openly in the Soviet press and public life. Dmitry Shlapentokh's chapter further analyzes anti-Semitism and related aspects of Soviet intellectual discussions.

Sidney Monas's survey of the peasantry in nineteenth-century Russian literature stresses the third estate's central and continuing significance for Russian national consciousness. Certainly the so-called Soviet village writers seem to have been at the forefront of the contemporary nationalist movement; the names of Astaf'ev, Belov, and Rasputin appear in many chapters of this volume. In the words of Harry Walsh, "Russian nationalism, one might say, has changed from a cottage industry to big business." Rasputin's *Farewell to Matera (Proshchanie s Materoi)* and *The Fire (Pozhar)*, seen by many as the high-water mark of village prose, display many aspects of contemporary nationalism, not least among them *pamiat'*, or memory (a word that has acquired sinister overtones following the takeover of the initially honorable Pamiat' movement by anti-Semites and bullies). As Dar'ia says in *Farewell to Matera*, "Truth is in remembering. He who has no memory has no life." If memory, like religion (more specifically Orthodoxy), now seems prone to distortion and exploitation, the ecological concerns of Rasputin at least are beyond possible reproach. Herman Ermolaev's study of the nationalities in Russian literature also discusses Rasputin's latest works as well as Astaf'ev's unpleasant *A Sad Detective Story (Pechaln'nyi detektiv)* and *Fishing in Georgia (Lovlia peskarei v Gruzii)*, together with a number of weaker but unscrupulous and influential writers like Pikul' and Shevtsov. However, his main concern is with the years between 1917 and 1934, when "for the sake of their survival and retention of power, Soviet leaders created an artificial symbiosis of two mutually exclusive elements—the international Marxist ideology and popular Russian patriotism." The latter has certainly provided a Johnsonian refuge for scoundrels, as the present-day anti-Semitism, hysteria, and bloodshed make abundantly plain.

Aleksandr Zinov'ev stands apart from all other Russian writers inside or outside the Soviet Union, a situation he himself considers entirely natural. Libor Brom's discussion of his vision of Soviet ideology shows Zinov'ev's understanding of it to be better than that of most western commentators, and therefore too important to ignore, particularly if one shares the author's view of that ideology's great durability. However, unlike the scholarly chapters in the present book, Zinov'ev largely disregards the influence of Russian history and traditions on Soviet ideology, as he does the role of Russian and non-Russian nationalisms in weakening it.

Milojkovic-Djuric's chapter stands apart from the others in that it deals with the impact of national problems on musicology. She argues that the Soviet critique of Igor Stravinsky's "classical" period was largely a result of the perception by Soviet Russian musicologists that classical tendencies weakened the presence of "national" motifs in music.

Contrasting aspects of the quest for Russian national identity are compared by George Gibian through what he considers to be two representative works of contemporary literature: P'etsukh's "New Moscow Philosophy" ("Novaia moskovskaia filosofiia") and Belov's *The Year of the Great Break (God velikogo pereloma)*. In the first one P'etsukh proclaims Russia's great mission but satirizes reality: literature emerges as the highest Russian connection to life, to a positive goal. Belov's latest work, on the other hand, is an earnest, pathetic lament: a memorial to mass murder, mass destruction. In Gibian's view, the painful self-defining, self-lamenting, self-eulogizing process in the Soviet Union today is the direct result of the suppression of nationalism over a period of seventy years. His fear that Russia has become a self-pitying nation will be shared by many who are following the current fortunes and travails of that country. In the future Russian nationalism will continue to play an important role in political and social developments. Nor can there be any doubt that for an understanding of Russian nationalism a knowledge of Russian history and literature is essential. Ewa Thompson's volume will be of interest to all who ponder the national psychology of one of the world's major nations.

ARNOLD MCMILLIN
University of London

Editor's Preface

While there are disagreements about the meaning and direction of changes in Russian culture in the 1990s, one fact is virtually incontestable: the Russians are experiencing a reawakening of their national consciousness. Not that it has ever been asleep; throughout their history, Russians have drawn on it remarkably often in their search for social cohesiveness and political success. A major reason for the intense concern with national identity in present-day Soviet Russia has been described by Uri Ra'anan of Boston University: "As the *Staatsvolk* (the nationality that dominates the state) of the USSR, Russians in general tend to identify not only with the RSFSR, but with the USSR as a whole. In other words, Russians have not only a national but also an 'imperial' identity." *

It is the uncertainty about where national identity ends and imperial identity begins that is a primary source of confusion and anxiety in Russia today. Once more, the Russians attempt to reconcile their imperial reality with the image of themselves produced by their literature, and they seem to be very far from reaching a consensus. It should be added that the Russian imperial identity was not invented by the Soviets but is a legacy of the tsarist Russian empire. Neither the tsars nor the commissars encouraged a free and open inquiry into its characteristics, and consequently literature has become virtually the only

---

*Uri Ra'anan, ed., *The Soviet Empire: The Challenge of National and Democratic Movements* (Lexington, MA: D. C. Heath, 1990), p.x.

forum where such an inquiry could be conducted. Hence the importance of Russian literature as a repository of self-knowledge and an expression of national aspirations and beliefs.

In recent years, the process of reasserting and redefining the Russian national identity has accelerated, at least partly because of the pressure generated by an unstable political situation. In the novels and stories by contemporary Russian writers, both Soviet and emigré, problems that preoccupied nineteenth-century Russophiles reappear with astonishing frequency and often in strikingly similar forms. In the Soviet Russian periodicals such as *Literaturnaia gazeta* and *Literaturnaia Rossiia,* diverse approaches to the Russian identity are seen.

It is this renewed interest in the national self-image of what might well be the last imperial nation on earth that led to the organization at Rice University of a conference entitled "The Uses of Nationalist Ideology in Russian Literature." The conference took place in September of 1989, and it brought together a number of scholars exploring both recent and nineteenth-century Russian literature. Selected papers from the conference form the bulk of this book.

As conference chair, I am convinced that the gathering addressed a topic that has been seriously underresearched in First World countries. Simply put, we tend to read nationalism out of Russian literature. Our American readings of Russian literature, our standard works of criticism, and our English-language Slavic literary journals tend not to notice the strong presence of nationalistic concerns in Russian letters, and they offer hardly any analyses of this phenomenon. The lack of a theoretical base in western discourse on Russian national identity explains the diversity of approaches adopted by the speakers at the conference.

It is my hope that this book will identify a number of problems and facts concerning the Russian national identity and that it will provide a groundwork for research into the national ideology of Russians and their self-image as an imperial nation. What seems particularly urgent is a reexamination of the Russian self-image in the light of such theoretical works as E. J. Hobsbawn's and T. Ranger's *The Invention of Tradition* (1983), Salo W. Baron's *Modern Nationalism and Religion* (1947, 2nd ed. 1971), and Alain Besançon's *The Rise of the Gulag:*

Intellectual Origins of Leninism (1981). Further analyses will have to accommodate the views of Russian culture held by non-Russian Soviet minorities, for without their voices a discourse about Russian self-definition would soon become a monologue untested by reality.

In preparing the conference and the book, I received financial and professional support from many sources. I would like to acknowledge the support of the Hoover Institution (Discretionary Grant Program, Department of State, Soviet-Eastern European Research & Training Act of 1983, Public Law 98–164, Title VIII, 97 Stat. 1047–50) and of the School of Humanities at Rice University in preparing and funding the conference.

Fellow Slavicists at various universities have helped in many ways. I would like to express my gratitude to Claire S. Allen, Henryk Baran, Arnold Beichman, Martha Bohachevsky-Chomiak, Olga M. Cooke, William B. Edgerton, Donald M. Fiene, Halina Filipowicz, Sheelagh Graham, Albina Serebriakova Hill, Danuta Z. Hutchins, Roy G. Jones, Simon Karlinsky, Igor Lukes, Ernest A. Scatton, Antoni J. Semczuk, Richard F. Staar, and Harry Walsh for their advice and encouragement. Thanks are also due to Ursula Keierleber and Connie Coleman, administrative assistants in the Department of German and Slavic Studies at Rice, and to graduate students Regina S. Clifford and Betty Heitzman, whose assistance in checking the references was invaluable. Last but not least, my husband, James R. Thompson, contributed generously to this book in ways that are too numerous to mention.

A Note on Transliteration

In transliterating Russian words, I have used the Library of Congress system for transliteration of modern Russian with most diacritical marks omitted. However, some Russian names and titles that have commonly been transliterated in other ways (e.g., Dostoevsky, Tolstoy, Trotsky) have been retained in their traditional form. In any multiauthored book that draws from many sources some arbitrariness of rules is inevitable. The titles of some contemporary periodicals have been retained in their popular form (e.g., *Ogonyok*), while others were transliterated according to the rules (e.g., *Literaturnaia gazeta*). For technical reasons, the apostrophe was used to transliterate the Cyrillic soft sign.

I The Quest for

Russian National Identity

in Soviet Culture Today

After the first eight volumes of Nikolai Karamzin's *History of the Russian State* were published in 1818, Prince Petr Viazemskii called Karamzin the man who "showed us that we have a fatherland." [1] Karamzin's *History* helped create an awareness of sharing a national identity. A similar process is going on in Russia now, but there is no Karamzin. There are scores, perhaps hundreds, of mini Karamzins or would-be Karamzins, presenting their versions of a history of the Soviet state, out of which millions of readers are trying to shape their sense of what they share, images of what their fatherland was and is, or why the Soviet Union is not their fatherland. The inhabitants of the Soviet Union are still searching, in many different directions, and their quest and construction of new myths is a significant aspect of the present scene in the USSR. Literature and culture are the media through which the process is being carried out, and the object of the inquiry is history plus ecology plus society in general.

A German scholar has written that the buzz words in Soviet poetry between 1954 and 1963 were "sincerity" (*iskrennost'*), "openness" (*otkrytost'*), and "boldness" (*smelost'*), with the works of Evtushenko and Voznesenskii offering the best examples. In the 1960s the themes began to be "memory" (*pamiat'*), "family" or "clan" (*rod*), "nature" (*priroda*), and "warmth" (*teplota*).[2]

Today Russian lyrical poetry may not have such dominant words or themes, but literature as a whole does. One major theme in Soviet Russian cultural life today is the question: What has happened to the Russians? To their society, their land, water, air? What will and what should happen to Russia? The topic of what is to be done is not new, but as a problematic theme applied to Russianness in the present manner, it is very new. There are several directions in which the search for national identity and national self-image is being carried out. The favorite images are very diverse.

In contrast to the controversies of the nineteenth century, participants in those of today have under their belts the awareness of seventy years of various preachings of internationalism, Bolshevism, and anti-nationalism. Being exhumed are mass murders, deportations, deaths, trials, and camps, from the Revolution and Civil War through the Stalinist years and afterward.

Writers of belles-lettres, poets, literary critics, and novelists are turning into historians. They do not call their writings factography or documentary prose, as they did in the 1920s and 1960s, but there is a strong pull toward exactly that: documentary prose, reportage, essays, letters to the editor, interviews in *Literaturnaia gazeta*, articles. Novels purport to be chronicles; prose fiction, *povesti* and *romany*, wear not sheep's clothing but the monkish chroniclers' vestments. A large nation has awakened, found out not that the king has no clothes, but that the general secretary of the empire's ruling party has been presiding over the dissolution of its ideology—not yet of the territorial empire, but of the ruling imperial ideology. The ideology imposed from above has evaporated, and the question of what is the nature and the future of the Russian nation has become paramount.

Let us look at some manifestations of this national fever in print. Because there are so many examples, we can only be very selective and brief. Then we shall look in more detail at two significant literary works, and, finally, draw some tentative conclusions.

The search for Russianness is not a new preoccupation, as several other chapters in this volume make clear. Its ubiquity in Russian consciousness can be illustrated from many sources. Let us cite only one example, Vladimir Nabokov's epigraph—itself a quotation—to his novel *Gift (Dar)*: "An oak is a tree. A rose is a flower. A deer is an animal. A sparrow is a bird. Russia is our fatherland. Death is inevitable (P. Smirnovskii, *A Textbook of Russian Grammar*)."

Preoccupation with the meaning of Russianness has existed on various levels of culture, from the realms of high culture to the subliterary world: jokes, quips, insults, proverbs—and these days as a major presence in the world of the media and literature.

What are the symptoms, outcroppings, of the contemporary concern? Let us list some of the various kinds of recent attempts to articulate Russian identity in a competition for the hearts and minds of Russian readers:

1. An umbrella category—the broadest, most prevalent, dominant category is the search (and nostalgia) for a usable past. This backward investigative turn, evident everywhere, is toward links with the past, toward tradition, toward continuity and bonds. See, for example, the passion behind such publications as the pamphlet *Lost Monuments of the Architecture of Petersburg-Leningrad (Utrachennye pamiatniki arkhitektury Peterburga-Leningrada)*, the catalog of a show of photographs held in Leningrad in 1988, compiled by V.V. Antonov and A. V. Kobak and published by the Leningrad Section of the Soviet Fund for Culture.

2. The focusing of attention on the destruction of nature and of natural resources (ecology of nature; they also speak of the ecology of society and the ecology of culture) in the "nonblack earth" districts, in Siberia and Lake Baikal. Much is being written and many films have been made about the destruction of the natural environment in the Soviet Union.

3. The return to respectability, even to a place of honor (instead of calumny and persecution), of religion, of the Orthodox Church, of

monasteries. Heavy and positive emphasis is placed on the Russian
religious tradition and on what had been repressed. It is sometimes
reminiscent of the 1920s, of N.A. Kliuev and B.A. Pil'niak. Russians
are trying to redraw the cultural-literary-historical map—in order to
shift and redirect their own future sense of themselves—in which direction? Sometimes it seems as if all the things that had been black are
now white. Is it a "photographic negative" procedure? That is one
conclusion we can draw from the situation in the USSR.

Let us consider the cover of Il'ia Glazunov's *Calendar* for 1990,
entitled "One Hundred Centuries" and sold openly in a department
store in Irkutsk, where I bought it in June 1989. In the first row of
this mass picture, which resembles an iconostasis on the one hand and
an Old Believer icon of the Last Judgment on the other, numerous
Orthodox saints are depicted, and in the rear, behind hundreds of historical figures, there are depictions of supposed Aryan origins, then a
monument to Perun, complete with a swastika on the pedestal, being
toppled by Byzantine Christians. Continuing on through Mongolian
and other figures, through the centuries to Trotsky and Lenin, is the
little boy Tsarevich in the center, like a martyr leading the procession
of Russians moving abreast toward their mysterious future.

Another characteristic piece of evidence is that *Literaturnaia gazeta* has been running a series of articles on Fedorov, Florenskii,
Leont'ev, and others. The series is called "From the History of Russian Thought"; it would seem from the writers featured that this history consists exclusively of religious and spiritual thinkers. A new,
resplendent art journal, *Our Legacy* (*Nashe nasledie*), has as its main
goal to restore links with the early twentieth-century journals emphasizing religiosity, the Middle Ages, pristine Russian traditions, and
such authors as Gumilev (executed) and others who had been censored
for a long time. The journals of the early parts of the century, which
this magazine seems to be reviving, were themselves an attempt at a
national revival (away from materialistic, revolutionary, socialistic,
rationalistic currents of Russian thought). We are seeing, then, a revival of revivals.

4. The repatriation or reimportation of emigrés. So much of this
has been going on that we may fear the public will come down with

emigré fatigue, or rehabilitation fatigue. The reaction, the backlash to the trendy self-flagellants, may come soon and strongly. One already detects some signs of victim fatigue and martyr fatigue, exposé-unmasking-revelation fatigue. Examples of newly rediscovered, previously neglected outstanding Russians are Kliuev, Gumilev, Vladimir Solov'ev, and Leont'ev. Here we could also list the anthology of the Esenin group of poets, recently published, edited by S. Iu. Kuniaev, with much praise for their pro-village, pro-countryside, pro-Russian orientation, and with much blaming of "the cosmopolitan-Trotskyist-Bukharinite" group, which allegedly stifled these poets and their views.[3]

Somewhat to the contrary of the examples we have been looking at, there exists an incredible, unabashed eagerness to hear foreigners' views. Surely this zeal to solicit foreigners' opinions, to get them to write articles and give interviews, asking the foreigners to be "bolder" (*smelee*) in their criticism of the Soviet past and present, listening to them as to authorities, has something to do with the Russians' opinion of themselves and their sense of themselves in relation to foreigners. It is either a contradiction or at least a mitigating factor to the charge that Russian national feeling is xenophobic and chauvinistic.

5. A tremendous amount of writing on historical tragedies—from Leninist terror and Gumilev's execution in 1921, through the Civil War, collectivization of agriculture, trials and executions, camps, World War II, postwar terror and trials and executions, to Rybakov's *Children of the Arbat*. And the haunting refrain is: Who is to blame? These are old Russian rhetorical questions: *Kto vinovat, Chto delat'*. The focus of today's searches is on which group was the chief victim. Intellectuals? Party officials? Russians? Jews? And who were the persecutors, the victimizers? The questions are still before them—and us. Who is responsible? Who did it? Did they do it to themselves? Or did others do it? Russians are only now finding out all, or almost all, about the collectivization of agriculture and the deportation and killing of peasants connected with the collectivization.

They seldom ask, What have we done to other people? but rather, What have others done to us?

When did which group (or which individual) start complaining? Is it the former party members and believers who belatedly are jumping on the bandwagon to blame someone? Who says *J'accuse*, about what, to whom, and when did he or she start accusing? Who is now running with the hares who had been riding with the hounds? People who are now pointing accusing fingers were doing and saying what when those crimes were being perpetrated? These are the hot questions today.

The old Russian answer (alas, not only a Russian answer) that it is the Jews who are to blame is now again popular. If a Jew was in charge in 1929, is or is not mentioning this fact now anti-Semitic? Of course, it depends on how the mentioning is done. But in this grey area reside the most vexed complications of the present questions of national consciousness.

Connected with this tendency is the Russian writers' perception of Russophobia: that of Estonians, Jews, and others. Some Russians feel that now the other nations have turned on them and that remarks are permitted by other nations about Russians that Russians are not allowed to make about others. Also, some Russians complain that they may not say anything in praise of their own nation while smaller nations can express pride or even boastfulness. There is a feeling of being put upon, of having become the butt of others' attacks. Such sentiments were expressed by Rasputin and Belov in their speeches at the Writers' Congress in Moscow in June 1989.

The Russians are now also facing the fact that their state, the USSR, is a multinational empire. They do not yet quite openly sort out the distinctions of what is Soviet and Russian or what is anti-Soviet and anti-Russian.

6. The rise of Georgii Gachev, a scholar of Bulgarian origin who devotes his energies to perhaps overstated but also neglected problems of the various nations' distinctive self-images and conceptions of others. His articles have appeared in many periodicals. His main book, *National Images of the World (Natsional'nye obrazy mira*, Moscow, 1988), had been known in some circles; fragments have appeared; but now the whole book is published and more has been promised of his free-wheeling and somewhat Bakhtinian marches through im-

pressionistic generalizations of national images of space and time and of national psychological predispositions. Books like Gachev's are now published and discussed in the press, and Gachev himself is often cited, interviewed, and asked to write articles. This is a by-product of the new boom in national consciousness publishing.

7. Voluminous and frequent public presentations of opinion on this topic, which may be divided into three main groups. We shall outline each of them as seen by their chief advocates.

First, there is academician Dmitrii Likhachev, who urges the broadest possible inclusion of other peoples within the concept of Russianness. His is a universal, tolerant, nonexclusive concern with being Russian. Likhachev has published many articles, interviews, and books on the subject of the Russian tradition, from the Middle Ages to the present, from styles of horticulture to the special characteristics of Russian architecture. He has become something of a television personality. The way in which his love of Russia links him to the most extreme advocates of free expression on the Soviet political scene is shown in the following passage in his article in *Ogonyok*, in the series "The Suffering of the Fatherland" ("Bol' Otechestva"):

Pamiat' and other extremists blame non-Russians and non-Orthodox people (*inorodtsev i inovertsev*) for all our troubles. This logic is well known. Everybody is guilty except ourselves! So that this nonsense will not be accepted, we must ascertain all the facts of the damage to our national culture. And we must state who is guilty. It is the system, the regime, entire institutions that are guilty. That of course does not take away personal responsibility. *Pamiat'* will fester in society as long as there is not a sufficient degree of *glasnost'*. And that has not yet been reached.

When we put the blame on other nationalities, the shadow of Stalin appears before me, the shadow of Stalinism. The Stalinist plan of moving nations and the defamation of entire nationalities. . . . Entire nations were "enemies of the people."[4]

Thus, Likhachev's desire for arousing Russian national consciousness is linked to, is part and parcel of, his desire to maximize *glasnost'*.

A second, centrist group is represented by Vadim Kozhinov, a staunch supporter of *glasnost'* and *perestroika*, who, however, also goes very far in the direction of rejecting all Marxism, Bolshevism, and the Bolshevik Revolution and who insists on commemorating the killings of Russian peasants and all others from 1917 onward, rather than concentrating on the sufferings of the intelligentsia, of party members, and of victims after 1937 only. He has made his views clear in many articles, particularly those criticizing Anatolii Rybakov's *Children of the Arbat*. Kozhinov tends to sympathize with historical figures who acted in the interests of Russian national values as they saw them—for instance with Tiutchev, whose biography Kozhinov published in the Gorbachev era, after many years of working on it and not being able to get it into print.

A third group, finally, would be represented by Viktor Astaf'ev's xenophobic rejoinder given in writing to the historian and literary scholar Natan Eidelman in an exchange of "Open Letters." [5] Astaf'-ev's resentment of non-Russian (Jewish or Georgian) scholars, editors, and commercial entrepreneurs, or black marketeers, is considerable. Views and feelings such as those revealed in his correspondence are usually confined to private conversations (or semi-closed meetings).

8. The fact of a *Russian* encyclopedia (*Russkaia entsiklopediia*) being planned. In an interview in *Literaturnaia gazeta*, March 22, 1989, O. N. Trubachev answered questions about this venture. What should a Russian encyclopedia include? What criteria will govern inclusion or exclusion? Will it be nationality, language, place of dwelling, or "belonging to Russian culture"? Trubachev said the last would be the criterion. His interviewers suggested a few examples: Mandel'shtam, for instance. Trubachev answered: "Mandel'shtam . . . wrote in the Russian language. He is an inalienable possession of Russian culture. How could one exclude him from the Russian encyclopedia on any ground?" By the same token Nabokov and Solzhenitsyn will be represented.

TWO RECENT PROSE WORKS

Let us now turn to two recently published works of prose fiction that raise questions of Russia's national destiny. The reason for choosing them is that they clearly represent contrasting attitudes toward and uses of Russian national awareness.

The first is a work of a newly emerged writer who has been called a member of the very latest, post-post-"thaw" generation of Soviet writers, Viacheslav P'etsukh. A self-made, self-grown, idiosyncratic writer, sprung from village teaching life, he published a collection of stories, *Alphabet (Alfavit)*, in Moscow (Sovetskii Pisatel', 1983), as well as various later stories, including "A Pessimistic Comedy" ("Pessimisticheskaia komediia") in the first issue of the almanac *Mirrors (Zerkala)*, edited by Aleksandr Lavrin and published in Moscow in 1989.

His "New Moscow Philosophy" ("Novaia moskovskaia filosofiia," *Novyi mir*, No. 1, 1989) is called a *povest'* in that issue of the journal, but the author said in an interview that it had been shortened, and he thinks of it as a novel.[6] It is a tongue-in-cheek story, humorous and comic in parts, but also puzzling, because we do not know whether to take certain passages seriously or ironically and because the light parts of the story may or may not reflect the earnest ones.

The story presents a group of heterogeneous characters (varying in age, educational background, and social standing) in a contemporary communal apartment in Moscow, engaged in a debate about distribution of the rooms. Two of them, Belotsvetov and Chinarikov, carry on a lengthy running polemic about the Russian spirit, Russian literature, and differences between contemporary Russia and the nineteenth century.

The slight plot involves two linked puzzles. First, an old woman living in the apartment disappears. She is eventually discovered, dead of exposure, sitting on a bench. Second, apparitions—perhaps ghosts—are seen in the apartment, possibly connected with the vanished old lady. So the story has a slight similarity to an Agatha Christie thriller plus neo-Dostoevskian or Chaadaevian debates on huge philosophical and national topics. It turns out that the apparitions are tricks played on the characters by a young boy, Mitia, projections done by means of a mirror and a hole in the wall of the bathroom.

There is also a parallel series of quotations from *Crime and Punishment*. References are made to the murder of an old woman in Petersburg, to Raskolnikov and Marmeladov, and to various aspects of themes, moods, atmosphere, and ideas of Dostoevsky's novel (and perhaps also to ghosts and incidents in Kharms's *Old Woman*). The Petersburg of Dostoevsky and the Leningrad of Kharms are invoked as contrasts to today's Moscow. The recurrent allusions to the analogies or differences between the nineteenth century and the present time further enrich the story. Are the Russians still the same? Are the old Dostoevskian themes still valid? These questions and debates about specifically Russian characteristics are not merely the unifying threads, they are the backbone of the story.

The garrulous philosophers who converse and argue in the story focus on the title phrase, "New Moscow Philosophy." They allude to Chaadaev and claim that there exist perennial constants, or invariants, in Russian culture. One of the characters, the most loquacious one, affirms that the Russians are marked by an unusually high degree of dependence on their literature for patterns, models, and prescriptions for their conduct. Their "real life" is exceptionally closely modeled on their literary exemplars. Another recurring theme is that of the problematics of the relationship of life and literature.

P'etsukh has been called "a researcher into the Russian national character" for his collection of stories *Happy Times (Veselye vremena)*. That is what S. Taroshchina, his interviewer in *Literaturnaia gazeta* (May 17, 1989), called him. According to the interview, L. Anninskii described him as one of those who come to succeed the literature "of both 'thaws' "; and he said that P'etsukh "researches especially the dissolution of the soil . . . [which brought about the existence of] an inwardly lost, spiritually weak person ready for anything," like the boy Mitka Nachalov, tenth-grade student, in the story. In the interview P'etsukh stated his faith in the Russian mission of "further moral building." He also said that he had the honor to agree with Chaadaev. He quoted not the late Chaadaev but his early remark, "I am firmly convinced that we are called to solve the major part of the problems of the social system, to bring to completion the major part of the ideas that originated in the old society and to pronounce the verdict on the most serious problems which occupy mankind." What an ambitious and messianic mission for P'etsukh to agree with.

His prose puts side by side archaisms and neologisms. He says he has a wife who is a medical specialist in the language of children, and she brings him children's expressions; and his son has, as it were, an "order" from his father to compile what almost amounts to a dictionary of Russian juvenile language.

In the story the ironic, chattering narrator throws out the paradox that in Russia people simply sit and compose stories about people who never actually existed—they play at life—and through their creations lead millions of honest readers into error. The Danes did not read their Kierkegaard for one hundred years, he claims; Stendhal meant nothing to the French until he died; but "east of the railway station at Chop" about half the Russian nation will sleep on nails if some priest's son from Saratov or a schoolteacher will tell them that they should learn how to do that for the sake of the future of the nation (p. 55). Whimsically, humorously, P'etsukh advances the platitude of western writing about Russian literature—that Russians look above all to the literary examples of Tatiana Larina, Alyosha Karamazov, Captain Lebiadkin, Evgenii Onegin, and others. It is P'etsukh's narrator, not one of his characters, who says, "We [the Russians] are an extremely literary people, and we trust life less than novels and stories." One might add that, therefore, the Russians also have a weakness for apparitions and ghosts, since "apparitions are the secret passion of our literature" (p. 69).

Belotsvetov and Chinarikov take up in their lengthy discussions such time-hallowed themes as the existence of evil, which they take back to Socrates but with clear allusions to its importance in Dostoevsky. They sound determined to evoke Russian nineteenth-century ancestry. They link evil to the question of the "I," of individuality *(lichnost')*, and of personality (p. 65).

"A militant nonacceptance of evil is the meaning of life," says Belotsvetov, whereas Chinarikov answers, "The meaning of life is a purely Russian invention. We invented it for the same reason Asiatics invented Buddhism: because of our shortages of the most essential objects. Eleven-twelfths of the population of the earth never heard of any meaning of life and, believe me, they feel just fine" (p. 77).

There is a law, the narrator reflects, that causes the popular (*narodnoe*) sense for truth to abbreviate philosophical teachings into proverbs, and abbreviates life into literature (p. 79).

Belotsvetov believes that if one does not love and believe in Russian literature, one will feel cold toward "our life." In other words—literature comes first. Love our literature, love our life. Russian life is truly fairytale-like (*skazochnaia zhizn'*), and is all based—as is Russian literature—on truth, conscience, and love. But now for the first time in the history of the Russian nation, a generation has appeared that knows no moral orientation. It does not know what is good, what is bad, what is necessary, and what is not permitted, as if it was the first ever on earth. "The Bible, Christ, Roman law, Spinoza, the encyclopedists, 'freedom, equality, fraternity'—all that is still to come" (p. 93).

Belotsvetov says that the [Russian] way of life (*stroi byta*) has played such a large role in forming the national character that historians will have to take it into account. The "family system" of our life is a fact and the communal system of life helped form it, even if it led to "kerosene in cabbage soup and fighting, and other ugliness" (pp. 105–106). They define this as simply "cave socialism." Chinarikov sings: "You too have suffered / and therefore have become Russified / My people who have fallen nobody knows where / Your people who were innocent and jailed" (p. 106). Belotsvetov further argues the polarity of individual wishes and needs versus social ones, and affirms—while explicitly invoking the New Moscow Philosophy—the mission of "our" society: a further moral advancement (p. 112). "In the search for further self-perfection . . . real life is the enjoyment of the possibilities of individual existence which is accessible only to pure souls."

The story mocks elevated ideals; it mocks the tradition of love triangles in Russian literature; it mocks Dostoevsky and all else—even *glasnost'*—but a kernel or after-taste of "real meaning" does remain behind.

The last two paragraphs state that one must read *Crime and Punishment,* and that "in the process of moral evolution of man, literature was assigned some kind of genetic significance, because literature is the spiritual experience of humanity in concentrated form. Literature is a most substantive ingredient or additive to the genetic code of rational being. Without literature man cannot make himself fully into man . . . some things are passed on from generation to generation, with the blood of our ancestors, and other things only by means of books; from this it follows that people must live taking literature into account, as Christians must take into account the Lord's Prayer."

The second prose work that addresses the problematics of Russianness is very different from P'etsukh's. Vasilii Belov's *The Year of the Great Break (God velikogo pereloma)* is as devoid of irony and multiplicity of points of view as P'etsukh is rich in them. This sequel to *The Eves (Kanuny)*[9] makes everything all too explicit. The beginning is couched in the manner of a Russian chronicle, the subtitle being "A Chronicle of Nine Months," and Belov tells us, in case we should have missed it, that the work is written in the manner of a chronicle. If a chronicler had lived at the time when Stalin was fifty, and when Lazar Kaganovich was made commissar of agriculture, he would have written the following—except that there were no chroniclers, we are told. The story follows the events taking place in the Kremlin and in a certain village from December 21, 1929, to the execution of the so-called kulaks.

Comrade Shilovskii is ordered to participate in the liquidation of "the criminal element, your class enemy, and the enemy of all the working people."[10] A rather plain narrative, a little dull perhaps, of persons under various forms of arrest—and of those who were arresting them—is interspersed with lyrical purple patches: "The earth bewitched by the winter and sleeping under its native snows perhaps did not even feel its new miseries. But how can we know? . . . The earth had hardly received into her womb millions of sufferers, and was she not getting ready for still more new, unusual labor? The force of awakened evil similar in its movement to a blizzard seized all new spaces, and again pulled into its crater the masses of people who suspected nothing. Russia perished over and over again, again, and again."[11]

At a January 31, 1930, meeting of administrators, a GPU representative from Moscow announces the arrival of transports of seventy thousand kulaks. Arrangements are made for various ways of disposing of them. Bergavinov wires Stalin, Kaganovich, and Molotov, giving them optimistic reassurances on the progress of dekulakization.

The story details the sufferings of peasants shipped north in trains, ill and dying, and it highlights a letter written by Patriarch Tikhon—all this against the background of St. Cyril's Monastery and Cathedral, the Time of Troubles, Lithuanian and Russian pillaging, and the Napoleonic Wars. The first message of the Patriarch sets the tone: "Hard times have befallen the Holy Orthodox Church of Christ in the Russian land. Open and secret enemies of this truth are persecuting Christ's truth." [12]

The story comes to life in moments of conflict. For example, the interest rises when the priest, interrogated by two GPU people, provokes them, like a medieval hero seeking martyrdom, or like a revolutionary hero in the formulas of socialist realism.

Most striking in Belov is the assumption of styles and mannerisms of ancient chronicles and of religious terminology—a Russian Orthodox cloak or halo, the religious garment, or *riza*.

The author presents a war waged by the city against the country, a war that is killing the peasantry. In Belov's imagining of the events, invaders and urban aliens are destroying the countryside. (All this is deeply enmeshed with ecological problems.) Russia is now being helped to regain its sight, to awaken, as in Esenin's imagery in "Advent": "He carries his cross / Out of awakening Russia." [13]

We are looking here at a reembodiment of an ancient Russian nativism, going back at least to Gleb Uspensky. [14] Belov uses archaic patterns, but not in the same way that Remizov had done earlier. The return to icons by Malevich and others, to the popular woodcut (*lubok*), was also different. In Belov it is ideological, creating an aura of nativism: it makes the destruction by the Bolsheviks not a time-hallowed but a time-cursed one. This presentation stresses that the patrimony of the peasants belonged to the Russian people, who are Christian, and casts the Bolsheviks and the Kremlin rulers in the roles of alien invaders destroying the country on a grand and almost biblical scale.

This is a book of prophetic doom, in the mode of a curse. The narrator reaches into the past and into the monks' chronicles the better to curse with. In order to teach the reader to hate more deeply, to show that the new enemies deserve an abhorrence of those with premodern roots, the book casts the narrator as a sacred prophet. He draws on chronicles and the past for that purpose. This is in contrast to Pil'niak—who had the village triumph over the cities and who distinguished between communists (foreign, bad) and Bolsheviks (Russian, good.) [15] In Belov, moreover, it is resident "foreigners" who have grasped power, not outsiders from beyond the borders of the country.

Pil'niak's Revolution was an elemental and Russian one: sects/ priestless religion/snowstorms are the primeval Russian principles, plus "the haze of home-brew" (*mut' samogonki*): that defines his Russian Revolution, which destroys European culture. But Belov agrees with Pil'niak in one tenet: the Revolution is a self-immolation by the Russian nation for the sake of international communism. Pil'niak viewed the Third International as cast out into the world beyond the borders of Russia. For itself, Russia kept cannibalism, the Bolshevik Time of Troubles (*smuta*), penury. Pil'niak's *The Third Capital* presents many attitudes toward the Revolution, even adulation of it, as well as many kinds of condemnation; but there is no understanding of it: "Russia lives with the will to want and the will not to see. This lie I consider a highly positive phenomenon, unique in the world."

P'etsukh's was an ironic, mixed, detached view, with earnest and messianic overtones, but also bemoaning losses and moral nihilism, deploring the terror, the lack of tradition, Soviet tabula rasa. He stresses the continuity of past Russian self-definitions, self-exhortations, the sense of mission, awareness of relations between Dostoevsky and today, Chaadaev and today. Yet he gives no sign of being aware of how these grandiose goals and ambitions might strike someone else—a non-Russian. He also has a keen feeling of diminishment, of loss, from Dostoevsky to today's communal apartments and petty crime. The mission proclaimed is grand, elevated. The reality is satirized. Literature emerges as the highest Russian connection to life, to a positive goal.

Belov's work is earnest, pathetic, a *plach*, a lament for the fate of the Russian land destroyed by aliens, by those from the alien-dominated center. His is a memorial to a mass murder, mass destruction.

CONCLUSIONS AND PROSPECTS

Pressures create counterpressures. Official internationalist, antinational Soviet ideology had been crushing discussions of Russian national feeling for seventy years; once *glasnost'* removed the prohibition against such debates in the media, the counterpressure that had been produced and quelched began to express itself. Hence, the voluminous concern with Russian national awareness and the concomitant self-defining, self-lamenting, self-eulogizing.

Great struggles rage: debates, polemics. A lively, energetic war of ideas is going on. It is not always a pretty picture. There is a strong element of xenophobia; there is much small thinking. Scores are being settled after many years of suffering, repression, injustices real and imaginary. A grand debate is going on, a tempest not in a teapot but on a vast battlefield with animosities and hatreds sufficient to make one feel like looking the other way, study some other subject—Pushkin or Derzhavin or Chekhov, perhaps. But the spectacle does go on, and there is some promise of health, and certainly much vigor, in the fact of this struggle.

There are some noble figures, Likhachev being the most outstanding. Such ignoble feelings and distortions of national consciousness as we do find are only one element, one ingredient. They are not the entire picture; let us not turn away and throw up our hands in complete despair. Appealing to national awareness may be the last best hope for Russia today. The alternative, the liberal western democratic Sakharov line, may have only a weaker appeal to Russians.

On an earlier occasion I divided the nationally conscious groups in Russia into the following five categories: [16]

1. Groups cherishing the national heritage: Russian identity as modesty, even humility, welcoming the otherness of non-Russians. Dmitri Likhachev represents this strain.

2. The Eurasian identity: Russianness in combination with Oriental (Asiatic) attitudes; anti-racism. Georgii Kuzmin stands for this definition.

3. Stress on religious faith, Russian Orthodoxy as a key element.

4. Neo-Dostoevskian: Russian universality.

5. Self-deprecating views: "Little Russia"; withdrawal to the Northeast; need for several generations of recuperation; prorural and Siberian, antiurban.

As the Russians now are facing (or evading or reacting to) what had happened in the recent past, they are cringing under the impact, assuming various contorted stances. They are in danger of becoming—temporarily one hopes, and contrary to their historical antecedents—a psychologically small nation. They are adopting the persecution mania, the victim's self-pity, of a small nation. What a dearth of magnanimity! It is sometimes hard to believe that this is a nation that in the past claimed for itself and for its national character a special talent for breadth of soul, for largeness. There is not an absolute absence of nobility: Likhachev is a fine example of dignity and greatness of soul. But more typically they are sorry for themselves. Like a small nation, they speak of being and having been the victims. Very often one hears the Russian phrase, "We fed them and we liberated them" (*My ikh kormili—My ikh osvobodili*), and now the other nationalities have all turned against us. We, the Russians, are poor because we have helped the others . . . we sacrificed everything for the others.

There are, of course, some reasons for their feeling of being besieged. For example, the *New York Times* reported on August 9, 1989, that Tiit Made, an Estonian economist, wrote in an article for a Swedish newspaper that Russians are an aggressive people whose primitive behavior can be traced back to centuries of breeding with Mongolian occupiers. "Their aggressiveness and violence is manifested even in love," Made wrote. "After rape comes a feeling of love and delight." *Sovetskaia Rossiia* republished Made's article as evidence of anti-Russian racism in the Baltic independence movement.

The Russians feel they were impoverished the most. This is a traditional Russian theme: we suffered the most; but instead of pride, they display resentment. Their land, their water, their air were the most seriously destroyed, as well as their forests and villages. The Russians no longer boast about the magnitude of their suffering, as they often did in the nineteenth century; they resent it.

There are also some startling absences in the current wave of self-definition. Russians seldom examine their role in expanding the borders of the Soviet Union. They do not claim a share of the guilt of having incorporated Lithuania and other countries.

Another feature, at first glance contradictory to what I have been asserting about the Russian danger of falling into small-nation psychology—is an occasional smugness, the self-importance of posturing and snobbishness, that one also encounters today in the Russian self-image. An example I witnessed myself in the summer of 1989 in Leningrad was a woman who was host at the *Kafe Literaturnoe*: she was self-conscious, verbose, and self-aggrandizing, and she made pretentious claims to a special Russian cultural continuity from Pushkin to the late 1980s Leningrad cafe.

Russians are wading through a mass of recriminations, trying to find a picture of what and who they are that squares with the new facts and with the self-respect and pride they want to feel. Debates on what is Soviet, progressive, and so on have collapsed. Now they talk about what is Russian, what it is, what happened to it.

After my talk at the American Association for the Advancement of Slavic Studies meeting in Honolulu, in November 1988, Maurice Friedberg said that Likhachev was a very bright and erudite man, but even he posited only positive things as being typically Russian. What is important is why the same old clichés that have been repeated for a hundred years are important now and in what contexts these clichés play a role in different times. They certainly play the role of arranging people in groups; they structure them; they are like a magnetic field that arranges metal shavings. The people feel incipient chaos and disarray. They look for lines of magnetic force along which to arrange themselves in new patterns, new structures. They feel besmirched and besieged by revelations of past and present crimes and they have the freedom to say what they feel.

There is no consensus on the mission of the Russian nation, on the essential features of its recent past, on the main characteristics of the nation, and on the chief needs of the near future. No informed public opinion exists. Instead of one or two views held by some kind of political-cultural community, there exists a *Gemeinschaft*—some kind of *obshchestvo*, society. Other than that, there is nothing but a splintering into numerous and shifting views. The artificial monolithic or monopolistic view of the party line and the regime (though changeable in direction through time) has been succeeded by a chaotic pluralism.

The relationships between being Soviet and being Russian, between being communist and being Russian, are confused, unclearly described, variously argued.

The most important conclusion is that no single national view (or even two or three competing but widely held views) has been formed yet, and that the reason for the fragmentation and diversity of the many separate views lies in the Soviet historical background, in past repression and control of the media, in the monopoly of official views, and in the results of that situation. Below the monolithic media, in the subliterary world of rumor, hint, and private conversation, there existed no intellectual audience formulating and refining views on national identity. There had not even existed any two or three distinct audiences or public opinions; what there was was a fragmented, in fact atomized, conglomeration of people, compartmentalized into tiny, private groups, expressing their attitudes within the small circle. Such small group talk took place not in the media, not in the literate world, but in the vast subliterary stratum of Soviet life—the world of proverb, quip, anecdote, slur, oral insult, oral comment, unstable, ephemeral, emotion-laden expression of national image or feeling, heavily dependent on (often growing out of, provoked into existence by) the immediate social context. This realm foments graphic formulations, vivid expressions; it does not favor nuance, shadings of opinion, and it particularly does not accept extended and reasoned formulations. Thousands of such temporary expressions of attitude never could jell, amalgamate, into one or two or three larger formulations; but they existed, atomized, in spurts, in little oases of informal life. They could not evolve and develop. What used to be the preserve of such oral, subliterary expression has now been permitted to hoist itself up into the world of TV, theater, film, print, political speech.

Now there do emerge, out of the fogs of national self-defense, self-flagellation, self-accusation, and self-praise—some rather indistinct, vague peaks speaking for several national conceptions or self-images. One says, do not blame us, the Russians—you Estonians and Caucasians and you others out there—we Russians (or we non-black-earth-area dwellers, as they sometimes say in print, clumsily and improbably) have been victimized more than you. Sometimes they say so boldly and from a straight-up position; at other times, whiningly, self-pityingly, as though the Russians had again been victimized and mistreated by others. And a voice from another dim peak seems to be saying, we are not to blame; on the contrary, it is you urban Jewish and other non-Russian Bolsheviks who have destroyed our land and our nation. The third, alas, least often heard, although spoken by the noblest advocate, says: To be Russian has always meant to be decent, tolerant, unracist, unxenophobic, universal; and let us adopt that ideal for ourselves now.

In the welter of various angles, different visions, around Russian national self-images of the past and present, it is easy for a westerner to dismiss the whole show as chaos, to become disgusted with some of the self-pity and turn away, to call the awakening and recovery of sight (*prozrenie*) not a regaining of sight but a distorted, self-serving, dangerous misperception and anti-Semitism. It is certainly not a neat, crisp spectacle. But we may be selling Russians short. Let us not underestimate their resilience, their ability to change, their creativity. After more than half a century of terror and repression, why should they not need a few years of free-for-all trial and error—perhaps to come up with fine works of literature again, and a settled, useful, positive view of their own national identity.

2 Portrayal of Nationalities in

Soviet Russian Literature

The portrayal of Russians and other nationalities in Soviet Russian literature has been to a large extent determined by the views and policies of the ruling communist party. In connection with shifts in party policy, one can distinguish roughly the following periods in the treatment of nationalities in Soviet literature: 1. 1917–34; 2. 1934–41; 3. 1941–45; 4. 1946–53; 5. 1953–64; 6. 1965–85; and 7. 1985 to the present.

In the first period, tsarist Russia was regarded as a backward, chauvinistic, and expansionist autocracy that subjugated and oppressed national minorities. Works dealing with the struggle of these peoples for liberation from the tsarist reign were welcomed. This was the case with Stepan Zlobin's *Salavat Iulaev* (1929), a novel concerned with the participation of the Bashkirs in the Pugachev rebellion. The official emphasis on equality of all nationalities allowed literature to depict realistically the role played by minorities in the Communist Party and the October Revolution. Thus, a character in Iurii Libedinskii's *A Week* (*Nedelia*, 1922) could say that half of the members of the Bolshevik party were non-Russians. In Aleksandr Fadeev's *The Rout* (*Razgrom*, 1927), the leading communist character is a Jew who has a real-life prototype.

Now and then we encounter censorial revisions purported to remove or replace words deemed offensive to national minorities. Already in 1924 the censors expunged from Artem Veselyi's story "Fiery Rivers" ("Reki ognennye," 1923) the appellation "Yiddish archbishop" (*arkhierei zhidovskii*) used by a character. Five years later, in Veselyi's uncompleted novel *Russia Washed in Blood* (*Rossiia, krov'iu umytaia*, 1927–), an unscrupulous Jewish quartermaster, Isaika Zuderman, was transformed into a Russian, Zudov, without a first name. But since 1932 he has been known under a neutral surname, Zudilovich. The word *khokhol*, which can be either a neutral or a derogatory name for a Ukrainian, was purged from the 1929 collection of Veselyi's works entitled *The Carousing Spring* (*Piruiushchaia vesna*) both in the authorial narrative and in the characters' speech. To my knowledge, this is the earliest elimination of *khokhol*, probably because the collection in question appeared in Khar'kov, then the capital of the Soviet Ukraine. In 1933 the authorial narrative of the first two volumes of Mikhail Sholokhov's *The Quiet Don* (*Tikhii Don*, 1928–40) lost all its *khokhols*. The 1932 censors of Veselyi's novel *My Native Land* (*Strana rodnaia*, 1925) eliminated a phrase about the Tatars' looting a town captured by anti-Bolshevik insurgents. On the other hand, descriptions of the ugly aspects of Russian life and behavior were virtually unchallenged by censorship. A notable exception was a rebuke given to Demian Bednyi by the supreme censor, Joseph Stalin, for publishing in 1930 a few poems portraying Russia as slavish, lazy, and savage. But the source of Stalin's ire was political rather than nationalistic. In his view, Bednyi slandered a people justly proud of its revolutionary heritage.[1]

The following period, from 1934 to 1941, was marked by the official revision of Russian history and the encouragement of Russian patriotism. The chief cause for this change was Hitler's rise to power and the associated threat of war. Stalin realized that his best and, perhaps, only chance to win this war lay in the appeal to traditional Russian patriotism. The focus of historical fiction moved from social revolutions to heroic battles of the Russians against foreign invaders. Sergei Borodin's *Dmitrii Donskoi* (1941) was devoted to the Grand Prince of Moscow who had crushed the Tatars in 1380. Konstantin Simonov's poem "The Ice Battle" ("Ledovoe poboishche," 1937) glorified the 1242 triumph of Aleksandr Nevskii over the Teutonic Knights and served as a warning to the Nazis not to attack the Soviet Union. Probably the most significant patriotic work of the period was a huge epic about the Crimean War, *The Ordeal of Sevastopol* (*Sevastopol'skaia strada*, 1937–39) by Sergei Sergeev-Tsenskii. The novel was characteristic of the late 1930s in the sense that its fervent patriotism was not coupled with antagonism toward other nations. Furthermore, it was quite outspoken about the general superiority of the West over backward Russia.

The accent on patriotism did not mean that the Marxist concept of class struggle was thrown out. A case in point was the revising done by Nikolai Ostrovskii in his *How the Steel Was Tempered* (*Kak zakalialas' stal'*, 1932–34). Concerned about having presented most of the Poles as enemies of the Bolsheviks, he added in 1935 Polish characters who side with their Ukrainian and Russian class brothers in the fight against the Polish aristocracy. In the same year, the censors played down Ukrainian nationalism by omitting from Ostrovskii's novel both the term "Ukrainian People's Republic" (which was hostile to the Soviets) and an appeal by Simon Petliura to fight the Bolsheviks who had destroyed a free Ukraine.

In the period from 1934 to 1941 the censors continued their sporadic liquidation of disparaging names for national minorities. Thus, in the 1935 edition of *Russia Washed in Blood* the word "Asiatic" was replaced by "horseman" or "mountaineer" in reference to members of the minorities in the Caucasus.

It was only natural that during the war the propaganda of Russian patriotism was greatly intensified. It is sufficient to mention Konstantin Simonov's play *The Russians* (*Russkie liudi*, 1942), Mikhail Sholokhov's unfinished novel *They Fought for Their Country* (*Oni srazhalis' za rodinu*, 1943–), and Sergei Sergeev-Tsenskii's three novels about World War I written between 1943 and 1945 and included in his novelistic cycle entitled *Transfiguration* (*Preobrazheniie*). The class approach to war gave way to the propagation of the struggle against the Germans as such. Simonov's poem "Kill Him" ("Ubei ego," 1942) called outright for the killing of a German. From the 1945 edition of *The Quiet Don* the censors banned the scene of fraternization between a Russian and a German soldier in World War I as well as an antipatriotic tirade of a Bolshevik that included the statements, "Workers have no fatherland. These words of Marx express the most profound of truths."[2] In the same novel, the nationality of the Bolshevik Shtokman was changed from German to Latvian, and some contemptuous remarks about Russia and the Russian people were excised. The Poles also benefited from the censors' actions. A character's comparison of the proud Poles with a well-fed pig, which appeared in 1940 in the last volume of *The Quiet Don*, vanished in 1945 because of the common war against Nazi Germany and the formation of the Polish communist government.

In the years between 1946 and 1953 patriotism degenerated into chauvinism. I see the chief reason for this development in the government's intention to neutralize the favorable impression made on millions of Soviet troops during their service abroad. The anti-western campaign was officially launched with the party resolution of August 14, 1946. It assailed a number of works for allegedly cultivating the spirit of servility to western culture. Elaborating on the resolution, Andrei Zhdanov asserted the absolute superiority of the Soviet way of life over that of the West. On May 13, 1947, Stalin, in a meeting with Simonov, Fadeev, and Boris Gorbatov, stressed the necessity to combat self-disparagement, suggesting that a novel be written on the subject.[3]

There is no point in dwelling on the numerous potboilers, particularly plays, that glorified the Russian past and the Soviet present and attacked practically everything in the West, except the people who sympathized with the Soviet Union. Even respectable writers, willingly or otherwise, joined the chorus of rabid nationalism and xenophobia. In Iurii Trifonov's *Students* (*Studenty*, 1950), American soldiers beat a black driver while their officers calmly look on. In addition, President Harry Truman and presidential candidate John Dewey are called scoundrels. Maksim Gor'kii is then said to represent the highest achievement of Russian realism, a writer without equal in any country. Americans and Britons in Emmanuil Kazakevich's novel *Spring on the Oder* (*Vesna na Odere*, 1949) are coarse, egotistic, and supportive of German capitalists. In 1952 Vsevolod Ivanov added to his play *Armored Train No. 14–69* (*Bronepoezd No. 14–69*, 1927) phrases alleging that Americans had established a concentration camp in Vladivostok where they killed, hanged, or starved to death their prisoners. While the British and Americans were maligned as the principal enemies of the Soviet Union, former wartime adversaries began to enjoy a much more lenient treatment, for the majority of them, including the East Germans, had by that time come under Soviet control. Already in 1949 in the first book-form edition of Valentin Kataev's novel *For the Power of the Soviets* (*Za vlast' Sovetov*, 1949) many designations of enemy soldiers as "Germans" or "Romanians" were either censored or replaced by "fascists," "SS men," or simply "enemies." Several passages about German atrocities in Odessa were also dropped.

A good insight into the impact of chauvinism on literature is provided by the nature of censorial intervention in the historical novels *Stepan Razin* (*Razin Stepan*, 1927) by Aleksei Chapygin and *The Ordeal of Sevastopol* (*Sevastopol'skaia strada*, 1937–39) by Sergei Sergeevich-Tsenskii. Both books underwent extensive revisions in 1948 and 1950. Of some two hundred deletions in *Stepan Razin*, most are connected with nationalism. Censors also removed numerous descriptions of the cruelty, ignorance, lewdness, and filthy living conditions of seventeenth-century Russia. To affirm the authority of Moscow, censors eliminated antagonistic statements made about it by the Don Cossacks. Moreover, the role of foreigners in the strengthening of the Russian state was virtually reduced to zero by suppressing information that they had formed the mainstay of the tsarist regime, serving it as military officers and master craftsmen and displaying more loyalty to the throne than the nobility did.

More than three hundred excisions in *The Ordeal of Sevastopol* were made for the sake of patriotic education. Gone were unfavorable comparisons between Russia and the West in terms of individual rights, freedom of the press, political tolerance, economic achievements, standards of living, and military might. There was no longer a place for chivalrous treatment of Russian prisoners by the French. The censors even deemed unprintable the fact that James Watt had invented the steam engine, or that English horses were as big as elephants. The same was done with passages about the obsolescence of the Russian navy, the panic experienced by Russian troops, and the aggressive policy of Nicholas I that led to the outbreak of the Crimean War.

The intent to Russify the Crimea was reflected in the removal of the adjectives "Tatar" and "Greek," formerly used to describe settlements on the peninsula founded by these minorities. Furthermore, the censors struck out phrases about the Tatars' hatred of Russians and their readiness to rebel. Likewise, the censors cut references to the desertion of the Poles to the Allied troops.

The tendency to downplay the mistreatment of minorities caused the elimination in 1948 of two and a half pages from *Stepan Razin*. The core of the deletion was a story about the rape, murder, and abuse of the Jews by the Razin and Ukrainian Cossacks. In the 1953 edition of *The Quiet Don*, more than half of the occurrences of the pejorative name "Yid" were either edited out or replaced. Made at the height of official anti-Semitism, these corrections might have been intended to camouflage the real attitude toward the Jews. The censors of the 1953 edition of *The Quiet Don* were apparently worried that the strong presence of foreigners in the Red Army might be indicative of a lack of pro-Bolshevik enthusiasm among Russians. Therefore, they saw it fit to erase the passages testifying to a large number of Latvians, Chinese, and other non-Russians in Red units.

During the first two years of Khrushchev's rule (1953–64), the ideological content of literature still had much in common with that of the preceding period. The year 1955 saw the appearance of new versions of Iurii Libedinskii's *A Week* and *The Commissars* (*Komissary*, 1926) and of Ivanov's novel *Armored Train No. 14–69* (1922), all of which were heavily revised in accordance with Stalinist canons. *A Week* was reprinted without a remark about the great number of non-Russians in the Communist Party; from *The Commissars* was struck a character's statement about the oppression of the Crimean Tatars by the Soviets in 1921. *Armored Train No. 14–69* featured numerous insertions concerning not only the intervention in the Far East of the British, Americans, and Japanese, but also the atrocities they allegedly committed there.

Under Khrushchev, the censors continued expunging words regarded as offensive to national feelings. The practice was vividly manifested in works that had not been reprinted for a long time. In the 1956 edition of Sholokhov's *The Don Stories* (*Donskie rasskazy*, 1926), the word *khokhol* was crossed out in the authorial narrative. Disrespectful designations of the Chinese vanished in 1958 from *Russia Washed in Blood*, along with a hostile characterization of the Czechs as vermin to be exterminated. In 1957 censors removed from Babel's story "Berestechko" (1924) the author's observation that the Russians, living side by side with active and businesslike Jews, Ukrainians, and Poles, have developed the dogged love for work that the Russian is capable of before succumbing to lice, drink, and despair.

Two important phenomena emerged under Khrushchev. One was the theme of Russian and Soviet anti-Semitism inaugurated by Evgenii Evtushenko's "Babii Iar" (1961); the other, represented by Solzhenitsyn's "Matrena's Household" ("Matrenin dvor," 1963), was inspired by the belief that traditional moral virtues are still retained in Russian villages, although their possessors are clearly in the minority.

Progressive re-Stalinization distinguished the period from 1965 to 1985. Publishing works about Soviet repression of Russians and other nationalities became impossible. Further erosion of the faith in Marxism-Leninism intensified a search for moral and esthetic values in the prerevolutionary life of one's nation. This could be seen in the works of minority writers like Chingiz Aitmatov and in those of "village writers," particularly Valentin Rasputin. Another kind of nationalism, exemplified by authors like Valentin Pikul' and Ivan Shevtsov, smacked of jingoism.

The party policy toward nationalism varied during this period. It was tolerated by Mikhail Suslov in the second half of the 1970s, probably because of its appeal to a sizable segment of the population. Iurii Andropov, on the other hand, considered nationalism to be a threat to Marxist ideology.

Characteristic of the 1965–85 period is the sharply different treatment of the Jewish question in literary works. One group of writers, following in Evtushenko's footsteps, portrayed the Jews in a favorable light. In this group belongs Andrei Voznesenskii, with "The Call of the Lake" ("Zov ozera," 1965), which evokes the Nazi executions of Jews. Anatolii Kuznetsov's novel *Babii Iar* (1966) relates not only the massacre of Jews in Kiev but also the attitudes of the local population, which ranged from indignation to approval and collaboration. Censors, however, excluded many remarks about Jews, both compassionate and hostile, from the Soviet publication of the novel; some scenes of German brutality also fell victim to the censors' heavy hand. Anatolii Rybakov's novel *Heavy Sand* (*Tiazhelyi pesok*, 1978) combines the theme of Jewish suffering under Nazi occupation with an active resistance offered by the Jews and Belorussians. The novel appeared in *Oktiabr'* after having been rejected by several publishers.[4]

On the opposite end of the spectrum, Pikul's novel *At the Last Frontier* (*U poslednei cherty*, 1979), set in the final years of the Romanov dynasty, presents the Zionists' attempts to attain political power by manipulating high-ranking officials and, especially, Grigorii Rasputin and the tsarina. To ward off charges of anti-Semitism, Pikul' writes that the Zionists do not represent the aspirations of hard-working and oppressed Jewish people. In Shevtsov's novel *In the Name of the Father and the Son* (*Vo imia ottsa i syna*, 1970), Zionism is equated with fascism, and Trotskyism is labeled as a brand of Zionism. Enemies of communism, all three strive for world domination. Stalin is credited with having correctly guessed Trotsky's true intentions, thus saving the country from a nightmare worse than Hitlerism. To lend credence to all this nonsense, Shevtsov puts it into the mouth of an old, loyal communist, a Jew.

Shevtsov's other novel, *Love and Hatred* (*Liubov' i nenavist'*, 1970), is aimed not at Zionism in general but rather at a particular character supposedly representative of a typical Jew. Naum Gol'tser, a spoiled brat and pseudointellectual, would commit any crime for the sake of money. To avoid sharing his father's inheritance with his mother, he stabs her to death with an awl; then he opens up her stomach, removes the entrails, and winds them around her neck. Fearing being reported to the police for a number of illegal activities, he murders a girl, dismembers her body, and scatters its pieces throughout the city. Needless to say, this piling up of horrors would provoke in any sensible reader a reaction quite different from that intended by the author.

Among the first works of the *perestroika* period are Rasputin's long story "The Fire" ("Pozhar," *Nash sovremennik*, No. 7, 1985) and Viktor Astaf'ev's novel *A Sad Detective*, (*Pechal'nyi detektiv, Oktiabr'*, No. 1, 1986). Both authors offer a depressing picture of the life of the Russian people. In "The Fire" the behavior of migrant workers illustrates the depth of their moral degradation. These uprooted people defile cemeteries, drink, fight, kill one another, and terrorize the population of a Siberian settlement. In *A Sad Detective* crime and savagery are presented through the experiences of a provincial militiaman, Soshnin. A gang rapes an elderly woman, drunkards attempt to murder Soshnin himself, an intoxicated driver kills several people with his truck, and a young man keeps beating a pregnant woman with a rock until she dies. The head of Glavlit passed the novel on the condition that the chief editor of *Oktiabr'*, Anatolii Anan'ev, take full responsibility for its publication.[5]

Glasnost' lifted the taboo from works dealing with the deportation of national minorities accused of cooperating with the Nazis during World War II. In February 1987, *Oktiabr'* printed Iosif Gerasimov's story "A Knock at the Door" ("Stuk v dver' "), written twenty-seven years earlier. Its subject is a partial expulsion from Moldavia of the Moldavians in 1949. Anatolii Pristavkin's novel *The Golden Cloud Slept There* (*Nochevala tuchka zolotaia*), written in 1981 and published in 1988 (*Znamia*, Nos. 3–4), provides some details of the total deportation of the Chechens in 1944. Both authors sympathize with the victims.

On the other hand, Astaf'ev's attitude toward contemporary Georgians in his story "Catching Gudgeon in Georgia" ("Lovlia peskarei v Gruzii," *Nash sovremennik*, No. 5, 1986) generated considerable controversy. Some Georgian writers and intellectuals complained about Astaf'ev's description of the black market activities of their compatriots and about his comparison of a stream of cars driven by young, affluent Georgians with a "monkey parade."[6] Most likely Astaf'ev had no intention of insulting the Georgians as a nationality. On the whole he shows them as decent, generous people with impressive cultural traditions. It was his admiration of an old Georgian temple that prompted him to create an abhorrent image of its Mongolian desecrators. They built campfires directly in the temple, skinned their horses, gorged themselves on bloody, undercooked horsemeat, and finally fell down themselves, "burying their slant-eyed snouts into stinking horse dung."[7] In his August 24, 1986, letter to Astaf'ev, the historian Natan Eidel'man called the portrayal of the Mongols racist and immoral.[8]

In 1988 the editors of *Oktiabr'* censored in Vasilii Grossman's *Life and Fate (Zhizn' i sud'ba*, 1960) a paragraph about deported national minorities and Jews. Grossman wrote that the battle of Stalingrad decided the fate of the Kalmyks, Crimean Tatars, Balkars, and Chechens as well as Jewish actors and writers, whose execution in 1952 was to precede a trial of Jewish doctors (which, fortunately, did not occur because of Stalin's death). The main reason for the deletion must have been the reference to the persecution of Jews in the Soviet Union. This explains the disappearance from *Oktiabr'* of Chapter 32, which analyzes anti-Semitism and its causes. The journal, however, printed the chapter several months later.

Anti-Semitism has become one of the most sensitive issues in the Soviet Union today. *Glasnost'* has made it possible to express both pro- and anti-Jewish sentiments with increasing frankness. Among writers sympathetic to Jews is Voznesenskii, whose poem "The Ditch" ("Rov," *Iunost'*, No. 7, 1986) condemns the looting of a mass grave containing the remains of Jews murdered by the Nazis in 1941. Sergei Kaledin's story, "A Construction Battalion" ("Stroibat," *Novyi mir*, No. 4, 1989) has an attractive Jewish soldier named Fishel' Itskovich. A carpenter by profession, he comes from the Carpathians, where many Jews lived in villages. To save the life of his fellow soldier, he kills a brutal military guard. In the end, it is a Russian soldier who betrays Fishel' to their commander. Wicked activity of an anti-Semitic writer is represented in Iurii Nagibin's story "The Internationalist" ("Internatsionalist," *Knizhnoe obozrenie*, September 1, 1989). At the end of the story, Nagibin speaks of today's growth of chauvinism and intimates the possibility of pogroms in the future.

Literary works promoting anti-Jewish feelings include Vasilii Belov's recent novels *Everything Is Still Ahead* (*Vse vperedi, Nash sovremennik*, Nos. 7–8, 1986) and *The Year of the Great Change* (*God velikogo pereloma, Novyi mir*, no. 3, 1989). *Everything Is Still Ahead* features an unpleasant Jewish character, a cynic and slanderer, devoid of patriotism. The second novel communicates a fairly common notion that it was the Jews who brought the worst calamities upon the Russian people. High-ranking Jews are shown to be the architects of the homicidal policy of collectivization. The destruction of the Russian peasantry, Belov suggests, was inspired not by class struggle, but by national or, possibly, religious considerations. This suggestion is preposterous: collectivization was carried out for political and economic reasons by a party whose leadership consisted of members of different nationalities.

Another negative view of Jews is displayed in the novel *Special Regime* (*Osobyi rezhim*), produced by an obscure writer, Boris Sotnikov. Quotations from this novel printed in a reader's letter to the editor of *Ogonyok* indicate that one of Sotnikov's aims is to demonstrate a variety of ways used by the Jews to gain control over the Soviet state.[9] Sotnikov harps on the fact that Stalin's children Iakov and Svetlana married Jews and presented their father with half-Jewish grandchildren. Wives of Bukharin and Molotov were Jewish, and Stalin himself cohabitated with Roza Kaganovich. Then Sotnikov makes Stalin share with Beria his ideas about Jewish ascendancy. Jews, the dictator says, have obtained important positions in the press, radio, and publishing houses, as well as in well-paying professions; to speed up their advancement, they resort to bribes and patronage. Trotsky, Zinov'ev, and Kamenev had a great number of Jews in their entourages. It is worth noting that Sotnikov's novel was serialized in *Dnepropetrovskaia pravda*, the organ of the party committee of the Dnepropetrovsk province. This bespeaks the presence of anti-Semitism in the upper strata of the party. The same applies to the military, whose publishing house, Voenizdat, reprinted in 1988 Shevtsov's *Love and Hatred* and *In the Name of the Father and the Son*. And in 1989 Pikul's *At the Last Frontier* was serialized in the Voronezh magazine *Pod"em* under the original and more expressive title of *The Evil Spirit* (*Nechistaia sila*).

No doubt Belov, Sotnikov, Shevtsov, and Pikul' can only exacerbate anti-Jewish feelings in a certain part of the Soviet population. The same type of reaction has been prompted by a completely different work, Grossman's tale *Forever Flowing* (*Vse techet*, 1963), published in the sixth issue of *Oktiabr'* for 1989. Grossman has no personal animosity toward the Russian people, but his concept of their history and character is likely to be perceived as unjust and offensive by a considerable number of Russians. According to Grossman, the Russian soul was formed during a thousand-year-long period of slavery. Moreover, he feels that Russians lack a sense of dignity. Lenin's intolerance, cruelty, fanaticism, and contempt for liberty, Grossman asserts, were rooted in the Russian history of *nesvoboda* (unfreedom).

In response to the publication of *Forever Flowing*, Igor' Shafarevich and two other individuals sent a complaint to the secretariat of the board of the Writers' Union of the Russian Republic about what they called "a consistently anti-Russian policy" of the journal *Oktiabr'*.[10] In addition to *Forever Flowing*, the letter mentions Andrei Siniavskii's book *Strolls with Pushkin* (*Progulki s Pushkinym*, 1975), a fragment of which was published in the fourth issue of *Oktiabr'* for 1989, and the announced publication of Aleksandr Ianov's writing. Anan'ev defended the publication of *Forever Flowing* in two recent interviews.[11] While he does not agree with all of Grossman's points, Anan'ev finds his ideas interesting, surprising, and stimulating.

For the sake of their survival and retention of power, Soviet leaders created an artificial symbiosis of two mutually exclusive elements—the internationalist Marxist ideology and popular Russian patriotism. The ultimate goal was the linguistic Russification of all other nationalities with the purpose of producing a new Soviet person, without national distinctions. The failure of this ill-conceived design is amply demonstrated by today's national tensions and bloodshed. I hope that this national tragedy will eventually receive a profound and impartial treatment in imaginative literature.

3 The Village Writers and

the Single-Stream Theory of

Russian History

The phrase "single stream" (*edinyi potok*) entered Russian thought as a by-product of the October Revolution. It is associated with efforts to assess the continuity or discontinuity of the pre- and post-revolutionary phases of Russian cultural and social institutions. That we, or anyone else, should be concerned with this concept so long after the event attests to the lack of consensus among the Bolshevik revolutionaries and their supporters as to the nature of national cultures during the "stage" of the "dictatorship of the proletariat," as well as to the terms of kinship and alienation between the new "socialist" order and the old regime. Just before the February Revolution, Lenin and Bukharin had a dispute about the nature of the culture that would arise after the demise of capitalism in Russia. Others disputed this as well. Organizations and movements emphasizing the break with the past arose in profusion following the October Revolution. The

Proletcult, the Russian Assocation of Proletarian Writers (RAPP), the Left Front in Arts, Pokrovskian historiography, N. Ia. Marr's "japhetidological" linguistics, and Michurinist genetics placed great emphasis on the chasm separating the new order from the old. Such views were sometimes expressed without the approval of the ideological sentries of communism, including V. I. Lenin. Lenin's remark regarding the necessity for recognizing two distinct cultures within any national culture under capitalism provided a useful yardstick for the division of important figures from the past into those who exhibited objectively progressive or democratic tendencies and those who did not.

When the dust from the cultural skirmishing of the 1920s had settled, it became clear that the prudent answer to this question of Soviet Russia's ties to the old order was more or less to avoid the question altogether. The sad experiences of thousands of intellectuals in the 1930s attest to the dangers of engaging in the controversy over Soviet Russia's links with the Russian past.

It is, therefore, not surprising that explorations of this question were first done outside the USSR. Emigré Russians, including the proponents of such movements as National Bolshevism and the Changing Landmarks (*Smena Vekh*) group regarded the October 1917 break with the past as incomplete and by no means final. The philosopher Nicholas Berdiaev, writing from Paris, also emphasized the cultural function of the Soviet state as the inheritor, however imperfect and unworthy, of Russia's past sins and past virtues. It is easy enough for us to see that the sentiments expressed from abroad had supporters within the Soviet state, particularly when we remember that the advocates of a clean break with the past were exterminated by the Stalinists in the 1930s. We should also remember the relative ease with which the Soviet leadership during its war against Germany reverted to the symbols and traditions of Russian patriotism.

The rejection of Russian patriotism as a guiding force in Soviet cultural policy during the postwar period is associated with the name of Andrei Zhdanov. The fragility of that "internationalist" policy becomes apparent when it is juxtaposed with the expanded boundaries of the Soviet Union after World War II and with the extension of Soviet influence to Eastern Europe. The post-Stalinist compromise, often associated with the name of the party ideologue Mikhail Suslov but doubtlessly the work of many hands, appears to have retained powerful symbols associated with Russian nationalism and an overwhelmingly Russian national content within a cultural policy designed to produce a "Soviet" culture closely controlled by party organs.

The story of the reemergence in Soviet writing of the single-stream theory of Russian history has been told comprehensively in other places and does not require retelling here.[1] It will be enough merely to recall that in the late 1960s and early '70s, the monthly *Molodaia gvardiia* printed a number of audacious articles by Viktor Chalmaev, Sergei Semanov, Mikhail Lobanov, and others, asserting in an uncompromising tone that the genius of the Russian commonwealth informed and guided the actions and thoughts of Lenin no less than those of Prince Pozharskii, Field Marshal Kutuzov, or Ivan Kireevskii. The nationalists at *Molodaia gvardiia* were evicted by the authorities from that particular bully pulpit and were silenced for a time, but, interestingly enough, those who combined their public displeasure with the single-stream nationalists with ridicule were also subjected to censure. Aleksandr Iakovlev, who delivered a strongly worded dismissal of the pretentions of the *Molodaia gvardiia* group, was himself rerouted from his Central Committee post to the embassy in Ottawa. After writing a cuttingly ironic dissection of the nationalists' patriotic fervor, Aleksandr Dement'ev was removed from the editorial board of *Novyi mir*. Furthermore, in spite of the severe and oft expressed disapproval of the single-stream theory by the highest authorities for its being at odds with the class analysis of social dynamics and therefore injurious to the multinational Soviet state, public expositions of views similar to those expressed in 1969 and 1970 by Chalmaev and Lobanov have increased exponentially since that time.

In a separate and perhaps coincidental development, the late 1960s saw a shift in the thematic orientation of the writers known as the *derevenshchiki*, or village writers. One perspicacious observer noted in the *Literaturnaia gazeta* in 1971 that this group of writers was shifting from concerns with "socioeconomic and economic-organizational problems" to "moral, ethical, psychological, and even philosophical" problems.[2] Looking back on this period from our present vantage point, we see that it is inevitable for this school of writing to also take up the question of the Russian village's links with the past, since, as one critic has observed, the early seventies saw basically two new and well-received trends in writing—fantasy and *istoritsizm*, or the incorporation into a fictive text of often fancifully conceived evocations of the Russian past.[3]

There is a temptation, when one is speaking about a group of writers who are called "Villagers," to imagine somehow that the Russian village is something entirely concrete and easily fixed in time and space. One often could read about such conventional villages in the writings of the "sketch writers" (*ocherkisty*) in the 1950s and '60s. Writers like Valentin Ovechkin, Efim Dorosh, and Gavriil Troepol'skii wrote rather straightforwardly about milkmaids, collective farm chairmen and agronomists, and adorable dogs. But the village of the 1970s and '80s can be as abstract as Dostoevsky's cities or Gogol's version of a provincial Russian town in *Dead Souls*. For writers such as Vasilii Belov, Valentin Rasputin, Evgenii Nosov, and Viktor Astaf'ev, the Russian village is a place where important ideas are acted out and where the actors clarify their understanding of their world. The phrase "little motherland" (*malaia rodina*) may be used to sum up the role of the mythical village in these writings, for the village truly represents there a little motherland.

While the Villagers often employ grandiose language in order to evoke the old lore and the informing genius of the *narod*, they do not as a rule excessively idealize the inhabitants of the village as a class. For the most part they are all still too conscious of Fedor Abramov's devastating critique of the "conflictless" depictions of the countryside in the stories of Semen Babaevskii and other literary footstools of Stalinism. Trotsky's derogatory term *muzhikovstvuiushchie*, denoting writers predisposed to glorify rural life, does not usually apply to the modern village writers as a consistent attribute. One exception is Nikolai Ustinov, Sergei Zalygin's wise oracle in the novel *The Commission* (*Komissiia*, 1975), who ruminates while plowing that God must be a peasant and probably hitches up the ox for a bit of plowing on His day off. The modern writer's Russian village has its fair share of homebred monsters. Vice, greed, and all manner of meanness are likely to be projected even into settings where modern contaminating agents such as the "administrative system" or non-Russian meddlers have not yet arrived. Yet the contemporary Russian village is held to be a tacit and unconscious guardian of a very powerful concept—the "historical memory of the people" (*istoricheskaia pamiat' naroda*), a phrase one often encounters in the outlets of nationalist, and particularly rural-nationalist, opinion. Valentin Rasputin uses the term "historical amnesia" to refer to the loss of this reservoir of national wisdom. Aleksandr Khvatov, a nationalist critic close to the Villagers, prefers the term "national nihilism" to convey this sense of loss.[4] This topic preoccupies many of the Villagers these days, among them Vologda writer Vasilii Belov. The title of his recent, controversial novel *Everything Lies Before Us* (*Vse vperedi*, 1986) is an ironic reference to Belov's belief that Russians are becoming perilously indifferent to the lessons and commands of their national past. This is a pet bugbear with Belov. One may recall that in his play *Kashchei the Deathless* (*Kashchei Bessmertnyi*), based on national myths, the tribes of *Rus'* are castigated by Kashchei for "needing yesterday," that is for their insistence on knowing and being guided by the past.

The derogator of the past has become a stock figure in village prose. A typical example is the archaeologist Stasik in Boris Mozhaev's story "The Three of Them" ("Troe"), who defends his lack of reverence for the past by saying, "I'm a scientist. For the scientist the past exists only for the interests of the present."

The instinctive guardians of the historical memory are a conservative and almost anachronistic body of positive heroes. They may be the last old-fashioned positive heroes to be found in serious fiction. Perhaps the most conspicuous achievement of the Villagers will turn out to be their effort to re-create the positive heroes in an artistic atmosphere that is neither vulgar nor servile. These good people possess the positive qualities of what Philippa Lewis has called the "traditional peasant." She writes of these men (alas, they are usually men, like their makers): "The traditional peasant knows what is good and bad, is a '*sovestlivyi chelovek*,' a man of good conscience, loyal to his family, people, and land (his sacrifices during the war are much emphasized) and strong in his loyalty and instinctive knowledge of life." [5]

I would add to those remarks the following additional qualities: these men are usually communists or at least sympathizers with the village version of Leninism; they are wary of the cant and slogans issuing from the cities; they esteem consciousness over reason as the highest of human endowments; and they possess through instinct and experience the ability to know when to exercise judgment according to a relative measure and when according to an absolute one. Fedor Abramov's Mikhail Priaslin in the tetralogy *Brothers and Sisters* is a predecessor of this type, and there is no shortage of examples.

Their emphatic insistence on the primacy of national experience over what is deprecated as "expedience" (*tselnosoobraznost'*) in service to the multinational Soviet state and over the shibboleths of the class struggle as the primal explanatory factor in human development, sets the nationalist writers on a collision course with those intellectuals and functionaries who advocate what has recently come to be called "democratic culture" or even "Soviet culture." The result has been a shrill battle of words, with the advocates of democratic culture firing off salvos from the pages of *Znamia, Novyi mir, Sovetskaia kul'tura,* and the like, while the nationalists return fire from *Molodaia gvardiia, Nash sovremennik, Moskva,* and the Sovremennik Publishing House established in 1970 by the Russian Republic's Union of Writers in order to trumpet the Russian nationalist position. Some of this trench-fighting has been carried out by writers of prose and poetry. Like their nineteenth-century *narodnik* predecessors, the Villagers devote much of their time to journalism. Catherine Nepomniashchii has noted that the Villagers often mix fiction and nonfiction in their writing. Her observations on the Villagers' indifference to traditional generic boundaries merit repeating here: "In their self-imposed role as chroniclers of the dying Russian village and guardians of the Russian cultural heritage, the ruralists have shown a marked preference for nonfictional narrative forms, and, in general, there is a thin line dividing fiction from nonfiction in rural prose."[6] Thus Rasputin, Astaf'ev, Belov, and Mozhaev have all appeared in *Pravda* and other newspapers in the past year expressing their views on questions important to them, while the poets Evgenii Evtushenko and Andrei Voznesenskii, the dramatist Mikhail Shatrov, and the novelist Anatolii

Rybakov in turn have warned against the dangers inherent in national particularism in extreme and exclusivistic form. Critics, historians, economists, and others have happily entered the controversy. Russian nationalism, one might say, has changed from a cottage industry to big business. *Nash sovremennik* has its own in-house historian in Apollon Grigor'evich Kuz'min, doctor of historical sciences, who adds to the rural-nationalist orientation of that journal the imprimatur of an academic personage. For some time now Kuz'min has been engaged in a polemic with Seten Kaltakhchiian, doctor of philosophical sciences, over the pros and cons of the single-stream theory of Russian culture.

Kaltakhchiian initiated this exchange with his article "Where Is the Single Stream Going?" in the newspaper *Sovetskaia kul'tura* in 1987.[7] His article bore the subtitle "Concerning the Leninist Conception of Two Cultures and the Distortions of It."

Kaltakhchiian attacks the alleged justifications for what he calls the "reanimation of the pre-Marxist theory of the 'single stream.' " These justifications, or "proofs," fall, according to the author, into such categories as "idealistic, biophysiological, and even religious-theological." Kaltakhchiian takes to the woodshed a number of ruralist and nationalist writers, including the Villager Vladimir Soloukhin, who propounds a theory of national immutability based on what he calls "encoding" (*zaprogrammirovannost'*) and who, furthermore, would welcome into the pantheon of worthy Russian thinkers such reactionaries as Vasilii Rozanov and Konstantin Leont'ev.

Kaltakhchiian examines and finds wanting several historians and critics whose works often appear in the journals frequented by the Villagers, including Aleksandr Khvatov, Petr Vykhodtsev, Vadim Kozhinov, and Apollon Kuz'min. The author charges that these thinkers wish to replace the Marxist formula that views humans and society as composed of accumulations of all social relations with an idealistic concept, namely that the prime factor in human life is immutable affiliation or bondedness with a given ethnic entity.

Apollon Kuz'min was quick to reply to Kaltakhchiian's charges with his article "Shoals in the Extraterritorial Stream" in *Nash sovremennik*.[8] Kuz'min writes that one must conclude from his opponent's reasoning that patriotism must perforce be identified with nationalism, and nationalism with chauvinism. He further charges that advocates of so-called democratic culture, and that includes Kaltakhchiian, are ideologically direct descendants of "Proletcult and RAPP anti-historicism," the product not of Marxist thinking but rather of the influence, exerted through Bogdanov, Lunacharskii, and others, of the philosopher Ernst Mach.

Kuz'min continues this line of reasoning in a subsequent article entitled "To Which Temple Are We Seeking a Road?" in which he states that Stalin, Trotsky, Rykov, and Bukharin were all imbued with the influence of Machism, the essence of which is, in Kuz'min's telling, indifference to life and to nationality. This spirit led to the assaults in the 1920s and '30s on "patriotism and its bearer, the peasant." [9]

Kuz'min also uses this article to reply to E. Losoto's earlier article in which Vasilii Belov and Viktor Astaf'ev are criticized for what Losoto calls, echoing Lenin's phrase, "flirting with Goddikins" (*koketnichan' e s bozhen'koi*) and in which the village writers are criticized for their loud protests over the destruction of churches in the 1920s and for their refusal to admit that the churches were not only cultural monuments but also "nests of clerical reaction." Kuz'min suggests that Losoto is merely a belated flowering of the spirit of RAPP and the Proletcult who wished to short-circuit the "historical memory of the people."

The dispute between Losoto and Kuz'min calls to mind the question of just what role religion—and in the present context we are speaking quite specifically of Russian Orthodoxy—plays in the writings of the Villagers and of Russian nationalists as a whole. Kuz'min, interestingly, appears to defend the interests of Russian Orthodoxy in this article, but in his historical writings he has taken pains to exclude himself from those who identify Russian culture as coterminous with the acceptance or imposition of Christianity in ancient *Rus'*, preferring instead to place emphasis on the relatively high material culture predating the mass Christianization of *Rus'* in the tenth century and enduring as a separate and unassimilated source of culture apart from Orthodoxy.

At this juncture it seems appropriate to address the question of whether Orthodoxy is in fact an integral and inexpugnable element in the version of Russianism embraced by the Villagers, or whether it is merely a botched Byzantine skin graft, an important but sometimes facultative adjunct of other, more fundamental features of Russian culture. It is sometimes said to be a central feature of Russian life and culture. Vladimir Soloukhin took this position in his lyrical ruminations called "Pebbles on the Palm" ("Kameshki na ladoni"). When the journal *Nash sovremennik* persisted in printing new selections of that work after being warned in the party organs that they were "flirting with Goddikins," the editorial board received a severe and formal reprimand from the party. This occurred in 1981–82. In the light of more recent developments in the USSR it is unlikely that such threats and reprimands would accompany the publication of Soloukhin's writings today. Boris Mozhaev has used stronger language to defend the role of Russian Orthodoxy twice in 1989 in *Pravda*. In February 1989, Mozhaev cited Christianity as the basic source of morality among Russians. He wrote: "Christianity, the millennium that established the ideals of the Russian people, was rejected and consequently forbidden in large measure by the official authorities. The first code of morality offered by them in place of the Christian code was exceedingly simple and easily understood: Whatever is useful for the revolution is moral. Sometimes it was expressed in even simpler terms: Plunder that which is the product of plunder (*grab nagrablennoe*)." [10] Five months later, Mozhaev returned to the pages of *Pravda* and to the subject of Russian Christianity. He wrote that Russians reacted strongly to the plundering and closing of churches, because these structures were not only places of spiritual communion but also "temples of history, where one generation was able to commune with their ancestors in a common rite and faith." [11] Mozhaev also called to his readers' attention the important role of the church as a rallying point for Russian patriotism, citing Sergii of Radonezh's services to the Princes of Muscovy and Kuz'ma Minin's inspiration to free Russia from the turmoils of the Time of Troubles while praying in the cathedral of Nizhnii Novgorod.

In the most recent installment of Vasilii Belov's long novel about the forced collectivization of the Soviet countryside at the end of the 1920s, it is left to a priest, Father Nikolai Perovskii, to utter the solemn dirge over Russia's ruin at the hands of party cadres overseeing the arrests, dispossessions, and dislocation of peasants, both prosperous and poor, righteous and wicked. Imprisoned in the town of Priluki in a cathedral now serving as a prison of "kulaks" and other suspicious elements, this priest rediscovers his lapsed faith as he reflects upon the persecution of clergy and worshippers, the desecration of altars and of graves—even that of Sergii of Radonezh—the theft of precious stones from venerated icons, and the removal of bells from churches. Of the last activity Father Perovskii observes, "The copper that once struck fear in the enemies of Orthodox *Rus'* is used by traitors to harm Russia." [12] Belov, true to form, then has the rededicated priest undergo martyrdom at the hands of the Jew and communist Semen Rufimovich Raiberg.

Even the village writer Petr Proskurin, whose portrait of Stalin in the epic trilogy published in the '70s and early '80s is as favorable as Belov's is censorious, combines with his nostalgia for the old tyrant an insistence on the recognition of Russian Orthodoxy as an imperative fixture of Russian life and culture.

Some village writers orient themselves toward Russian Orthodoxy from a kind of ditheism (*dvoeverie*) wherein the rituals of paganism share honors with Christian rites. This may be seen in Valentin Rasputin's novel *Farewell to Matera* (*Proshchanie s Materoi*), which celebrates the continuity of Russian folk culture from an unreal, pantheistic perspective. Yet another wrinkle in this subject is provided by the recently published first part of Arsenii Larionov's novel *Lida's Ashes* (*Lidina gar'*), in which Russian Orthodoxy is treated with respect but with less reverence than the rites of the Old Believer sectarians. The novel is set in the North, east of Arkhangel'sk, where many schismatics were driven in the seventeenth century. The novel's hero, Seliverst Kuz'min, calls the Archpriest Avvakum the "first genius and first Russian intellectual to come from the people." [13]

One may also find within the establishment of Russian nationalism and among the Villagers sentiments lacking in sympathy for the proposition that Russian culture is indissolubly intertwined with Christianity. Julia Wishnewski recently observed in *Survey* that a branch of the nationalists clustered around the *Pamiat'* and *Otechestvo* groups find their mystical forebears among the legendary heroes of pre-baptismal *Rus'*. They are said to have engendered a cult of the late artist Konstantin Vasil'ev, who once painted a canvas portraying the victory of Il'ia of Murom over "the Christian plague." [14] One can also find this trend among the volumes of historical fiction that the Molodaia Gvardiia and Sovremennik publishing houses have been turning out in profusion. Gennadii Osetrov's novel *Death of a Sorcerer (Gibel' volkhva)* is a very anti-Christian work, in which the intolerant and alien cult of Jesus is shown in decidedly unflattering hues, while the animistic paganism of the hero sorcerer Vseslav is depicted as the natural outgrowth of aspirations and folkways expressing the genius of the tribes of *Rus'*. [15]

A strong anti-Christian bias may be found in the recent novels of the young Siberian writer Sergei Trofimovich Alekseev. Although Alekseev hails from a small, now deserted village in the Tomsk *oblast'* and shares most of the interests, convictions, and animosities of the best-known village writers—anti-westernism, environmentalism, anti-cosmopolitanism, and ancestor worship on a par with Japanese Shinto—he stands somewhat apart from his peers in his outspoken rejection of Christianity as a defining factor in the development of Russian culture.

In his novel *The Word (Slovo)*, the story passes between the years 988 and 1961. One story line is devoted to the life and work of Nikita Gudoshnikov, a philologist who has dedicated his life to finding and saving for posterity the ancient manuscripts of the eastern Slavs. In one respect Gudoshnikov fits the profile of heroes in village fiction (even though he happens to hail from the "big" village of Moscow): he becomes enraged when reminded of the antihistorical bias of New Era organizations such as RAPP, Proletcult, and the Left Front of Art (LEF). Gudoshnikov is unlike many of the Villagers in his refusal to identify Old Russian culture with Christian rites. For Gudoshnikov Christianity and Russian culture are not merely separate, they are opposed.

In one of the novel's episodes set in the early 1920s, Gudoshnikov has left his position at Petrograd University in order to seek an ancient manuscript, written in pre-Cyrillic script allegedly used before Orthodoxy's establishment as a state religion in *Rus'*. The quest takes him

to the Sever'ianov monastery, situated on the Pechora River in the far
north. The monastery has been closed by the communists, its sole
inhabitants being old Petr Lavrent'ev, who had been kept a prisoner
in the monastery's dungeon for sixty years and flogged by each suc-
cessive abbot for having expressed atheism as a young student and
never recanting, and the stray dogs that are invoked several times
throughout the novel as a symbol, one must assume, of the rupture of
natural life by the dogmas of the church. As Gudoshnikov gazes in
admiration at the beauty of a church in the derelict monastery, we read
that "he forgot that the church was standing on the ground, with its
foundations sunk into the hard earth. And there, in the depths, stands
a dungeon with rusting chains, slime-covered walls, disgusting red-
dish rats, with its stench, and the blackness of eternal night. This
elegant, magnificent church and, for that matter, the world of Christianity, could also be seen in this subterranean image, which also was
created for man's benefit." [16] When later Gudoshnikov thinks of old
Petr, who, freed by the revolution, has become a quite literal icono-
clast, chopping up holy relics and posing for atheistic magazines, he
thinks to himself, "Old Petr is right. Religion had made beggars of
men, had forced them to bow down before the mighty and beg for
mercy." [17]

Sergei Alekseev's negative orientation toward Christianity may be
seen also in his latest novel, *Strife* (*Kramola*), which appeared in 1989
in the first four numbers of *Nash sovremennik*. Although the novel is
set mainly in the years before, during, and after the October Revolution, three chapters are devoted to a very original retelling of Prince
Igor's campaign against the Cumans. Igor is shown to be torn between
the new Byzantine cult of Jesus and the old Slavic faith. As in Osetrov's novel, Alekseev's sympathies come down decidedly on the side
of East Slavic paganism as a faith consonant with the aspirations and
lifestyle of the tribes of ancient *Rus'*. [18]

Of those Villagers who do and those who do not include Russian
Orthodoxy as a keystone of Russian morality and national continuity,
it may be said that they reject the notion of a clean break with the past.
And, of course, a necessary corollary of such a position is the dimi-
nution of the explanatory power of the class struggle and of class distinctions in general and an at least partial replacement of class by an

interpretation of *narodnost'* as an existential state of elect affiliation, rather than as self-consciousness, which Iurii Surovtsev and other advocates of "Soviet culture" or "democratic culture" have put forward.[19]

The question of the "unity" (*tselnost'*) of Russian culture before and after the October Revolution leads one inevitably to consider the question of how the Villagers relate to the culture of the period preceding 1917. Here we see, or seem to see, the adoption of the nationalist position worked out by Sergei Semanov, Mikhail Lobanov, Viktor Chalmaev, and the other adherents of Russian cultural fusionism in the late 1960s. The nationalists' position on the nineteenth century can be expressed by paraphrasing the title of Jean-François Revel's book *Without Marx or Jesus*: it might be called "With both Dostoevsky and Saltykov." In fact, Aleksandr Khvatov, a literary historian and stablemate of the Villagers at *Nash sovremennik*, does attempt to show in his *Paths of Nationalism and Realism* (*Puti narodnosti i realizma*, 1980) that Dostoevsky and Saltykov were united in their love of the narod even though this love might have been expressed with different nuances of affection. There is no shortage of examples of such reductionism. A couple of years ago the Sovremennik Publishing House issued a collection of stories by Sergei Lykoshin entitled *Behind the White Wall* (*Za beloi stenoi*). This book drew criticism from antichauvinist critics but also won a Young Communist Youth award. The book contains an essay that begins with a quotation from the Slavophile writer Ivan Kireevskii: "Believe in humanity, in the power of genius, in the future, in yourself. Know where you come from in order to know where you are going." (*Verui v chelovechestvo, v silu geniia, v budushchee, v samogo sebia. Znai otkuda ty iskhodish', chtoby znat', kuda stremish'sia.*)

Lykoshin then immediately, in the very next line, launches quite implausibly in my view into an interpretation of Vissarion Belinskii as a model of what a Russian nationalist-minded critic should be.[20] In a similar vein, Mikhail Lobanov's biography of Aleksandr Ostrovskii states that, contrary to what the radical critic Dobroliubov thought he discerned in Ostrovskii's cast of characters, there never was any dark kingdom in the mid-century Russian merchantry.[21]

A truly remarkable occurrence over the past twenty years has been the shift toward Dostoevskian positions in considerations of Russianness. It is most significant that the Villager Boris Mozhaev chooses to tell a story of Stalin's collectivization drive with a subtext taken from Dostoevsky's *The Possessed*. Mozhaev's most important spokesperson in *Peasant Men and Women* (*Muzhiki i baby*) is the schoolteacher Dmitrii Uspenskii, who easily rivals the writers of the "Landmarks" group (*Vekhovtsy*) as a critic of the prerevolutionary tradition of radical intelligentsia.

Recently, Valentin Rasputin gave an interview in which he insisted on the civic necessity for Russians to read the literature of their past. The only writers he listed in this regard, for whom he says Russians should set aside "free, almost sacred time," are Dostoevsky, Tolstoy, and Nikolai Fedorov. The threesome is rather telling, especially the inclusion of Fedorov, the eccentric philosopher whose dream for Russia envisioned life in museum-like villages focused on the village cemetery.[22]

The mind of the village writer easily assimilates the Russian nationalist bifurcation of the October Revolution into its positive and negative parts. The negative parts are likely to include the full-throated titanism and worldly cosmopolitanism found among the enthusiasts of the New Epoch in the aftermath of the October Revolution and before what may be called the Stalinist synthesis. The term "the twenties" in the vocabulary of the nationalists usually conveys the idea of a decade in which many things went wrong. Among the Villagers two common grievances left over from those days are, first, a concern over the failure of the authorities to revere or take into account Russia's past and, second, the predisposition of the ideological leadership of the state not to recognize the peasantry as an enduring institution worthy of respect and care. The critic Vadim Kozhinov has written about the "antihistoricism" of such literary associations as RAPP and the Proletcult. Apollon Kuz'min has suggested that internationally minded intellectuals and state officials sought to erase the historical memory of the people in the 1920s. Others are likely to blame the OPOIAZ (Society for the Study of Poetic Language), some of the more enthusiastic slogans of the Left Front for the Arts, or Viktor Shklovskii's statements about the need for a clean break with the past.

Sergei Zalygin, who is, of course, not an extreme nationalist by any means and who has been critical in his fiction of Russian chauvinists, nonetheless introduced into his novels about the 1920s, *The Commission* (*Komissiia*) and *After the Storm* (*Posle buri*), representatives of the attitude wherein all of Russia's past and traditions are to be swept into the dustbin. In *The Commission* the village eccentric Kudeiar espouses a sort of rustic gnosticism that includes the belief that all that exists is fatally tainted with the past and should be put to the flame. He even suggests to the novel's hero, the wise and resourceful Nikolai Ustinov, that they leap together into the flames of a burning hut.

The Villagers generally maintain an unforgiving attitude toward any inclination or even tolerance for modernism in any form. But this feeling goes even deeper than that. They tend to assume that a widespread and enduring conspiracy against the "historical memory" and against village life has long existed and continues to exist in the USSR. There is an unwillingness to impute to any decision or recommendation about altering agrarian life or conditions a merely economic motivation. This attitude is now being projected back in time by the Villagers in order to reconstruct the rationale for that most fateful process in the life of the Russian peasantry—the period of forced collectivization, commencing in the year 1929.

Vasilii Belov's novel *Eves* (*Kanuny*, 1987) has generated much discussion in the Soviet Union. It is said that two recent resignations from the editorial board of *Novyi mir* were the direct result of that journal's decision to print parts three and four of the novel. In March 1989, *Novyi mir* printed the most recent installment, which bears the ironic title of *Year of the Great Change* (*God velikogo pereloma*). The title is taken from a speech by Stalin commemorating the twelfth anniversary of the October Revolution. The word used by Stalin for the revolutionary change is *perelom*, which also conveys the idea of a break or fracture. The meaning here is that of a break of faith by the party leadership with the Soviet peasantry. The novel is expansive, as recent village fiction has tended to be, but is mainly concerned with the onslaught—and that is the appropriate word—visited upon two villages of the Vologda *oblast'* . The actions of the authorities and the fate of the Villagers are set against the background of Russian history through frequent evocations of events from the distant past and by the use in some passages of a narrative tone reminiscent of the Old Russian chronicles. The first three parts of the novel bear the subtitle "A Chronicle of the End of the 1920s," whereas *Year of the Great Change*, has the subtitle "A Chronicle of Nine Months." At the beginning of the latter installment the narrator, who is not loath to reveal himself to be Vasilii Belov, regrets the lack of a faithful chronicler of these events, and so supplies his own beginning: "In the year one thousand nine hundred and twenty nine, on the Feast Day of St. Filip, and with the assent of God, Iakov Iakovlev, the son of a Grodno pharmacist, was in the Kremlin in Moscow established as Commissar over all Christians and toilers of the soil." [23] Thus, the stage is set: it is Iakovlev, whose real name, we are informed, was Epshtein, a non-Russian and non-peasant, who is deputed to the Jew Lazar Kaganovich, identified by the narrator as an "executioner of nations" (*palach narodov*), who in turn will be the instrument for destroying the free peasantry for the non-Russian Stalin. The countryside, we are told, is about to be attacked by "fanatical internationalists" bent on ending a world alien to their spirits and experience.

Stalin, who figures interestingly in the novel's cast of characters, is in Belov's telling a man bearing a grudge against the peasantry for a beating suffered as a young man at the hands of soldiers, whom Stalin sees as peasants in different clothes. Stalin refers to peasants as "dung bags" (*meshki s der'mom*). But even Stalin is seen as something of a victim. At the beginning of *Year of the Great Change* it is hinted that the ultimate culprit behind the slaughter and dislocation of the peasants is Trotsky, who, it is noted, has left Russia, but not before leaving behind malevolent seeds that "fear neither the frosts of Siberia nor the drought of the steppe." Thus, Trotsky is the ultimate initiator of the plans Iakovlev carries in his briefcase, plans which, according to the narrator, "portended a ruinous path for a great country that would in considerable measure determine the future of the entire world."

If there are many large villains in Belov's novel, there are also a few small villains, and foremost among them is Ignashka Sopronov, a lazy but opportunistic peasant, a former and future member of the Communist Party, an envious denouncer of upright and reasonable villagers, and lately a source of some conflict in Soviet journalism over whether such a lump of an ignoramus could figure out the first thing about Trotskyism. Even the academic journal *Voprosy istorii* recently carried a piece criticizing Belov and other Villagers for trying to shift the blame for the collectivization drive onto Communist Party figures such as Trotsky and Zinov'ev, who were by then far away from the levers of control.

Belov's sympathetic characters are by no means all peasants, but they share a deep affection for national traditions and a loathing for the cant and vengefulness of the collectivizers. His Dr. Preobrazhenskii speaks of Russia's self-destruction and says it is not the result of class struggle but of an assault on nationalism and religion. The engineer Vladimir Prozorov, former member of the gentry and former revolutionary, is imprisoned as a saboteur for having questioned the sturdiness of a structure's foundation. There are also dedicated, compassionate communists in the village, one of whom quits the party in disgust. Others are turned out of the party for "lack of vigilance."

When the time comes to arrest and dispossess the kulaks in the village, none are to be found. It then falls to Ignashka Sopronov to have arrested those villagers against whom he bears grudges. When two peasants are arbitrarily seized are executed, Belov uses an uncharacteristically subtle irony by having the order signed with a red and blue pencil produced at the Sacco and Vanzetti pencil factory.

Both Belov's *Eves* and Mozhaev's *Peasant Men and Women* experienced difficulty getting into print. The last half of Mozhaev's novel had to wait seven years before publication, and then it appeared in the regional journal *Don*, having been rejected by *Novyi mir* and even by *Nash sovremennik*. These difficulties in finding a publisher undoubtedly resulted from the radical treatment of the collectivization period, the powerful indictment of the party's actions in those years, and the open appeal to Russian national experience as the guiding spirit for the nation. It is often the case that the Villagers seeking to capture the countryside in historical perspective omit or gloss over the period treated by Belov and Mozhaev in their recent novels. This was the case with the first volume of Petr Proskurin's potboiler *Destiny* (*Sud'ba*), and with Larionov's *Lida's Ashes*, too. It is also clear that the Villagers literary community is not pleased with Belov's and Mozhaev's efforts. In an article printed in *Nash sovremennik* in April and

May 1989, an article, incidentally, noteworthy for the ferocity of its liberal-bashing and Jew-bashing in a journal notorious for both activities, Mozhaev is criticized for his failure to assess objectively the forces at work in the countryside. The author, Nikolai Fed', then discusses a novel that does provide such an analysis:[24] Sergei Alekseev's *The Swarm* (*Roi*), which happens to pass over the period of forced collectivization with no hint of the enormity of the suffering it caused.

Outside the Villagers literary community may be encountered harsher criticisms of Mozhaev and Belov, such as L. Vil'chek's article "Going Downstream with Village Prose" in the periodical *Voprosy literatury*, in which the author dismisses the hue and cry over 1929 as so much water under the bridge. Vil'chek compares the collectivization controversy with Pushkin's *Bronze Horseman*: there were two truths involved—the truth of Peter the Great and the truth of the wretched Evgenii.[25] In *Novyi mir*, Igor Kliamkin also objects to the imputation by the village writers that collectivization was somehow avoidable. It was, writes Kliamkin, the inevitable clash of two incompatible economic theories, resolved in the inevitable way.[26]

Lately, particularly with the recent publication of Anatolii Rybakov's novels *Children of the Arbat* and *1935 and Other Years*, those who see 1929 as the year in which Soviet power broke faith with the Russian people appear to view the Communist Party purge commencing in 1937 as revenge against those party cadres who were willing to assist in the destruction of village traditions during collectivization. A recent article on this subject is subtitled "1929 versus 1937." The author of this article quotes from a poem in this vein written by the Villager Stanislav Kuniaev:

> The souls from the Arbat wish not to know,
> That dying in Narym's ice and snow
> Are the Russian priest and the beggar kulak.
> For the children of the Arbat life is still good,
> But for vulgar folk human flesh is human food,
> And on Solovki's Isles is born the Gulag.[27]

Vadim Kozhinov and Apollon Kuz'min have written pieces in *Nash sovremennik* that are very critical of Rybakov's works and in which so-called liberals are said to be hypocritical for demanding a monument commemorating the victims of the purges while ignoring or understating the much greater suffering occasioned by forced collectivization in the late 1920s and early 1930s. It is also true that a number of the writers associated with the Villagers have played prominent roles in opposition to certain of the reforming tendencies of the current party leadership, although here there is no unanimity. Belov, for instance, who was elected to the Congress of People's Deputies on the slate chosen by the Central Committee of the party, has strongly endorsed the policy of greater openness.

We have come to the present day in this examination of the Villagers' understanding of Russia's past. And for the purpose of assessing Russia's present status in the continuum of its history, the village writers have offered a withering appraisal of Russia's present condition and a shrill warning against prospects even for survival unless the progressive attenuation of the country's bonds with the past is somehow reversed. Viktor Astaf'ev's *The Sad Detective Story* (*Pechal'nyi detektiv*) presents a shocking picture of societal collapse in a Siberian town, where alcoholism, violence, corruption, and civic indifference are seen as the inevitable consequence of the loss of ties with the age-old morality of village life. But perhaps a greater impression is made on the reader by Valentin Rasputin's last two novellas, *Farewell to Matera* (*Proshchanie s Materoi*) and *The Fire* (*Pozhar*), since Rasputin's writing, especially in the former work, is endowed with literary gifts enjoyed by few living Russian writers. Tolstoy said that all great art is simple, but he did not say it had to be hackneyed, yet Rasputin has taken a plot with whiskers—the contrast of the harmonious, tradition-inspired lives of Matera's villagers with the rootless, opportunistic newcomers unleashed on the Siberian forests by a power that makes war on nature for sport—and has woven with this unpromising fabric a classic for the ages. These newcomers, who worship no god, have no loyalties, and swear fealty to no motherland, are more frightening than Mozhaev's scourging collectivizers, for they were obviously inspired not by Dostoevskian fiction but by observation of their very real surroundings. Rasputin's transient roughnecks are merely products of an environment in which a sense of time and place have been lost. Old

Dar'ia Pinigina expresses this equation as she visits Matera's three hundred-year-old graveyard just before the village is inundated by the Ust'-Ilim hydroelectric station's effluent: "Truth is in remembering. Who has no memory has no life."

By Rasputin's admission *The Fire* is a sequel to *Farewell to Matera*. Written in a journalistic style reminiscent of Astaf'ev but without the supernatural effects of its predecessor, it is, if anything, even gloomier. Ivan Egorov is very nearly the last honest and civic-minded citizen of a hastily thrown together logging settlement. It is through the eyes of this former resident of one of the flooded villages in the Angara region in eastern Siberia that we witness the reactions of his fellow residents to a conflagration in the poorly designed and maintained storage warehouse. By now the transient roughnecks dominate all aspects of the settlement and fear nothing, their only deity being the vodka bottle. Of the intemperance of these newcomers Ivan thinks to himself: "Drunks were rife—whenever weren't they rife in Holy Russia?—but to gather into a circle, to grow up within it into an open force that fears nothing, that has its own *ataman* and council, to become a ruling power—there had never been anything like that before. This is an achievement of our own." [28]

The impermanence and untidiness of the settlement could stand for post-Brezhnevian Russia:

> Uncomfortable and untidy, the settlement was neither of city nor of rural, but of bivouac type, as if the people had been wandering like nomads from place to place, had stopped for a rest while waiting for bad weather to pass, and had become stuck. But they were stuck in expectation of the time when the order would come through to move on and so, without putting down roots, without prettifying anything and without organizing themselves with a view to children and grandchildren, but merely content to get through the summer and then the winter. [29]

How similar this is to Astaf'ev's character Ivan Trofimovich in the story "To Live Your Life," who compares his old now-flooded village on the river Enisei with the thrown-together town that succeeded it. He asks himself: "We lived and worked on our own Izagash land from generation to generation, we feel sorry for it, and it's frightening to think what kind of people are springing up on that gray concrete, without land, without their own shore, without a meadow or forest stands or green glades. What will settle in their souls? A bureaucratic wall! What sort of work are they going to do? Whom are they to love? For whom will they feel sorry? Whom will they remember?" [30]

Egorov looks around him at this makeshift settlement of Sosnovka, surrounded on all sides by clearcut stumps left waist high in violation of a law no one has the courage to try to enforce, and thinks of the three centuries-old villages flooded and turned into this place, which is a non-home to residents who do not possess a real home. Ivan recalls his own village and embarks on this panvitalistic rumination: "Home is home, naturally; every stone before your birth had foreknowledge of your coming and waited for you, every blade of grass in the new spring brings you something for the preservation or support of former times, and a subtle ancestral watch is kept over you everywhere and in everything." [31]

Ivan Egorov has discovered the key factor that accounts for the breakdown in morality, courage, and civic pride among these "barracks folk" (*barachnye liudi*): it is the "turning aside and breaking free of the harmonious communal existence reinforced with customs and laws that had not come into being yesterday."

The narrator then tells us of Ivan Egorov's final conclusion: "If a man was to feel that his life was bearable, he must be at home. That was it: at home. Before everything else, at home, and not in dormitories; but in himself, in his personal inner world, where everything has its definite, established place and function since times of old. Then at home—in a log house, in an apartment, whence you go one way to work and the other way into yourself. And at home on your native soil." [32] This last point underscores the Villagers' conviction that one should, as Boris Pasternak's Doctor Zhivago put it, share the fate of one's country.

A couple of months ago there appeared in *Nash sovremennik* a short story, "The District Miracle-worker" ("Uezdnyi chudotvorets"), by Iaroslav Shipov. In the story, told in mock-Leskovian fashion, the local landowner (*barin*) returns to his family's estate after the October

Revolution and asks the local *feldsher,* a rustic, self-taught genius, to accompany him in exile to Paris, where he will through his healing art become rich and famous. The *feldsher* turns the young master down flat, saying, "What sort of life would that be? To suffer, go through torments, endure insults. And then to end with an absurd and empty death." [33] The *feldsher* reasons that any fate is more tolerable than separation from the motherland. We have seen so many Russian writers emigrate to the West that they are sometimes referred to as the intelligentsia of the sixteenth Soviet republic. In contrast, the Villagers do not emigrate or defect. Even when they merely travel to the West their impressions are likely to call to mind Dostoevsky's venomous *Winter Notes on Summer Impresssions.*

Rasputin makes the claim that the "harmonious communal existence" with its own laws and customs got Russia through the war and the difficult time that followed it. In making this assertion he follows Fedor Abramov's statement to the Sixth Congress of Writers that the village and the "type of person created by it" would not "allow Russia to perish in the years of its hardest trials." One of Belov's characters in *Everything Lies Before Us* puts this proposition very bluntly: "Over and over again it was the peasant hut that saved Russia." This conviction of the Villagers serves as a support for that peculiar amalgam of "alternative ideology" put forward by some of the Villagers as a means of reversing the moral atrophy of their nation. For want of a better term this doctrine might be called diachronic ecologism.

In a recent issue of *Soviet Economy*, Robert Darst has observed that the environmental writings of the Villagers differ from those normally encountered in the West in that the Russians make no distinction between nature and human culture. [34] In fact, the maintenance of traditional villages, especially since the government's announcement of the plan to consolidate "unprofitable collectives in the non-black-earth zone" into new and more profitable aggregates, is an integral feature of the Villagers' version of environmentalism. Hence their advocacy of family farming and small-scale collectives. How different this is from the western conception of saving nature which most often involves getting humans out of it.

Diachronic ecologism, which is one outcome of the single-stream approach to history, does not merely emphasize the peasantry's respect for nature, it projects this attitude into the past. Zalygin's villagers in his novels about the early Soviet years have a worshipful attitude toward the *taiga* that provides them with their livelihood. Zalygin even pays a compliment to the tsarist authorities for their policies of protecting the forests along the river Irtysh. In Alekseev's novel *The Swarm*, similar claims are made for the oldtimers (*starozhily*) in the Tomsk *guberniia* and the Old Believers (*kerzhaki*) who look with horror at the deep-draft plows brought to Siberia by the Stolypin resettlers from Viatka. In the later chapters of *The Swarm*, the Viatka settlers' grandchildren are equally appalled by the government's decision to use wasteful and ruinous methods of farming to feed the influx of oil-field workers. It is significant that in Belov's *Everything Lies Before Us* the villain Mikhail Brish repeats with approval Turgenev's saying that nature is a workshop (*masterskaia*) and not a temple (*khram*).

Finally, an examination of the historiographic foundations of the Villagers leads to the consideration of two principal questions: can their vision of a Russian future rejuvenated by rediscovery of salutary features of a rural past be realized, and can this vision build and sustain an artistic movement? I can more readily accept the possibility of partial success in the social sphere of the Villagers' endeavor, where their concerns are shared with much of the citizenry and include opposition to the river diversion plan, desire for reclaiming Lake Baikal and the Aral Sea, and sentiment for curtailing investment in nuclear energy and space exploration.

On the other hand, there is something self-limiting about village writing as a movement in art. One is reminded of an episode in Alekseev's *The Swarm*, which has as its main setting a Siberian village called Stremianka, after the village of the same name in Viatka province whence the central family, the Zavarzins, migrated with many of their fellow villagers after the promulgation of Stolypin's agrarian reforms. For decades the older residents of Siberian Stremianka had harbored the desire one day to return to Russian Stremianka, which some of them had left as children. When one of the Zavarzins, a young university lecturer tired of city life, decides to return permanently to his native village in Siberia, he decides to make a detour to visit the old Stremianka, which had been home to his forebears. He finds there only a plowed field, empty of habitation. The only trace of the centuries-old village of Stremianka is the discoloration of the soil where the foundation posts of the huts had been pulled from the ground.[35] The vision of the Villagers is to a certain extent like that desire of the Siberian settlers to return to a style of life that is no longer there. And while Valentin Rasputin is condemning Russia's contamination from western institutions, as he did at the Fifth Congress of the All-Russian Society for the Protection of Monuments of History and Culture (*Vserossiiskoe Obshchestvo Okhrany Pamiatnikov Istorii i Kul'tury*), and inveighing against the destruction of monuments, one has the feeling that his own *Farewell to Matera* may turn out to be the greatest monument of village prose and that nothing quite as good is likely to follow in this movement aimed at reuniting Russia's present with its past.

4   A Conflict Of Visions:

Vasilii Grossman and the

Russian Idea

*No, it is better in Russia: here, at least, one can blame
others for everything, and justify oneself.*

—Svidrigailov

No literary works published during *glasnost'* have aroused as
much vociferous reaction in the Soviet Union as Vasilii Grossman's
two novels, *Forever Flowing (Vse techet . . .)* and *Life and Fate
(Zhizn' i sud'ba)*. Evidently typed on Bulgakov's fireproof paper, each
manuscript was smuggled to the West and published in 1970 and
1980, respectively. An unknown number of copies of the books were
then resmuggled back into their country of origin, but the two novels
first entered Soviet public consciousness a quarter century after their
author's death in 1964 by appearing in the Moscow journal *Oktiabr'*.[1]
They received much praise, from both officials and the liberal intelli-

gentsia.[2] On the other hand, political conservatives, including many of the country's leading establishment writers, condemned Grossman's comparison of Hitler's Germany and Stalin's Russia in *Life and Fate*, and his fundamental attack on Marxism-Leninism, and on Lenin personally, in *Forever Flowing*. Angered as they were by these political and ideological sins, members of the Russian nationalist-conservative coalition saved their most intense wrath for Grossman's sophisticated and multifaceted analysis of Russian nationalism.[3]

Grossman had transgressed by refusing to follow a time-honored tradition in modern Russian literature, which owes much to Herder's prediction that vigorous new German and Slavic cultures were destined to push the decadent culture of Western Europe into the shade. In countless Russian works from Fonvizin on, we find amorphous but supposedly unique Russian virtues contrasted to the lesser virtues of non-Russians living within the multinational empire, or, more frequently, to the vices of foreign neighbors in Western Europe. As Valentin Kiparsky justly remarked, "A Russian novel without a West European or, at least a Polish, Ukrainian, Jewish or Caucasian character, is almost as rare as a West European novel containing a Russian character."[4] In the works of some Russian authors, most notably Dostoevsky, the assertion of exclusive Russian virtues leads to the conviction that Russia has a special mission to improve and complete western civilization; to this goal Dostoevsky even advanced the notion of a "Russian Christ." But his is only the most extreme case of Russian literary chauvinism over the past two hundred years. Since the late eighteenth century Russian writers have tended to define national virtues against a background of various West European (later western) iniquities.

It is rare indeed to find a Russian writer bold enough to take exception to the comforting platitudes of national preeminence—Turgenev and, later, Chekhov are noteworthy exceptions. But Grossman's has been a lone voice crying out in the Russian literary wilderness during the twentieth century, when the efforts of both Germans and Russians to assert their supremacy have led to catastrophic results, both for themselves and their neighbors. Under Gorbachev's campaign for *glasnost'* Russian literary chauvinism has risen to a new fever pitch, as the Soviet press has been opened up to a variety of opinions long submerged in society. The ostensibly "literary" debate over the esthetics of Grossman's novels, particularly of his masterpiece *Life and Fate*, is Aesopian language covering an important political conflict. With great skill those who oppose modernization of Soviet society have defined the terms of the debate to their own advantage: anyone who disagrees with them is automatically condemned as a Russophobe, and very likely part of a Jewish-Masonic plot to destroy what remains of Russian culture.

Their success is a measure of chauvinism's taproot in the Russian character. Andrei Siniavskii has noted the strong traditional Russian preference for "us" and "ours" (*svoi*) versus "the other" and "theirs" (*chuzhoi*) long before the Petrine reforms and the rise of modern Russian literature and society. Glossing this deeply ingrained dichotomy, he argues: "One of the peculiarities of the Russian national character is the propensity to be content to judge a man solely on the basis of his Russian nationality—if he is Russian, he is good. Conversely, Russians mistrust other peoples; this finds expression in national intolerance and even xenophobia." [5]

The simplistic equation, "ours is good, theirs is bad," is by no means limited to Russians. After all, we owe the word chauvinism itself to a Frenchman and the phrase, "My country, right or wrong," to the English, who have not always taken to heart Samuel Johnson's warning, "Patriotism is the last refuge of the scoundrel." What is remarkable in the Russian context is that the equation should have been accepted by so many creative writers, whether westernizer or Slavophile, Soviet or dissident, who tend to define Russianness against a foil of negative alien values and characteristics.

Set against this background, Grossman's challenge stands out in sharp relief. Instead of granting Russians a privileged reading of their own history, Grossman dared to question some of their most cherished assumptions. He distinguished between the patriotic feeling of the individual, which he admired, and an aggressive chauvinism sponsored (or better, manipulated) by the state and the ruling party, which he detested. He argued that certain intellectual and cultural streams had had a deleterious effect on the nation's political well-being and had led to the fanaticism of Lenin and Stalin. And he saw, without the benefit of hindsight that has enabled western historians to understand the essential similarity between Hitler and Stalin, that both dictators based their appeal on a powerful stirring of nationalism in their populations.[6]

German nationalism was the basis of the National Socialist German Worker's Party, soon to become better known as the Nazi Party, condensed from the first two syllables of *Nazional*. National Socialism rose to prominence by promising "to ensure for the German man a happy and industrious existence, for the German woman a beautiful and worthy life, for German children a bright future." [7] Excluded from this bright future were virtually all other nationalities, for the Germans set themselves up as the *Herrenvolk*, a master race to rule other peoples, whom they carefully graded and ranked according to Hitler's crackpot "Aryan" racism. Very soon after Hitler assumed power as chancellor, the German judiciary codified the disenfranchisement of Jews in September of 1935. The first of the two infamous Nuremberg Laws legally restricted citizenship only to those of "German or related blood." The second law defined the Jews as *not* of German blood.[8] Down this road lay the gas chambers and ovens of Auschwitz and Treblinka.

As Grossman argued in *Forever Flowing*, while Hitler proposed a racism of blood, Lenin had already advanced a racism of class. But Stalin's policy of "socialism in one country" in the mid-twenties and the resurrection of the emotionally charged word *rodina* for the new socialist motherland in 1934 laid the foundations for the appearance during World War II of a Soviet version of German National Socialism, based on Russian nationality, Russian language and culture. In *Life and Fate* Grossman noted the critical change that took place as the tide turned against the Germans: "The war accelerated a previously unconscious process, allowing the birth of an overtly national consciousness. The word 'Russian' once again had meaning" (463/665).[9] Grossman was well aware that "national consciousness is a powerful and splendid force at a time of disaster," but argued that this positive potential had been swallowed up in Stalin's proclamation of his ideology of "state nationalism." Grossman shows in *Life and Fate* that this state-sponsored Russian nationalism could lead to results very similar to German National Socialism.

To make his own case against national intolerance Grossman weaves an opposition of freedom and slavery into *Life and Fate's* major plot line, the course of the battle of Stalingrad. The dangers of extreme nationalism are examined through a comparison between the assault on human integrity mounted by the warring states, Nazi Germany and Soviet Russia, and a focus on individual moral choice in the face of terrible suffering and violent death. After the scene set in the gas chamber where we are taken inside the minds of Sofia Levinton and the boy David as they die, the narrator speaks directly to the reader, saying, "What constitutes the freedom, the soul of an individual life, is its uniqueness" (383/555). Such a statement shows the emptiness of a central tenet of the Nazis, that the simple fact of Jewishness defines a human being's worth (or in that perverted ideology, worthlessness) and should determine one's fate. For Grossman the gas chamber is the final, extreme expression of chauvinism, a vicious patriotism that excludes "the other" from the human race.

In *Life and Fate* the most extreme Russian nationalists are the political commissars, anxious to follow the new Stalinist line. Thus, the super-patriotic political commissar Dementii Trifonovich Getmanov is portrayed as a chauvinist, as well as a treacherous hypocrite. He is assigned to work with Colonel Novikov, the epitome of the courageous and competent Russian officer, who significantly finds himself intimidated by party apparatchiks. When Novikov proposes the promotion of a Kalmyk officer within his tank brigade purely on the basis of military performance, Getmanov angrily objects, using phrases that prefigure exactly the language of the extreme Russian nationalists during *glasnost'*:

Quite frankly, all this makes me want to puke. In the name of the friendship of peoples we keep sacrificing the Russians. A member of a national minority barely needs to know the alphabet to be appointed a people's commissar, while our Ivan, no matter if he's a genius, has to "yield place to the minorities." The great Russian people is becoming a national minority itself. I'm all for the friendship of peoples, but not on these terms. I'm sick of it. (142/221)

Getmanov's bold condemnation of non-Russian nationalities reveals assurance that it will have no political consequences; a man with a keen nose for the sources of power, he has sniffed out the new Stalinist "Russia first!" line. Grossman intends for Getmanov to illustrate the ugly side of Russian nationalism, which was fast becoming a state-sponsored obscurantism that even disregarded the war effort and the main task of defeating the Germans on the battlefield.

For Grossman the *reductio ad absurdum* of both German and Russian chauvinism is anti-Semitism. In a brief section of *Life and Fate* Grossman distinguishes three levels of anti-Semitism. At the lowest level there is the "relatively harmless everyday" type, which "bears witness to the existence of failures and envious fools." At the second level he discerns a "social" kind that manifests itself in the reactionary media and in commercial boycotts. But it is a third level that Grossman considers the most dangerous: "In totalitarian countries, where society as such no longer exists, only State and anti-Semitism can arise. This is a sign that the State is looking for the support of fools, reactionaries and failures, that it is seeking to capitalize on the ignorance of the superstitious and the anger of the hungry" (335/487). Grossman is speaking ostensibly here about Nazi Germany, but everything he says applies also to the other major totalitarian state of the time, the Soviet Union: "Ignorant people blame the Jews for their troubles when they should blame the social structure of the State itself." [10]

Grossman's justifiable concerns about state-sponsored anti-Semitism in both Nazi Germany and Soviet Russia did not prevent him from portraying some Jewish characters in a negative light. In *Forever Flowing* one of the fiercest persecutors of Jewish scientists during the anticosmopolitan campaign in the late forties is in fact a Jew, Margolin. And in *Life and Fate* Shtrum's mother, penned into the ghetto and doomed to extinction, manages to smuggle out a letter to Shtrum in which she confesses that there are "many bad people" among her companions. Even though Shtrum is Jewish and certainly embodies certain elements of Grossman's own background, he is by no means portrayed in heroic colors throughout the novel.

Grossman even takes pains to show a Jewish political commissar cynically manipulating Russian patriotism. In a discussion occurring in Lieutenant Viktorov's fighter squadron a pilot, Solomatin, praises a fellow officer, a man who had saved his life, "Korol's not a Jew . . . he's one of us." But when Korol confirms that indeed he is a Jew, Solomatin insults him. The pilots are trying to guess where they'll be sent next, and Solomatin says, "I suppose you want us to go to your own capital, Berdichev" (105/169). Berdichev, a prerevolutionary center of Jewish cultural and intellectual life in the Ukraine, was Grossman's birthplace and the site of yet another mass murder of Jews, including his own mother, during the German occupation. But the scene does not end there, for the fighter squadron's political commissar, the Jew Berman, handles the argument between the two pilots in the following way: "Everyone knew that Solomatin had deliberately offended Korol, but there was Berman confidently explaining that Korol had failed to overcome his nationalist prejudices and that his behaviour evinced a contempt for the friendship of peoples. And Korol should remember that it was the Fascists who exploited nationalist prejudices." [11]

Thus, a Jewish political commissar speaks for the Soviet state, which is itself shamelessly exploiting the very nationalism that it suits Berman here to decry. Hundreds of pages later, Grossman arranges for the Russian pilot Viktorov and the Jewish commissar Berman to die on the same day at Stalingrad.

Grossman's even-handedness is such that his Jewish readers, both in the Soviet Union and in the western emigration, have failed to embrace him unconditionally. They do not acknowledge him as a Jewish writer, let alone a Zionist spokesman, since in his novels he refuses to grant Jews a privileged reading of history as God's "chosen people"; his Jewish characters reveal the same mix of good, bad and indifferent qualities as those of the Russians or of any other national or ethnic origin. Grossman is like a judge who in writing a dispassionate brief has managed to infuriate both prosecution and defense.

As an assimilated Jew, Grossman appears to have been obliged to think of his own Jewish background by the Nazi atrocities he witnessed at first hand during the war. [12] In the Soviet journal *Znamia* (October 1944) he published the first report of a Nazi death camp based on eyewitness accounts, "The Hell of Treblinka" ("Treblinskii ad"), and he cooperated with Il'ia Erenburg in compiling the so-called

Black Book (*Chernaia kniga*), a collection of materials on Nazi atrocities against Jews in the occupied territories of the western Soviet Union; but the book was banned by Stalin in 1946 and has never been published in the Soviet Union.[13] Grossman himself very nearly became a victim of the new wave of anti-Semitism unleashed by the "doctors' plot" at the beginning of 1953; only Stalin's death saved his life.

Nevertheless, as a frontline correspondent who saw constant action throughout World War II, Grossman realized full well that other peoples in Europe were also being brutalized and murdered. In his story, "The Old Schoolteacher" ("Staryi uchitel'"), published in 1942, Grossman has Boris Isaakovich Rozental', the teacher of mathematics and philosophy, state that the Germans have created an "enormous staircase of oppression" to keep all the captive peoples of Europe obedient. The Slavs, as *Untermenschen* in Nazi ideology, were on the penultimate step of this staircase—beneath them yawned the abyss of hell reserved especially for the Jews. All the other peoples behave circumspectly so as to avoid the Jews' fate. Rozental' calls this the result not of "spontaneous hatred, but simply the arithmetic of bestiality" (*prostaia arifmetika zverstva, a ne stikhiinaia nenavist'*).[14]

The *Herrenvolk* thus felt justified in treating Slavs as less than human, with the result that conditions for millions of Slavic soldiers taken prisoner in the war were absolutely appalling. It should not be imagined that Grossman exaggerates the horrors of the Russian POW's predicament under the Germans. One of the finest historians of the eastern front, Alan Clark, described the POW camps in these powerful words: "Dark compounds of misery and anguish, where the dead lay undisturbed in heaps for weeks on end, they were often ravaged by epidemics so virulent that no guard would enter—except with flame throwers when, in the interests of 'hygiene,' the dying and corpses were set alight together on their beds of verminous rags."[15]

In describing their plight, Grossman focuses on the conflict between individual patriotic feeling and state-sponsored nationalism. Russian prisoners were faced with the agonizing choice of dying a slow death in the camps or joining the anti-Soviet forces of General Vlasov, the former hero of the battle of Moscow who became a German collaborator after he and his whole army were abandoned and doomed to encirclement by the Soviet high command. As a man who rose to the rank of lieutenant-colonel in the Red Army, Grossman was probably well acquainted with the overall nationalist base of the anti-Vlasov propaganda advanced by the Soviet authorities. The large numbers of Russian soldiers who chose to fight in the army of General Vlasov posed a very serious threat. Vlasov claimed that he was fighting against Stalin, and up until the victory of Stalingrad and beyond, many of the six or seven millions of captured Red Army soldiers, offered the draconian choice between collaboration or a slow agonizing death of disease and starvation, chose the "mug of soup" and "warm greatcoat," as *Life and Fate* puts it.

Like Solzhenitsyn in *The Gulag Archipelago,* which was written after *Life and Fate,* Grossman sympathized with the dilemma of these Russian prisoners, but he could not agree with those who sided with Vlasov. Grossman's views are made clear through the statements of Chernetsov, a Russian POW and a former Menshevik who is portrayed more sympathetically than the Bolshevik prisoners: "It's just not right. . . . It's dishonorable. . . . Don't do it. Don't join Vlasov!" (205/307).

The most dispassionate professional historian of the eastern front has probably been John Erickson. He provides in *The Road to Berlin,* the second volume of his magisterial study, documentation which corroborates Grossman's analysis of *Stavka*'s treatment of Vlasov and his potential army of defectors. Erickson quotes from a collection of Soviet anti-Vlasov leaflets and materials, and distills their essential thrust into several key points:

- The German aim was the enslaving of Russia;
- The Vlasov army was a German tool;
- The Soviet system has already conceded a number of popular demands, including the recognition of the church and the displacement of the commissars;
- Soviet leadership had now decided that only the Great Russians had passed the test of war;
- The postwar "Soviet Union" would merge the separate republics under Great Russian rule;
- The postwar political system would be drastically modified, with

the republics dismantled and with the Communist Party turned into a people's party with a broad educational mission;
• Stalin himself would be removed in favor of Andreev (a Russian, unlike Stalin) and the collective farms disbanded (the main desire of the peasants, who made up the great majority of the Soviet army).

As Erickson succintly remarks, "This had lavish patriotic appeal and a chauvinistic twist to Russian feelings—Russia for the Russians, minus Stalin and stripped of its collectivization." [16] Of course, we know it worked beautifully. Stalin made superb use of Russian nationalism to strengthen loyalty and to encourage the redefection of Vlasov supporters. In Erickson's words, "At home, on both sides of the line, and also abroad, the nationalist line with its strong chauvinist overtones pursued by Stalin paid handsome dividends." [17]

Grossman understood perfectly how Stalin used Russian chauvinism as a means to arouse the very Russians he had persecuted to fight for the Soviet state, that is, as a tool to maintain political power. A character in *Life and Fate*, the prerevolutionary aristocrat Prince Vladimir Shargorodskii, says, "The founders of the Comintern proved unable to think of anything better in the hour of war than the old phrase about 'the sacred earth of Russia'. . . . Just wait. The war will end in Victory and then the Internationalists will declare: 'Mother Russia's equal to anyone in the world'" (82–3/134). And so it happens.

The dividends were many, but the cost in human terms was enormous. For, in the basic paradox of *Life and Fate*, Russian soldiers delivered to Stalin the crucial victory of World War II, and that victory enabled him to reign as a dictator until his death in 1953. Grossman was present at Stalingrad, and he knew that the Soviet state denied freedom and democracy at precisely the same moment Soviet soldiers in Stalingrad fought and died for those very goals. He brings out this cruel irony in the scenes set in Grekov's house—modeled on the historical Pavlov's House and other encircled ruins where Soviet soldiers cobbled together from various units held off superior German forces for days and weeks, buying time with their blood until Soviet reserves could mount an encircling assault that resulted in the destruction of Field-Marshal von Paulus' Sixth Army.

When Commissar Krymov is sent by the divisional commissar to Grekov's house, he is told to "establish Bolshevik order" and if necessary relieve Grekov, because "a state within a state is something we can do without" (287/419). What offends the party is that inside Grekov's tiny "state" all decisions are taken democratically. Grekov tells Krymov that they must talk openly, not privately: "My men and I fight together. We can settle whatever needs settling together" (291/425). As a longtime Bolshevik and member of the Comintern, Krymov is appalled since he has grown up guided by the Bolshevik code of *partiinost'*. He does manage to engage Grekov in a private discussion, asking him what he wants. Grekov responds, "Freedom. That's what I'm fighting for." Seeing that he cannot persuade Krymov to leave them alone, Grekov grazes the commissar's head with a shot while he is sleeping, then has him removed back to the other side of the Volga. Krymov promptly writes a report denouncing Grekov.

And what happens to Grekov's tiny state? It is completely obliterated by the Germans in a massive bombardment that Grekov knows is coming: no one survives. Having tried to bring Grekov and his comrades to heel during the battle itself, once they have all been killed, the party decides to make them heroes and to condemn Krymov for failing to perceive their true value. He is arrested shortly afterward by the People's Commissariat for Internal Affairs (NKVD) and then brutalized in the Lubianka because he refuses to confess in the approved manner. Had the Germans not succeeded in destroying Grekov's miniature state and his dangerous democratic procedures, the party would have done so.

The issues in the conversation between Grekov and Krymov are picked up by the narrator as he describes the eve of the counterattack at Stalingrad:

Some of the Russian regiments [in Stalingrad] now only numbered a few dozen soldiers; it was these few men, bearing all the weight of the terrible fighting, who confused the calculations of the Germans [who thought the Russians had committed all their reserves]. . . . The remorseless cunning of History, however, lay still more deeply hidden. Freedom engendered the Russian victory.

Freedom was the apparent aim of the war. But the sly fingers of History changed this: freedom became simply a way of waging the war, a means to an end. (336/488)

The counterattack itself is successful because of the heroics of men like Colonel Novikov, his friend Lt. Colonel Darenskii, and Major Berezkin, who treat all men as equals; their only concern is competence. When Darenskii sees a Russian colonel brutalizing a German prisoner-of-war, he tells him, "Russians don't kick a man when he's down." The colonel responds, "What do you think I am then? Do you think I'm not a Russian?" And Darenskii has the courage to tell him to his face, "You're a scoundrel" (498/713). Darenskii's nobility is contrasted to the vindictiveness of the colonel, who promises him, "You will be hearing from me."

Darenskii, who cries to Novikov in a drinking bout, "I'll love Russia till my dying day!" (502/720), demonstrates through his actions Grossman's belief that true Russian patriotism must be defined in terms of humanity, not the state-sanctioned nationalism of Stalin, nor the traditional chauvinism of many Russian writers. For Grossman, the true path of Russia, the path of freedom and democracy, is exemplified in the works of Anton Chekhov. References to Chekhov's works occur throughout the novel and elsewhere in his writings. In a personal interview (Moscow, August 1989), Semen Lipkin, Grossman's lifelong friend, confirmed that Chekhov was the writer whom he most admired.

Grossman puts the basic theme of *Life and Fate* into the mouth of a minor character, Mad'iarov, who is given some of the best lines in the book, including the immortal comparison of socialist realism with the wicked queen's magic mirror in *Snow White*—its purpose is to reassure the party, "You are fairest of all." Mad'iarov disappears after leading a series of unusually frank discussions among scientists evacuated from Kazan to Moscow during the first year after the German invasion—later we learn that he has been denounced by one of those present and arrested. But during his brief moment in the sun Mad'iarov zeroes in on the dangers inherent in "our Russian humanism," which he declares "has always been cruel, intolerant, sectarian.

From Avvakum to Lenin our conception of humanity and freedom has always been partisan and fanatical. It has always mercilessly sacrificed the individual to some abstract idea of humanity" (187/283).

Mad'iarov contrasts this mainstream Russian tradition with another, which he associates directly and solely with Chekhov: "Chekhov is the bearer of the greatest banner that has been raised in the thousand years of Russian history—the banner of a true, humane, Russian democracy, of Russian freedom, of the dignity of the Russian man."

Note here the repeated use of "Russian"—Grossman is not advocating a non-Russian, let alone an anti-Russian view, but one that he sees as based in a submerged native Russian tradition, which does not merely pay lip service to universal love and forgiveness, while dividing people up according to class or ethnic origin. The essence of Chekhovian democracy, as Mad'iarov puts it, is that Chekhov portrayed his character as "a true Russian democrat":

He said—and no one had said this before, not even Tolstoy—that first and foremost we are all of us human beings. Do you understand? Human beings! He said something no one in Russia had ever said. He said that first of all we are human beings—and only secondly are we bishops, Russians, shopkeepers, Tatars, workers. Do you understand? Instead of saying that people are good or bad because they are bishops or workers, Tatars or Ukrainians, instead of this he said that people are equal because they are human beings.

The repetitions and clumsy phrasing here are surely deliberate. Mad'iarov is excited and struggling to explain a cherished thought that he knows could easily be regarded as subversive and might get him into trouble—as indeed it does. The scene, with its lengthy discussion by scientists of various Russian creative writers, may at first seem to be extraneous to the plot, but it is crucial to the explication of Grossman's warning against state-sanctioned intolerance.

Significantly, it is a *Russian* officer, Colonel Novikov, who brings this philosophy into the plot. Novikov does not pigeonhole people according to nationality. He understands the uniqueness of each of his soldiers' personalities, even though they are dressed in the identical black uniforms of tank troops and have all been selected because of their low stature. As Novikov looks at his men, the narrator enters his mind.

> Human groupings have one main purpose: to assert everyone's right to be different, to be special, to think, feel and live in his or her own way. People join together in order to win or defend this right. But this is where a terrible, fateful error is born: the belief that these groupings in the name of a race, a God, a party or a State are the very purpose of life and not simply a means to an end. No! The only true and lasting meaning of the struggle for life lies in the individual, in his modest peculiarities and in his right to those peculiarities. (148/230)

Colonel Novikov, himself a man without intellectual pretensions (he prefers standard Soviet literature to Chekhov) has arrived at this wisdom in some mysterious fashion, but he is unable to verbalize it directly; the narrator must come to his aid.

In *Life and Fate*, and even more directly in *Forever Flowing*, Grossman argues that Russian claims to superiority over their neighbors led them to ignore Chekhov's modest proposal and instead trapped them in a fallacious "either-or" approach to history. Many Russians in the immediate prerevolutionary period felt that the only two choices they had were either to side with vicious political radicals such as Lenin or to seek refuge from political questions in purely literary and artistic concerns. In *Life and Fate* the former Bolshevik Abarchuk, now imprisoned in a Soviet camp in the far North, overhears a conversation posing the dilemma. After another prisoner, Prince Dolgorukii, recites his latest mystical poem, Stepanov, formerly a professor in an economics institute, responds, "Pure decadence!" Dolgorukii replies, "Look where all your Chernyshevskiis and Herzens have got us!" But Stepanov refuses to narrow the discussion to the old opposition: "I detest you and your mystical obscurantism as much as I detest the organizers of this camp," replied Stepanov in a schoolmasterly tone. "Both they and you forget the third and most natural path for Russia: the path of democracy and freedom" (119–20/187).

For once Abarchuk, listening to this, is silent. To underscore the point, a few pages later, Grossman arranges for Abarchuk to meet up again with his old mentor, Magar, the man who introduced him to the party. Magar confesses that he and the other old Bolsheviks "made a mistake." And what was their mistake?

> We did not understand freedom. . . . We go through the camp, we go through the taiga, and yet our faith is stronger than ever. But this faith of ours is a weakness—a means of self-preservation. On the other side of the barbed wire, a sense of self-preservation tells people to change—unless they want to die or be sent to a camp. And so Communists have created idols, put on uniforms and epaulettes, begun preaching nationalism and attacking the working class. If necessary, they'll revive the Black Hundreds [*chernosotenstvo*]. (123–24/193)

Like Mad'iarov, Stepanov disappears from the novel after calling for the path not taken. Like Darenskii, who is headed for a reckoning with the hate-filled colonel who kicked the German POW, Novikov too will face the epigones of Stalin after the victory is assured: "One day I'll be in trouble myself" (502/720). Magar's prediction that Stalin would preach nationalism and anti-Semitism came all too true in the "anticosmopolitan" campaign when the war was won. But in the voices of characters who disappear from the text without a trace or whose terrible fate we know—such as the doomed Grekov and his men—is the voice of Vasilii Grossman, condemning both extremes of the Russian intelligentsia, decadence and Bolshevism, and pleading for the path not taken, that of democracy and freedom.

Today, a quarter-century after Grossman's death, it is not the party that is threatening to revive the Black Hundreds, but the people themselves, and most notably members of the writing community. In an irony that Grossman may not have foreseen, the chauvinistic remarks of his commissar Getmanov prefigure almost word for word the sorts of comments being made by extreme Russian nationalists in the period of glasnost'. Today's Russian nationalists, and particularly the anti-Semites among them, are the true epigones of Stalinism, or perhaps we should say they are victims of the state nationalism he introduced during World War II. These people have tried to pigeonhole Grossman as a Jewish writer, and thus by definition, anti-Russian. Such an approach merely offers an illustration of the very nationalist bias that Grossman was at such pains to condemn. In a classic Stalinist maneuver, conservative writers in the Russian Republic branch of the Union of Soviet Writers have responded to the publication of Grossman's two novels by demanding, on the grounds that he had approved their publication, Anatolii Anan'ev's removal from his position as chief editor of *Oktiabr'*.[18]

The hostile Soviet reaction to Grossman's two novels echoed an earlier negative response of several Russian emigré groups, who charged that Grossman "did not really love Russia."[19] But the reaction to Grossman's works in the Soviet Union was all the more harsh because the two posthumously published novels appeared at a time when— ironically enough—*glasnost'* led to an outburst of grassroots Stalinism among the cultural elite, as well as to the publication of long-suppressed works such as the novels of Grossman himself, Pasternak, and Zamiatin. Freedom of speech and a fading of censorship permitted open expression of an extreme Russian nationalism, which quickly became an important social phenomenon. In the summer of 1989, following the appearance of *Forever Flowing* in June, conservatives and Russian nationalists in the Soviet Union began to complain more openly about what they called the *grossmanizatsiia* of Soviet Russian culture. This neologism was popularized by such flacks of the Russian nationalist-conservative coalition as the Leningrad chemistry teacher Nina Andreyeva, whose attacks on the writer reveal nakedly the gnawing anti-Semitism that sophisticated literary critics like Vadim Kozhinov have tried to bury beneath rhetoric. They are not always successful, even when on their best behavior. In an interview with an American journalist, the highly respected writer Valentin Rasputin charged that the Jews were responsible both for the Revolution (i.e., the Bolshevik coup in November 1917) and for the terror that followed: "They played a large role, and their guilt is great. Both for the killing of God, and for that."[20] In his excitement Rasputin let slip the medieval claim that the Jews (unlike the Italians, descendants of the Roman legions) should still be held responsible for the crucifixion of Jesus

Christ. His remark says as much as any amount of commentary about the state of mind of even the more intelligent and talented members of the nationalist-conservative coalition in the Soviet Union today. Vitalii Korotich, a Ukrainian who writes in Russian and editor-in-chief of the important weekly *Ogonyok*, said in a personal interview in August 1989 that the main danger of the Union of Soviet Writers is that "it is a terribly chauvinistic organization," dominated by Russian nationalists. These people, he said, are not interested in those who write in Russian, but only those who are of "pure Russian blood." He joked that to follow the Russian nationalists would be to exclude half of Russian literature: Pushkin, on the grounds that he had an Abyssinian grandfather; Gogol', since he was Ukrainian; Dostoevsky, since he was of Polish ancestry; Babel', since he was "terribly Jewish," and so forth.

The Soviet press provides plenty of evidence to back up Korotich's claims. For example, the term "literature in Russian" (*russkoiazychnaia literatura*), rather than simply "Russian literature" (*russkaia literatura*), is increasingly used to designate works written by non-Russian Soviet writers, and particularly by Russian Jews, such as Grossman himself and Boris Pasternak. In some cases, Russian works by Russian Jews are not part of Russian literature. For example, in a recent dialogue with Anatolii Bocharov, published in *Literaturnaia gazeta*, Mikhail Lobanov ruled out the Civil War novel *Red Cavalry* (*Konarmiia*) by Isaak Babel' because "its explicit descriptions (*fiziologizm*) and cynical attitude towards those unlike himself (*ne svoi*) have nothing in common with the spirit of Russian literature."[21] Lobanov justifies his separation of works merely written in the Russian language from those that are truly Russian by insisting that the essence of Russian literature is "spiritual, not biological"—an interesting twist on Nazi German racial theories. Professor Bocharov, who holds the chair in Russian literature at Moscow University, responded that apparently one needs a very sensitive nose indeed to sniff out truly Russian works these days, and went on to question the tendency of the Russian nationalists to be inclusive, as evidenced in the substitution of the term *rossiiane* for the standard "population of the RSFSR" (Russian Socialist Federative Soviet Republic) and the terms *rossiiskaia literatura* for the standard "literature of the peoples of the RSFSR." Bocharov insisted that the adjective masks "an illusory concept." [22]

It is easy to see why Grossman has aroused intense hostility among such fierce anti-Semitic critics as Lobanov and Vadim Kozhinov, but his works constitute a serious challenge to Russian nationalists of all stripes. Grossman tries to show that the mythology of Russianness has led to a kind of moral blindness and to an impoverishment of Russian (and now Soviet) social dialogue. He warned that Russians must do more than search for scapegoats; they must acknowledge their own responsibility for the evil in their country, and not blame Jews and foreigners. Grossman has few predecessors in Russian literary history. In some respects he may be compared to Petr Chaadaev, to whom he alludes only briefly in *Life and Fate*, and more substantially in *Forever Flowing*. Grossman played the subversive and unpopular role that Chaadaev did with his first *Philosophical Letter*. But there are at least two important differences between the two men. First, unlike Chaadaev, Grossman did not "repent" of his harsh views of the Russian past and did not revert to the traditional view of a special Russian role in the future. Second, Grossman was a Jew; what was reprehensible coming from a Russian is viewed as *lese-majesté* coming from a Jew.

Grossman continued to advocate the value of each individual human being even during his last years, when he was suffering from terminal cancer. In his final completed work, *I Wish You Well!* (*Dobro vam!*), an account of his two-month visit to Armenia during the winter of 1961–62, he condemned chauvinist comments and jokes about Armenians, reminding his readers that it was Hitler and the Nazis who had focused particular attention on "questions of national hatred, national contempt, and national superiority." [23] In fact, like the Russians and the Jews, Armenians were the product of countless other cultures; hence the many different facial and personality types in Armenia. Grossman himself asserts that the basis of national character is human nature itself; therefore, we should rejoice in this common heritage and at the same time in the extraordinary variety within and among nationalities. [24]

Such views did not prevent Grossman from loving Russian culture, which he regarded as his own. Just a few lines after arguing for cultural pluralism, Grossman himself could not resist referring to Russian literature as "the greatest literature in the world." His works show that he appreciated as much as anyone the natural desire of Russians to treasure their heritage. But he spoke out courageously against the misuse of Russian patriotic feelings for political purposes. Ironically, some Russian nationalist writers, led by Iurii Bondarev, have called for "another Stalingrad" to throttle the energies released by *glasnost'* and *perestroika*. Grossman's *Life and Fate* calls for another Stalingrad, too: one with a different outcome. "Freedom had engendered the Russian victory," he said, but he had to lament that "freedom became simply a way of waging the war, a means to an end." Were he alive today, Vasilii Grossman, himself a veteran of Stalingrad, would be calling to his compatriots to take the "third and most natural path for Russia: the path of freedom and democracy." As the fiftieth anniversary of the German surrender at Stalingrad draws nigh, history waits to see if his call will be answered.

5 "Self" and "Other" in

Russian Literature

What books have you read? Which ones had the deepest meaning for you? Which did you dislike? And what were your criteria for meaning and for dislike? We have all asked these questions of friends and acquaintances and on the basis of the answers—not just the substance of the answers, but their manner as well—bridges are built or destroyed, ties of kinship are established, or barriers of alienation are emplaced. Perhaps in our technotronic age the importance of literature as such has receded, but as it has withdrawn film and video and television have been highly literatized. We cannot live without the images, the symbols, the myths of self that have inhabited literature, and if we find them now in other media and take our styles of presentation and representation from elsewhere, that is surely a secondary matter.

Literature does not create these signposts of self. It finds and arranges, presents and represents them. But once found and represented, they tend to have a staying power that outlasts their "real life" sources. And, of course, literature so very often finds them in other literature—after the work of Ernst Robert Curtius we can scarcely underestimate the inertial power of the *topos*, the commonplace[1]— just as the more recent media tend to find them in literature or in folklore. At some point in space and time these signposts have an origin in social life outside of literature. But that point may be more or less remote. And from literature the signposts have a disconcerting way of returning to social life. Iurii Lotman has shown most eloquently how, for example, the Decembrist movement in Russia was permeated by a romantic theatricality originating in readings of Schiller, and how strikingly the events of December 14, 1825, and their aftermath fell into the plot-line of Don Carlos.[2]

Literature "works," but not always in simple or daylit ways. It works in a way that brings the present into relationship with the past; it fosters a shared experience, brings the nature of that experience into a play of colored lights, some of them glamorizing and enhancing it, others subjecting it to a harsh critical glare. It probes as well what is frustrating and inhibiting in that experience and seeks a possible escape. To bring a little clarity to Fredric Jameson's turgid book, *The Political Unconscious*, literature is the political unconscious; or, rather, the political unconscious finds its way to consciousness in and through literature.[3]

Literature consists of more than fiction and poetry; it includes within its institutional network criticism, reviewing, a certain presence within all public media of communication and universities and foundations; it also includes the practice of censorship, governmental and otherwise, and the practice of translation; above all, it implies the existence of a literate public eager to receive it, one that is something more than merely a class public. In modern Europe, the coming into being of literature involved a translation and transformation of the classical and medieval heritage and coincided with and was closely tied to the emergence of the nation-state. Just as the nation-state achieved a certain distinctness and personality in its interplay with other nation-states in a system of rivalry and emulation, hostility and alliance, that we call "Europe," so in each nation-state a literature emerged that had distinct characteristics yet at the same time partook of a larger "European" entity. Russian literature began at the same time that Russia entered the European state system, with the reign of Peter the Great, yet throughout the eighteenth century it remained merely a class literature, possibly even merely a court literature; it was only in the 1830s and 1840s that something like a Russian reading public came into being that transcended very narrow class lines— indeed, "class" was almost too broad a definition for it, since the court circle and its immediate entourage were what defined it. In these cultural-historical terms, nineteenth-century Russia bore a certain resemblance to the sixteenth century in Western Europe. Just as the emergence of a national literature was accompanied in Western Europe by a severe yet in some ways also complicitous political censorship in the sixteenth and seventeenth centuries, so it was in Russia in the nineteenth.[4]

Having indicated my belief that literature in general has served as an important element in the growth of national self-consciousness and that it has served as one of the significant signposts of self by which identities and alterities are brought to consciousness, let me add also my belief that Russian literature has played this role to an unusual degree. Russian culture is permeated by literary reference. The history of Russian thought, for instance, cannot be studied apart from the history of Russian literature. Russian philosophy, at least until 1917, has been thoroughly mediated by a screen of literary reference. In Russian, traditionally since the nineteenth century, self-awareness and self-consciousness have expressed themselves best in literary form.

What I propose to discuss in this chapter are some of the marks of identity and alterity that seem to me striking and characteristic of classical Russian literature for a period of about a century, from the 1820s to the 1920s roughly speaking, with a few words on the present. I also wish to indicate certain striking absences—themes and signposts one might reasonably have expected to appear in such a rich literary output, given the nature of Russia's historical experience during this period, but which are not there, or are only fleetingly or wanly there. I mean to limit myself to the canon of classical Russian literature as it is commonly conceived in both Russia and the West. That is, I do not mean to include minor writers like Grigorovich or Uspenskii or Korolenko. There is inevitably a very strong element of subjectivity and impressionism in such an enterprise, and my intention here is to be suggestive rather than definitive.

First, let me mention "class" as a signpost of self—though "class" is perhaps not the right word, and I should use the Russian word *soslovie*, which means an "estate" to which one is ascribed by law.[5] In a nation in which the vast majority of the population was ascribed to the peasantry, it is striking that the peasant plays so faint a role in classical Russian literature. Of course, there is a genre-literature that centers on the peasant village, from Grigorovich to Korolenko and the Uspenskii brothers. These are for the most part, however, works of considerably less literary magnitude than the classics, though some of them had great impact in their time. There is also an important peasant-folkloric element in Russian poetry, in the poems of Nekrasov, for instance, outstandingly in one of his narrative masterpieces, "Moroz, Krasnyi Nos" ("Frost the Red-Nosed"). The peasant as an ideological element, the idea of the peasant as the *narod*, "the people," is, it needs to be said, an important theme, probably the most important theme in Russian national thought and certainly an important presence in Russian literature, and I shall return to that aspect later. But the peasant as a foregrounded character, a personality, a sensibility with which the reader is moved to identify is notable by his or her absence. There are a number of well-drawn peasant characters, to be sure, and some interesting and vivid descriptions of peasant life, from *The Captain's Daughter* to *Anna Karenina*, and even something of the peasant's point of view and sensibility are conveyed—but almost always in the background, as an adjunct to the sentimental education of central figures who are of a different class entirely. There are, however, some apparent exceptions to this generalization.

There is Pugachev in Pushkin's *The Captain's Daughter*, a historical figure, a peasant by origin, though he appears as the leader of a rebel army and claims to be "the true tsar." Though he is not a central figure in the novel, the plot hinges on him, and he plays a surprising and rather disturbing role in the life of the main protagonists. The rather bland and stereotyped hero, Grinev, twice owes his life to him. The more interesting villain, a sinister nobleman named Shvabrin, who has betrayed his class and joined forces with the rebels, is in his service.

Shvabrin and Grinev are such antipodes, the reader can hardly escape the conjecture that they form the bright and the shadow side of a single implied character; that the author, perhaps at a deep level, identified more closely with the character of Shvabrin than with that of the insipid and too-good-to-be-true hero, Grinev, who, although fully in Pugachev's power and at risk of his own life, retains his class loyalty. Or does he? Surely the most extraordinary scene in the novel is Grinev's dream in which a figure he takes to be his father rises up out of his mother's bed and turns out to be Pugachev. True, the figure then threatens him with an axe and he wakes in a cold sweat, but something of an identity has been suggested, though it is one that provokes much anxiety.

In Gogol's *Dead Souls*, Chichikov wanders around the countryside buying up dead souls—male serfs who have died between the last census taken and the next, on whom the landowner must still pay taxes. Chichikov's purpose is to compile a list of serfs he owns that would entitle him to free land in the newly Russianized Caucasus. The serfs are nonexistent, but Chichikov means to sell the land and accrue a nice profit. In his travels he meets with the local landowners, who respond to his proposition in characteristic ways. They are an appalling lot. Between stops he reads aloud the names of the dead souls he has bought to his coachman, Seliphan. As he reads he speculates on the personality the name suggests:

> Stepan the Cork—Carpenter; of exemplary sobriety. Ah, there he is, Stepan the Cork, there's the mighty giant who was fit to be in the guards! Guess he covered all the provinces on foot with his axe stuck in his belt and his boots slung over his shoulders; he'd eat a copper's worth of bread and two of dried fish, yet in his purse, like as not, he'd lug home a hundred solid silver rubles every time, and maybe even sew a government note in his linen breeches or put it in the toe of his boot. . . . Maksim Teliatnikov—Shoemaker. Ha, a shoemaker! Drunk as a shoemaker, says the proverb. . . . You learned your trade from a German, who fed all of you apprentices together, beat you over the back with a strap for slovenliness, and wouldn't let you out into the streets to skylark and carry on. . . . Grigorii Try-to-get-there-but-you-won't! What sort of man were

you? Did you go in for hauling and did you get yourself a *troika* and cart covered with matting. . . . and started transporting merchants to the fairs? . . . Habakkuk Phyrov! What are you up to, brother? Where are you, what regions are you knocking about in? Has fate carried you off to the Volga, and have you fallen in love with a free life, having joined the brotherhood of barge-haulers? . . .[6]

In this manner, somehow the dead souls spring to life. In any case, they assume a liveliness and a play of possibilities that the so-called "live" souls of the obsessed and obsessive landowners Chichikov has been interviewing do not possess.

The narrator in Turgenev's *Hunter's Notebook* describes the peasants he encounters on his hunting expeditions, and the *Notebook* is a kind of survey of peasant types and their lot under serfdom. The beauty of the natural landscape and the joys of the hunt are contrasted subtly and quietly with the hard lot of the peasant and the arbitrary mechanism of the serf system. Yet the narrator is strangely removed from everything that he describes. There is a certain passivity to his presence, which at times seems almost spectral, although it is his person that links the stories and provides what unity there is to the "notebook." Turgenev did write a few later stories that featured peasants, but in his novels, the work by which he is known, peasants fade again into the background. I would note, however, that in one of his later stories, "Mumu," the central figure is a mute serf who suffers the persecution of his owner, a tyrannical woman not unlike Turgenev's mother—whom he nevertheless survives. It is a story of endurance and survival that elaborates on some of the motifs suggested in the *Hunter's Notebook*.[7]

A story of Tolstoy's, also set in the time of serfdom, that deals with a different kind of interference on the part of a woman landowner in the lives of "her" peasants might almost serve as counterpoint to Turgenev's "Mumu." The story is called "Polikushka." In this case, the landowner is well-intentioned, even sentimental, though ignorant of peasant life and incurious and incautious as to the possible consequences of her acts. Her intervention to prevent the military recruitment of a favorite serf, Polikushka, causes mayhem and tragedy in the peasant village, and she is left frightened, upset, and frustrated by what she has wrought, yet still uncomprehending and "at sea" with regard to the system she nominally commands.[8]

In *War and Peace*, peasants are a very important part of the background, from Pierre Bezukhov's failed attempt at "reform" to the threatening peasant revolt on the Bolkonsky estate as the Napoleonic invasion nears. Among the central characters, only Nikolai Rostov, in the later parts of the novel, is described as working closely with peasants, understanding them and their way of life, grasping the link between their prosperity and his own as landowner, and therefore succeeding in bringing the economy of his estate into the black. He is also described, however, as dealing with the peasants in something of a peasant way, striking at them with his fists, for instance, when he loses his temper, rather disregarding the fact that they cannot strike back.

The only peasant in Tolstoy's great novel who steps into the foreground is less a "character" than an emblematic figure—Platon Karataev. He evokes echoes from Turgenev's *Hunter's Notebook*—even his surname appears in the title of one of those sketches—but his intended meaning is rendered much more explicitly. The hero of the novel, Pierre Bezukhov, meets him at a time of danger and despair. Both have been taken prisoner by the French and are being marched to some uncertain destination. Pierre becomes aware of Karataev first as a smell: "Besides Pierre in a stooping position sat a small man of whose presence he was first made aware by a strong smell of sweat which came from him every time he moved."[9] Characteristically for Tolstoy's mode of introducing a character, he is doing something, removing his leg-bands before turning in for the night. "Pierre was conscious of something pleasant, comforting and well-rounded in these deft movements, in the man's well-ordered arrangements in his corner, and even in his very smell, and he looked at the man without taking his eyes from him."

Karataev is described as rounded in his figure, almost maternal. His resemblance to the latter, maternal Natasha is difficult to escape. Though small, he has a body shaped something like the earth itself and it is part of his earthiness that he makes no hierarchical distinctions either among his captors or among his fellow prisoners or between them, or for that matter between men and horses and dogs, all of whom he includes in his prayers. He regards them all with respect and sympathy, and his talk with and about them has a kind of earthy poetry. Before dropping off to sleep, he prays: "Lay me down like a stone, O God, and let me rise up like new bread." He faces his death by firing-squad with the same acceptance that he shows to all forms of life.

Pierre, as Tolstoy's surrogate, admires Karataev's capacity to accept his fate. He admires, too, his capacity to adapt himself to all circumstances, to be able to do a little bit of everything as circumstance demands, though he does no one thing with any outstanding or unusual skill. In short, what Tolstoy admires in Karataev, and what he depicts him as emblematic of, is a holistic culture, one that integrates the individual into a sense of kinship with the world. This respect for what he regarded as the holistic nature of peasant culture manifested itself as well in his educational efforts, the school he founded and his essays on pedagogy. It is, of course, also evident in *Anna Karenina* and his other works. In a superb short story, for instance, entitled "How Much Land Does a Man Need?" Tolstoy focuses on a "successful" prosperous peasant, whose very success has estranged him from his peers and the world. He hears that the Bashkirs are offering free land, and he travels to Bashkiria, where the inscrutable native inhabitants say they will give him as much land as he can traverse in a day. This whets his greed with increasing intensity as he makes his way. He moves faster and faster across larger and larger areas, until at the end of the day he drops dead of exhaustion.[10]

It has been commonly observed of Russian literature that it deals with a limited social milieu, the landowning gentry or nobility, with Dostoevsky's work a partial exception to the rule, since he deals largely with the urban intelligentsia. Foreigners, and even the non-Russian inhabitants of the Russian Empire, are scarcer in the pages of Russian literature than peasants. Gogol' was Ukrainian and his early works are full of Ukrainian folklorics. Then they disappear. Anna Akhmatova, Ukrainian in origin, makes little of this in the presentation of her lyric persona, though others, like her husband, the poet Nikolai Gumilev, occasionally emphasized it.[11] There was a whole romantic genre of Caucasus literature, both prose and verse, to which such major poets as Pushkin and Lermontov contributed. Susan Layton, in a fine recent article, has pointed out a whole "imaginary geography" of the Caucasus which bore a much closer relationship to romantic notions of the sublime than it did to any actual physical landscape, least of all that of the Caucasus.[12] In his wonderful novella "The Cossacks," Tolstoy did not try to deflate the romantic notion of Caucasus, but rather attempted to show that the Caucasus is spiritually inaccessible to the Russians.[13] In his very last novel, *Hadji Murad*, Tolstoy's central figure is a Circassian warrior who, attempting to protect his family, is caught between the fanaticism of Shamil and the mindless imperialism of the Russians. Although the central figure of the novel, around whom the action revolves, Hadji Murad nevertheless remains largely in the background as a character.[14]

Both Russian prose and verse of the first half of the nineteenth century are sprinkled with innumerable French tutors in Russian landowning households, comic figures generally, rather alike, whose ineptitude tends to provoke a certain wonder that the Russian educated classes ever learned to speak French at all. Germans fare little better. Gogol's are burgherly artisans or shopkeepers, figures of fun. Pushkin's Germann in "The Queen of Spades," a Russianized German of considerable vividness if of dubious morality, is a rare exception.[15] Turgenev and Tolstoy have an occasional sympathetic, melancholy German music master lurking in the background, brooding on the harsh facts of exile, but in *War and Peace* the Germans are predominantly those who believe in "military science," which Tolstoy means to disparage. There is, of course, Shtolts in Goncharov's *Oblomov*, who is half German.[16] He represents European competence and efficacy in contrast to Oblomovian sloth. His real distinction, however, consists in his tacit recognition of Oblomov's spiritual superiority and his determination (ultimately unsuccessful) to get Oblomov moving and out of bed.

Poles fare worse than either the French or the Germans. They are curiously absent from Tolstoy's *War and Peace*, though as we know one-fifth of Napoleon's army was Polish. Dostoevsky's Poles always turn out to be nasty at the core. Grushenka's former lover in *The*

Brothers Karamazov is the outstanding example. Handsome and cultivated, with the bearing of a soldier and a gentleman, he turns out nevertheless to be a cad—a liar and a cheat, and above all incorrigibly vain. It is generally vanity, hauteur and contempt for things Russian, a feeling of ethnic and cultural superiority that he attributes to them, by which Dostoevsky characterizes Poles.[17] Jews occupy a sparser and socially lower place, and are not any pleasanter. There is the Kapernaumov family in *Crime and Punishment*, who sublet a room to Sonia and all of whose children have hare-lips. There is the fire-watch before whom Svidrigailov commits suicide, in part at least in response to the expression on his face—"that expression of long-suffering querulousness that has been stamped without exception on all Jewish faces."[18]

Classical Russian literature is almost exclusively about Russians and it deals with a distinctly limited social milieu. Nevertheless, for its major protagonists social class is a secondary consideration, if it is in any way a signpost of self. Dostoevsky's central figures are for the most part *raznochintsy*; if they are gentry, they are either impoverished, déclassé, or arriviste. But even Tolstoy's and Turgenev's landowners are more marked by the books they have read, by their reflections and speculations on life, by their education, than by the other marks of class. This is not true of the urban aristocratic milieu in which the Karenins and Vronskii move; it is not true of Oblomovka or the appalling estate of the Golovlevs. But by and large it is true in Russian literature that education and ideas are stronger markers of self than other aspects of social class.

But about this education there is a deep-seated ambivalence. "With the mind, one cannot grasp Russia," wrote the poet Tiutchev, and by the mid-nineteenth century "grasping Russia" had somehow become a central project of Russian literature. The protagonists of the Russian novel, the so-called "superfluous men," are passionate seekers after the meaning of life, they are deeply introspective and reflect constantly on the meaning of their experience, yet their very intellectuality isolates and disarms them. They are "all sicklied o'er with the pale cast of thought," and it is not for nothing that Hamlet has been interpreted in Russian criticism as the representative *intelligent*, not very good at action to be sure, but the hero of conscience. And "grasping Russia" meant above all identifying with the peasant and the "bleak landscape and impoverished huts" of village Russia. In his rather bad and atypically tendentious novel *Smoke*, Turgenev has at least this striking passage in which one of the characters, Potugin, depicts a scene in which educated landowner and impoverished peasant confront each other, each with the plea, "Save me!" [19]

As early as 1829, Chaadaev had tried to express what was to become a central intelligentsia theme and mood as characteristic of Russia *per se*. He wrote to an acquaintance:

Look around you: don't we all have one foot in the air? We all look as though we are traveling. No one has a definite sphere of existence; no one has proper habits; there are no rules for anything; there is no home base; everything passes, leaving no trace either outside or within us. In our homes we are like visitors, among our families we are like strangers, in our cities we are like nomads, more nomadic than those whose animals graze on our steppes, for they are more attached to their deserts than we are to our cities. [20]

It was this theme of homelessness, of not belonging anywhere, of a kind of orphanhood that attached itself to the "superfluous men," the heroes and protagonists of Russian literature.

The heroines were somewhat different—in their loyalty and fidelity to the heroes, to name but one simple thing. But above all in their integrity, their wholeness of being that contrasted so strongly with the feeling of fragmentation and alienation that characterized their male counterparts. In his brilliant essay "On Socialist Realism," Abram Tertz characterized the strong, integral Russian heroine of classical fiction as a kind of substitute for the lost sense of purpose among the educated classes, a kind of substitute for God and the civilizing mission of the state which they could no longer believe in. [21] It might be more correct to say that the image of the peasant rather than the heroine served that "purpose." It should be remembered, though, that the image of the peasant was that of a rounded body, a holistic culture, a capacity for endurance, a certain passivity and blankness that needed to be filled in, a distinctly feminine image.

In the ideological controversies of the 1840s between westernizers and Slavophiles, the Slavophiles took the position that Russian culture had been severely disrupted and fragmented by Peter the Great and his efforts at westernization, that the educated classes suffered that fragmentation, while the peasantry retained what was authentic and integral in Russian culture, especially their Christian faith and the communal way of life, the mystical *sobornost'* (communal spirit) that was a product of that faith. That faith and its manifestation in a communal way of life made Russia fundamentally different from Western Europe and indicated a different path of development. Indeed, the Slavophiles saw the secularization of Europe, the falling away from faith, as leading to an intellectual impasse, which only a culture still rooted in faith, like the Russian, could resolve.[22]

The westernizers did not deny there were differences between Russia and the West, but, they pointed out, the countries of Europe were also different from each other, even while they shared a common civilization. Russia was essentially like the other countries of Europe, only more backward. In a sense, there was something comforting in this notion because it seemed to make the future predictable and secure—Russia's future could be understood in terms of the European present. Yet there is also a streak of messianism that runs through westernizing thought, in which the very notion of backwardness is turned into a pledge for the future. This is already evident in Chaadaev, who had called Russian history a "blank page" that had produced nothing for the enrichment of human culture other than the occupation of space. In his unfinished essay, "The Apology of a Madman," he turns the very blankness of that page into a promise for the future—for a blank page remains to be written on.[23] The archwesternizer Belinskii, in a totally different mood and tone to be sure, proclaimed in 1842 that Russia had no literature, but regarded this lack almost as a kind of triumph, as an indication that it soon would have a vigorous and vital one. And it was Belinskii in 1846 who anticipated by thirty-five years Dostoevsky's message in his famous Pushkin speech that the Russians were a "God-bearing people," a people who combined within themselves the talents of all the other nations.[24]

Aleksandr Gertsen separated the peasant's communal way of life from what the Slavophiles considered to be its grounding in Orthodox faith and attempted to find a role for the educated Russian against a background of disillusionment with European developments based on the failure of revolutionary movements rather than what the Slavophiles considered to be the impasse of secularization. He tried to find a historic, perhaps even a cosmic role for the highly developed, talented, creative, educated individual in developing the social conscience and felt communal responsibility of the peasant village while disposing of its barbarous superstitions, its ignorance, its backwardness, and its occasional cruelty.[25]

All these ideas, both in their 1840s form and in their later development in the 1860s, play an important role in Dostoevsky's later novels. Dostoevsky was never a Slavophile, nor did he, after his return from Siberian exile, share Gertsen's vision of a socialist future. Ironically, his experience of the peasantry at hard labor and in exile had been a bitter one—they had rejected him. Among his few friends had been the Polish exiles, with whom he could at least talk. Yet Dostoevsky, like the Slavophiles, sensed something of great value in the peasant's retention of a kind of primitive Christianity. In some respects he felt that the faith had been preserved in its purest form among some of the non-Orthodox sectarians—the *molokane*, for instance. In spite of the brutal and primitive nature of peasant life, in spite of ignorance and superstition, in spite of the temptations of greed and hunger, he felt that faith kept alive in the peasant conscience a hope for the future from which intellectuals had much to learn. It was the image of Christ and the faith in Christianity as it had been to such a remarkable degree preserved in the peasant milieu that Dostoevsky saw as central to Russia and Russia's future.

In Dostoevsky's most densely ideological novel, *The Possessed*, I wish to dwell briefly on the character of Shatov and his ideas—not that I identify them completely with Dostoevsky's own, but rather because his is the character the author seems to stand closest to, and because these ideas play a certain role in the future.

Shatov is of peasant birth but long alienated from his origins. He is entirely an intellectual. He has been to America, where, we are told, he lay in a barn for three days and thought deeply about life. In Dostoevsky's novels, "going to America" is a kind of death, and return from America has almost the force of a resurrection. Shatov has begun to rethink his ways. At the time of the novel, he welcomes back his estranged wife, in spite of the fact that she is pregnant by another man. He is in a state of high excitement and tension as his wife is about to give birth. One has the sense that his mood, fueled by love, compassion, and forgiveness and producing an almost comical level of excitement and exaltation, is going to produce great and fundamental changes in his soul. He has removed himself from the band of revolutionary conspirators led by the sinister Petr Verkhovenskii, who now plans to murder him. He speaks of his beliefs to Stavrogin, the man he regards as their inspirator, but who now responds coldly and indifferently to his impassioned representation. Shatov's belief is in the *narod*, in the people; that is to say, the peasantry, because it is in the people that a compassionate, humane, living religion has been preserved; it is the narod that keeps Christ. "And God?" Stavrogin asks him, "do you believe in God?" Shatov stammers, pauses, then answers: "I will believe in God." In other words, his faith is in the people, the Russian peasantry, in the hope that their faith in God will lead him to his own, which he still lacks. In the meantime, his faith in the people is a faith in God. But Shatov is murdered and the transition never takes place.[26]

Aleksandr Blok's unfinished long poem "Retribution" and the essays he wrote at the time of the Revolution and Civil War project a curious image of self and other, because in these he fully identifies himself first with the high culture of Western Europe as it developed since the Renaissance, and second with the Russian educated classes of the late nineteenth century that absorbed that culture. At the same time, he sees that culture as not only doomed but morally condemned. It is damned because it has forcibly excluded from its benefits and delights the vast, ignorant masses. In Russia, where the masses have been especially brutalized and ground under, they have now arisen and begun to take their revenge. The *narod* is formless and chaotic but it moves with a will that is the will of God. The Bolsheviks are the expression of that will—and it portends the complete destruction of the old order, including its culture. On the one hand, Blok is contemptuous of the *narod* and sees himself as separate from it; on the other, he exalts and identifies himself with its destructive mission.[27]

In conclusion, let me dwell briefly on a recent school of Russian writers who have been the focus of considerable interest, and among them there are undoubtedly writers of talent. I refer to the *dereven-shchiki*, or village writers. Probably the school has its origin in a book published around 1960 by Vladimir Soloukhin called *Vladimirskie proselki*, or *Vladimir Trails*. In format as well as, to some degree, in style, it resembles Turgenev's *Hunter's Notebook*. It is an account of a walking tour in the Vladimir region, and it describes a ravaged countryside. Churches in disrepair, old manor houses in ruin, and above all peasant villages depopulated and old peasant skills and crafts abandoned—the grim toll of collectivization, urbanization, sovietization; though it is never explicitly labeled as "grim," still less as "Soviet," the picture is clear. Soloukhin has since become known as a nationalist in the Slavophile tradition, with just a tinge of xenophobia that was foreign to the Slavophiles of the 1840s. The nucleus of the later "village prose" school, however, was a group of writers who came from Siberia, where some peasant villages hung on longer than elsewhere to the old ways—the playwright Vasilii Shukshin, who died in 1974, and the best-known writer of the group, Valentin Rasputin.

No less a figure than Solzhenitsyn has stressed the importance of the fact that Rasputin is of peasant origin. Sergei Zalygin, editor of the prestigious journal *Novyi mir*, himself the son of a prosperous peasant "dekulakized" during collectivization, and from Siberia as well, has also shown some tenderness for Rasputin's career. At a time when so few authentic Russian peasants are left, when the traditional life of the Russian village has been ground and decimated and reground over a period of sixty years, the holistic culture of the peasant village has emerged once more as an ideal of order and a signpost of identity.

Rasputin's novel *Farewell to Matera* deals with a peasant village on an island that is about to be flooded in the construction of a dam. Only a handful of old people and eccentrics are left, but their sense of community, their rootedness, their integration with nature, their sense of place in a larger and suprahuman cosmos are dramatically contrasted with the unreflective, brusquer, brasher ways of those who have been ordered to remove them. The imagery is so strong that it seems the island is not going to be flooded so much as uprooted or unmoored.

The Master—an unspecified animal that roams the island at night—
sets up its last funeral wail that seems to mourn the final separation of
humanity not only from nature but from the natural order of things.[28]

A great Russian philosopher, Mikhail Bakhtin, is reported to have
said in 1929 when he heard some of the reports about collectivization
and the bloody way it had intervened in the traditional life of the Russian village—"They have killed Russia." But Russia, it would seem,
and its long identification with the life of the traditional peasant village, no matter in how melancholy and retrospective a form, is still
alive. What is even more intensely alive, however, is the image of the
peasant as "Russian self," at a time when an authentic peasantry, a
rooted peasant way of life, exists only in vague traces—if it ever did
really exist in the idealized, Christianized form of which the Slavophiles dreamed, and still dream, their fondest dreams.

6   Stalin's Legacy:

Populism in Literature

To the unfading memory of my friend Thomas Blakeley.

During the last years of Stalin's long and tiresome reign, Russian nationalism in Soviet Russian literature, criticism, and the arts became a palpable reality, at once grotesque and mythical. The goal of this chapter is not so much to describe various aspects of this disconcerting phenomenon as to trace, in a provisory manner at least, when, why, and how this tendency was introduced and enforced by Stalin and his ideological helpers, what the reaction of Soviet writers to this edict was and how the tendency modified itself after Stalin's death.

Despite the enormous and continually expanding volume of literature and memoirs dedicated to Stalin, especially in the years 1984–89, we are still unable to come to a viable conclusion about Stalin's personality. This is an important issue because Stalin had concentrated in his hands a power undreamt of by any tyrant in world history, and he was personally responsible for the ways in which official Soviet literature and the arts developed. Step by step, from the early 1930s on-ward, Stalin influenced literature and authors, "the engineers of human souls," and a populism tightly interwoven with nationalism was maintained throughout, to remain one of his most powerful ideological weapons.

Who was Stalin? A devoted Marxist, in love with Lenin, whose portrait he was said to have carried with him to his numerous residences and palaces? A great scholar, scientist, and intellectual whose mind could overshadow that of Aristotle himself? A shrewd cutthroat, a Caucasian bandit, in the words of an American ambassador, who apparently did not experience any pangs of remorse for the millions of his victims?[1] An unparalleled sadist, extremely well-read in the relevant historical literature describing Nero-like cruelties, the tortures of the Inquisition, and the massacres of Tamurlane and the Turkish sultans? A madman enchanted by Ivan the Terrible displaying, like the Muscovite tsar, an insatiable bloodthirst and paranoia, and diagnosed as such as early as Christmas 1927 by Vladimir Bekhterev, for which the great psychiatrist immediately paid the ultimate price?[2] An evil-minded powermonger who disregarded, in Volkogonov's words, gold, wealth, comfort for the sake of power and power alone?

Stalin boasted of his iron will, which looked more like an inflexible stubbornness to others. He was aware that to perpetuate his power he needed to make use of many factors, such as a strong, deified leader, a detailed ideology bordering on absurdity yet still blindly believed in by his people, shrewd use of Russian history and habits, and, last but not least, a relentless terror accompanied by a total lack of compassion and an incessant flow of blood. It is misleading to visualize him as a mediocrity or an ignoramus; having survived until age nineteen in the Tiflis Theological Seminary, he knew perfectly well the laws of hypocrisy and double-mindedness. He knew in fine detail the lives of the world's tyrants, his personal mentors being Machiavelli and Talleyrand.

He had built up his praetorian guard, surrounding himself with a circle of aides capable of committing any crime at an order from their boss. He used modern technology both for eavesdropping and for indoctrinating millions of people. He had tested his theory based on

Marxism, mythology, and absurdity in a series of trials around 1929, the turning point of his reign. Trotsky and his followers were deported or exiled. The necessity for world revolution was downplayed while "socialism in one country" was pushed ahead. Hitler, viewed by Stalin with a mixture of envy and admiration, was climbing to power: his ideas about the party, the Gestapo, the masses, and *Volksliteratur* were studied by Stalin's experts. The western world, its leaders, and prominent intellectuals such as Romain Rolland and Bernard Shaw could be shrewdly manipulated. Stalin's attitude toward the West might be summed up by Il'ia Repin's masterpiece, "The Zaporozh'e Cossacks Writing a Letter to the Turkish Sultan," a reproduction of which was displayed in one of his living rooms. From the early 1930s, the historical past of Russia received a better, though one-sided interpretation in Soviet arts, but at the same time further suppression and brutality toward Russian peasants and the Church continued. Stalin was by no means oblivious to Russia as the Third Rome, and he acknowledged that Dostoevsky, who was virtually banned in those years, was a genius in psychology but "harmful for our youths."[3] Dostoevsky's *The Possessed*, in particular Petr Verkhovenskii's and Shigalev's utopian schemes, were treasured by Stalin as the models to imitate. It was said that Nechaev's archive was kept in Stalin's personal file until his death.

In the early 1930s, particularly in the first months of 1932, there occurred profound changes in "official" Soviet literature. By that time, Maxim Gor'kii had been tested by his well-publicized testimonials about the new, happy conditions in the Soviet prison camps, and he had settled in Moscow comfortably, feeling kidnapped, imprisoned, and exploited. However, he did not fail to serve Stalin's initiatives in developing Russian literature, and to that purpose he used his worldwide positive reputation. In April 1932, Stalin sponsored the elimination of the Russian Association of Proletarian Writers (RAPP) and the banishment of Leopol'd Averbakh, and he personally met with a group of leading Soviet Russian writers. The proletarian principle defended by the dissolved writers' association was replaced by socialist realism, ultimately based on various concepts, including the three most important theoretical categories: party-mindedness, ideological commitment, and populism (*partiinost'*, *ideinost'*, *narodnost'*). The

First Congress of Soviet Writers held in Moscow in August 1934 made socialist realism and its concepts the law of Soviet literature.

Stalin's policy on literature and the arts was dictated by various factors. Generally speaking, it began to take shape when Stalin decided to centralize his power even more, to isolate Lenin's guard with their slogan of internationalism, and to bring into reality Koz'ma Prutkov's "total uniformity of thought," in contrast to what he himself maintained in 1912: that "full conformity of views can be achieved only in a cemetery." [4] By introducing "populism" in the arts, Stalin took note of Hitler's policy in regard to the arts with its *Schlagwort* "Die Kunst dem Völke," the arts of the people. Hitler's *Volkskunst, Volkskultur*, and *Volksliteratur* did not go unnoticed by Stalin's ideological collaborators, a point seldom noted by western researchers.

From 1934 on, party-mindedness and ideological commitment were injected into the conscience of writers along with the advantages of "people's creativity" and populism in general. But Stalin needed time to enforce the concept of populism. He could not ignore the decades-long traditions of Russian revolutionaries, the Decembrists, Gertsen, Chernyshevskii, and others, who had been permeated with western ideas and were opposed to Slavophilism. Millions of Soviet Russians learned by heart Lenin's words:

We remember that Chernyshevskii, the Great-Russian democrat who dedicated his life to the cause of revolution, said half a century ago: "A wretched nation, a nation of slaves, from top to bottom—all slaves." The overt and covert Great-Russian slaves [slaves of tsarist autocracy] do not like to recall these words, yet in our opinion these were words of genuine love for our country, a love pained by the absence of a revolutionary spirit in the masses of the Great-Russian people. . . . We are full of national pride because the Great-Russian nation, too, has created a revolutionary class, because it, too, has proved capable of providing mankind with great models of the struggle for freedom and socialism, and not just with great pogroms, rows of gallows, dungeons, famines and humble servility to priests, tsars, landowners and capitalists. [5]

Being an attentive observer of common Russians before the October Revolution and afterward, Stalin, unlike Chernyshevskii and Lenin, was not exceedingly upset by "the absence of the revolutionary spirit in the masses of the Great-Russian people." Stalin by no means regretted the lack of revolutionary spirit at the time of landslide collectivization and industrialization, and in his own way he appreciated the Russians' servility toward the reborn and reattired "priests, tsars, landowners and capitalists," in other words toward the much more powerful and ruthless party, state, and secret police officials appointed by Stalin and his collaborators. More than that, by having uninterruptedly encouraged a bloodbath for the revolutionary class whom Lenin had praised as the conspicuous achievement of Russian history and the Russians, Stalin seemed to satisfy the thirst of Soviet thugs for "great pogroms, rows of gallows, dungeons, famines and servility."

The three dominating concepts of socialist realism and Marxist-Leninist esthetics, party-mindedness, ideological commitment, and populism, developed in the 1930s and 1940s, remind us of Sergei Uvarov's well-known triad proclaimed under Nicholas I a hundred years before the major shifts in Soviet literature: "Orthodoxy, autocracy, populism." It seems relevant to emphasize some of Uvarov's words about this triad:

> In the midst of the rapid collapse in Europe of religious and civil institutions, at a time of general spreading of destructive ideas, at the sight of grievous phenomena surrounding us on all sides, it was necessary to establish our fatherland on firm foundations upon which is based a people's well-being, strength and life; it was necessary to find the principles which form the distinctive character of Russia, and which belong only to Russia; it was necessary to gather into one whole the sacred remnants of Russian nationality and fasten to them the anchor of our salvation.[6]

These three principles of Orthodoxy, autocracy, and populism could have had some meaning in the first half of the nineteenth century, even though the Russian intelligentsia did not always treat them seriously. But what the principles of Soviet aesthetics meant to writers and artists is not easy to say with any precision. First of all, each unit of the triad of socialist realism is difficult to translate into English, and the independent position of each is in doubt. Stalin's future historians will probably treat this subject against the background of the tyrant's religious education. Can one translate "Orthodoxy, autocracy, and populism" into "party-mindedness, ideological commitment, and populism?" Does party-mindedness correspond to Orthodoxy? In 1928, filmmakers Eisenstein and Pudovkin appealed to "the Party Commission on Cinema Affairs" to provide them with a "Red culture instructor" and "a strict ideological dictatorship." A hero in V.M. Kirshon's play *Bread* (*Khleb*, 1930) says: "The party . . . is a ring, an iron fetter uniting the people. . . . This fetter sometimes wounds the body, but without it I cannot live."[7] Does ideological commitment correspond to autocracy, and do its vague semantics mean a blind devotion and commitment to the present-day monarch, even though not officially crowned? Or does it replace the creative gift, and does ideological commitment to the high priest suffice?

In Mikhail Heller's words, in the first half of the 1930s the culture was nationalized, and N.R. Erdman's *Suicide* (*Samoubiitsa*, 1928), banned in 1932, calls the culture "a Red slave girl in the proletariat's harem."[8] But the nationalization of culture mentioned by Erdman in 1928 implies one more important characteristic: the presence of populism.

If it is complicated to differentiate between party-mindedness and ideological commitment, it is no easier to give a proper interpretation of populism.

Soviet culture in general, and Soviet Russian literature in particular, do satisfy the principle of populism. One cannot deny that the term *narodnost'*, often used by Zhdanov in his efforts to improve the quality of Soviet literature, appeared to be a cry of "Eureka!" It linked Russian literature not only with Uvarov's debatable triad, but with the nobler traditions of Russian literature, beginning with Viazemskii through Dobroliubov, Nekrasov, Tolstoy, and Gor'kii. It repeated, reflected, corrected, and at the same time resisted Goebbels' *Volksliteratur*.

In accordance with Stalin's appeal to authors: "Write the truth!" the concept of populism urged the engineers of human souls to serve the people, to be understood by them, to reproduce the people's desires and dreams, to lead the people and learn from them. It seemed incredibly meaningful to strike root in this promising principle at a time when millions of peasants, the core of the Russian people, were uprooted, starved to death, exiled to Siberian snow deserts and taigas; when millions of workers were physically and mentally chained and enslaved. It was at that time that Mikhail Bulgakov asked Stalin to do anything to him, even make him a street-sweeper, as Andrei Platonov would do some years later, because he was sentenced to the capital punishment of silence. Zamiatin, with his knowledge of the Russian *muzhik*, had to emigrate, while Babel' accomplished his heroic deed of silence, and Pasternak suffered insomnia and feared the loss of his sanity. Undoubtedly Osip Mandel'shtam, having written his satirical poem on Stalin, and Anna Akhmatova, seeing herself living in the time of the Apocalypse, had every reason to see the party's appeal as wise and candid.

Stalin's *narodnost'* , or populism, should be interpreted first of all as praise for the Russian people, its history and culture. The books and films about Aleksandr Nevskii and Peter the Great, Ivan the Terrible and Stepan Razin were created, read, and seen. At the same time, the physical extermination of the Russian people went on unabated, the best Russian intellectuals, poets and artists, scholars and scientists were stifled. Until his death Stalin never softened his iron rule, which prescribed as much killing as necessary to maintain and perpetuate his power. Nikita Khrushchev's recollections of Stalin, published in 1989 in *Ogonyok*, shed additional light on this aspect of Stalin's activities. At one time, Stalin and his aides watched a foreign movie about a famous pirate on a special mission from the British crown. In order to fulfill his mission, the pirate killed a good number of his close aides one after another. Beria afterward whispered to Khrushchev that Stalin had praised the pirate as a smart fellow, and Beria now urged Khrushchev to question Stalin about the pirate's actions. At the table Khrushchev, according to his own testimony, asked Stalin if he considered the pirate an awful scoundrel for slaying his own close friends. Stalin gave no verbal answer but cast an angry glance at Khrushchev.[9]

Populism in Russian literature and the arts was launched by Stalin as part of an expedient policy. Bukharin was said to have characterized Stalin as "a great provider of measured doses" in the time preceding the mass-scale massacres. According to P.I. Chagin and A.V. Antonov-Ovseenko, as early as 1927, frying his favorite kebab in the fireplace of Kirov's apartment in Leningrad, Stalin philosophically answered Kirov's remark concerning the need for a collective leadership: "Well, of course, the Central Committee, the collective leadership—all that is very fine. But the Russian *muzhik* is a tsarist, he needs only one person at the top." And saying this, he raised his index finger. A pause followed this remark. Everybody present was spellbound.[10]

To understand Stalin's motivation, one must be acquainted with an observation made by Karl Radek, an *Izvestiia* editor and Stalin's victim in 1937. Once in the circle of his close friends Radek is said to have recalled something that happened the day before, after a lengthy and tiring meeting in Moscow in the suburban part "Morozovka." This took place a few years after the October Revolution when Stalin was still relatively unknown. While they were sitting relaxing on a grassy meadow, eating good food and drinking fine wine, someone asked the eternal question, "What is the best thing in the world?" Kamenev answered at once: "A book!" Radek: "Nobody and nothing can give greater joy than a woman, your woman, the soul of your existence!" Bukharin then rose to his feet: "Nothing compares to the feeling of being on top of the people's mighty wave." Rykov answered with a joke: "Why should we go anywhere when we've just finished this delicious cognac." But Stalin's answer was firm in his mind: "The sweetest thing is to ponder deeply, to keep it in your heart, to wait; to watch your man carefully; to catch him—and take revenge!"[11]

A ridiculous aspect of this paradox of insisting on populism in Soviet Russian culture might be seen in Stalin's being a Georgian-born tyrant on the Russian throne. He spoke Russian with a formidable Caucasian accent and he liked spicy Georgian food in contrast to the rather bland Russian cuisine. Lavrentii Beria, a member of the Mingrelian minority in Georgia, alone was allowed to enter Stalin's bedroom and living room. To the dismay and horror of his Russian-speaking associates, Stalin preferred all too frequently to speak in Georgian to Beria and his bodyguards. Svetlana, his daughter, complained that in his habits and tastes he remained essentially an old Caucasian. In Radek's words, "Crawling stubbornly for days and weeks, hiding behind rocks and looking for their enemy, Caucasian people have an undeniable feature: the acute sense of mountain beasts. 'The Great Leader' inherited Caucasian qualities instinctively: cunning, malicious cruelty, vengefulness, wrath, the sharp eye of a predator, ability to sniff things out, skill, stubbornness. And the law of the forest has been adopted: force alone reigns, as well as the horror spread by it. And in addition, beastly shrewdness."[12]

At the same time, however, Stalin was well familiar with Russian history. Like the Tatars, he impoverished Russian villages. Like Catherine II, a German, he wanted to be seen by the people as a Russian; but unlike the False Dmitrii, one Grigorii Otrep'ev who aspired to the Muscovite throne in the early seventeenth century, and his Polish-born wife, Marina Mniszek, he was scrupulously careful not to overly injure the Russophile emotions of the enslaved and raped nation.

Among the scores of books and articles about Stalin, the memoirs of Konstantin Simonov (1915–79)[13] and Aleksandr Avdeenko (b. 1908)[14] are especially significant for our understanding of Stalin's legacy in promoting populism in Soviet literature. Both of them were famous in Russia: Avdeenko in the 1930s, Simonov in the 1940s. Each had the privilege of observing Stalin personally: Avdeenko, in 1940, during the five-hour discussion of his film *The Law of Life*, Simonov, in 1947 and after, when as a leading official of the Soviet Union of Writers he saw Stalin many times in hours-long conversations on Soviet literature and the Stalin Prizes.

Simonov was of noble origin, while Avdeenko was born to a miner's family. Both began publishing in 1933–34. Avdeenko found immediate success and fame, whereas Simonov had to wait a few years. In early 1935, at the All-Union Congress of Soviets and in the presence of Stalin, Avdeenko made an emotional speech ending with the following words: "When my son is born and starts to speak, the first word he will pronounce will be 'Stalin'."[15] Not surprisingly, this pleased Stalin. Simonov wrote his first popular play, *A Story of Love* (*Istoriia odnoi liubvi*), in 1939, and starting with 1941, he began to receive almost annually Stalin's Prize for his literary achievements.

Simonov had a difficult childhood, with several of his close relatives having been arrested. He was all the more grateful to Stalin and the party, which he joined in 1942, for sponsoring him in the new society. When in 1947 Zhdanov severely criticized Simonov's novel *The Fatherland's Fume*, doing so on the personal instructions of Stalin, Simonov behaved as an obedient member of the party, and then until Stalin's death he seemed to have no major setbacks with Stalin. He followed Stalin's suggestions and, of course, was more than happy when Stalin personally rewrote Simonov's critical article about President Tito.[16]

As to Avdeenko, initially life seemed more than just plain success. Having received Gor'kii's blessing, he published abundantly; he was given two houses, one of them in Moscow, as well as a summer house and a car; he was allowed to go abroad, and even to visit Stalin's prison camps in the worst years. He had a beautiful young wife and a lot of privileges. He was working for the Soviet movie industry and his film, *The Law of Life*, was to be seen by millions of Soviet people in their scant hours of leisure. Avdeenko was cheerful, happy-go-lucky; he enjoyed friendly ties with many distinguished intellectuals and officials of the time, including Meyerhold and his wife, Marshal Tukhachevskii, Beso Lominadze, and Aleksandr Fadeev. When some of them were arrested for treason, Avdeenko was able to help their families financially. The trouble came all at once, when on August 12, 1940, *Pravda* published an unsigned, stunningly critical review entitled "A False Film." Strangely enough, the film sounded quite patriotic and it followed the well-known ideological prescriptions of the party. Avdeenko was immediately summoned to Moscow to the Central Committee headquarters, where Stalin, in the presence of Zhdanov, Malenkov, Fadeev, Trenev, Aseev, and many others took Avdeenko to task in a five-hour long discussion. The accusations reached a dangerous point, but Avdeenko failed to agree with those who were accusing him. Stalin himself looked awful and ugly: there was almost no resemblance to his well-known portraits. He was full of wrath and the terrified Avdeenko expected to be killed in the Central Committee building once the meeting was over. But the last words spoken by Stalin were: "I may be mistaken with regard to comrade Avdeenko. You cannot crawl into a human being's soul."[17]

Among the many allegations against Avdeenko were his hypocritical behavior; his redundant praises of life in the Polish city of Czerniowce, "liberated" quite recently by the Soviet army; but most of all, the allegation that the Communist Party member Avdeenko had failed to rush headlong to his Party regional committee with an unconditional repentance of his wrong positions. Eisenstein and Shostakovich did repent in similar cases. Expecting the worst, Avdeenko collapsed at the end of the meeting, but to his amazement he was neither arrested nor killed, unlike many of his friends in similar situations. Within several days, however, he was deprived of his privileges, including his prestigious job with *Pravda*, his luxurious houses, his party and Writers' Union memberships. While daily expecting his own arrest, he started to work as an ordinary miner in the Ukraine.

With Simonov, almost everything was safer and happier. When German troops besieged Moscow in the autumn of 1941, Simonov wrote his famous "Comrade Stalin, dost thou hear us? Thou must hear us, we know this. In this fatal hour it is neither Mother nor her Son, but Thou art whom we recall as first." In other words, Stalin was recalled as God the Father, and the address to Stalin as *thou* was quite appropriate. Undoubtedly Stalin appreciated this poetically camouflaged metaphor. Simonov accepted Stalin's Prizes with gratitude and created his new works to please Stalin. After having written *The Fatherland's Fume* about hardships in postwar years and feeling frustrated over the unjust criticism of the novel, the criticism supported by Stalin, he canceled the agreement on the book, which was otherwise ready for publication. At the same time he worked hard on his play *The Alien Shadow* (*Chuzhaia ten'*), about Russian nationalism and patriotism along the lines prescribed personally by Stalin, and made all the changes suggested by the latter.[18]

With Simonov, Stalin's opinions about his literary works and their details were decisive. However, Simonov was by no means devoid of some kindness and even elements of nobility. In his capacity as editor-in-chief of *Novyi mir* he initiated publication of Mikhail Zoshchenko's short stories after Zhdanov's devastating criticism of Zoshchenko in 1946. He was known later to have helped generously and secretly some writers who had been ostracized and defamed. But in the time of Stalin, while almost at the top of the Soviet literary hierarchy, Simonov impeccably implemented each desire and whim of the leader. He wrote his passionate article against the renegade Kravchenko, about and against his former Yugoslav communist friends, including Marshal Tito. He was instrumental in luring Russian emigrés living in France back to their dear Russia without mentioning prisons and Siberian exile in their long talks. Simonov almost never resisted Stalin's decisions to give literary prizes to obvious mediocrities. As a non-voting member of the Central Committee, he listened with horror and fear as Stalin, a few months before his death, read a death verdict to his close and longtime associates, Molotov and Mikoyan.[19] In the same period, Simonov received intelligence from his high-positioned friends that his enemies at the top were weaving dangerous webs for him. But at Stalin's funeral, and alone in his study, Simonov sobbed desperately for the deceased *Vozhd*.

Avdeenko survived as a miner and later as a military correspondent during the last part of World War II. In 1943, Stalin personally forgave him his "trespasses," apparently after reading his article "Redemption by Blood." In those and succeeding years, in Avdeenko's words, he was more afraid of Stalin's wrath than of an enemy bullet.[20] What Avdeenko wrote was full of praises for Stalin and his inseparable bond with the people. When Stalin died, Avdeenko was asked to be present at his funeral, to describe it for the popular magazine *Ogonyok*. In those days he could not stop sobbing and was unable to listen to his comrade-in-arms' words about the death of their uncrowned bloodsucker.[21]

Avdeenko writes in his *Memoirs*: "I was afraid during *his* life. I am afraid after *his* death. From there, from another world he threatens me with the sword of Damocles."[22] In 1963, he wrote a novel about the Hungarian uprising of 1956 from the Soviet point of view. He concludes his *Memoirs* with words about life after the Twentieth Party Congress: "Life has reevaluated and emancipated us from the slavish cult of the 'Khoziain'. About this a separate book should be written, but, alas, I do not have sufficient strength for that—I am more than eighty years old." As to Simonov, he did not admit that he was a Stalinist, either during Stalin's life or in the three years after his death.

But in those years he saw, of course, a great man in Stalin, and he said so numerous times. Weeks after Stalin's death, he stated in an editorial in *Literaturnaia gazeta* that "the sacred duty of a writer is . . . to create in all its grandeur and fullness, for our contemporaries and future generations, the image of the greatest genius of all times and all nations—the image of the immortal Stalin." [23] He added that nobody forced him to write in this manner and that Khrushchev, having read the editorial, wanted to dismiss Simonov from his position immediately. In 1954, Simonov hung on his study wall his favorite portrait of Stalin, "with the strong and clever face of an old tiger." In the succeeding twenty-five years he rethought Stalin, the incipient disintegration of his personality, "his cruelty, his morbid suspiciousness," and came to the conclusion that Stalin was "a great and at the same time horrible man." [24] But having written these notes about Stalin (they were published posthumously), he seemed unable to revise his opinion more radically; nor was he able to remake himself into a person that had not been molded by Stalin's influence.

To sum up, Stalin's demand for populism in literature was no less sincere than his appeal to writers to "write the truth." His taste in literature was not unlike his "erudition" in music, and it has been described in detail by Dmitrii Shostakovich. Stalin was fond of simplicity bordering on mediocrity. It is true that his favorite authors were Gogol' and Saltykov-Shchedrin, especially in their satirical attitude toward ordinary Russians. Anything complicated or ambiguous could not win his literary sympathies. The symbolists, acmeists, futurists, imaginists and Seraphion Brothers, Kliuev and Pil'niak, Bulgakov and Babel', Mandel'shtam and Zoshchenko were unable to proceed safely on the road they had embarked on as writers. Stalin had his own yardstick for judging what suited the people and what was understood by them. Remaining essentially a person of Caucasian culture, he knew how to play on the meanest strings of Russian chauvinism, bigotry, and anti-Semitism. Goebbels' *Volkskunst* and *Volksliteratur* did not go unnoticed by him, nor did the tradition of Uvarov's "Orthodoxy, autocracy, and populism" escape his attention. His demand for *narodnost'* along with party-mindedness and ideological commitment provided him with a wide range of possibilities for interpreting literary works in accordance with his personal whims and his long-term policy. Quite surprisingly, he was confident of his almost divine prerogative to dictate to writers what and how they should write. Although he was never totally satisfied with Soviet literary achievement, he seemed to be relatively happy with the many works awarded the Stalin Prize with his consent. And his engineers of human soul accomplished their duty with enviable zeal. When Stalin's ideological handyman Polikarpov complained that the leading Soviet writers were too much engaged in petty intrigues and mutual denouncements, and had too little enthusiasm for creating new and praiseworthy masterpieces, Stalin responded with the air of one hurt and annoyed: "I have no other writers for you, Polikarpov. Go and supervise them." [25]

7 Aleksandr Zinov'ev's Vision

of Soviet Ideology

Former head of the Logic Department at Moscow State University and later an exile, Aleksandr Zinov'ev has been described as one of the most provocative thinkers of our time. He has written numerous semifictional works that depict the application of Soviet ideology in the USSR. His description of a new type of man whom he calls *homo sovieticus* in a book under this title is a truly original analysis of Soviet life. In this book and elsewhere, Zinov'ev concentrates on two themes: the relation of Soviet ideology to logic, science, and religion and the consequences and perspectives of Soviet ideology. At present, Zinov'ev's analyses seem particularly timely as the Soviet system under Mikhail Gorbachev gains new credibility through reforms.

SOVIET IDEOLOGY: THE TERM

The term "ideology" has undergone many reinterpretations since Karl Marx and Friedrich Engels brought it into popular usage.

In *German Ideology* and in other works, the founders of Marxism do not apply the word "ideology" to their own views.[1] Instead, they understand it as an idealistic concept by means of which the world presents itself as the embodiment of ideas, thoughts, and principles to people who do not understand the role of class struggle in history. Ideologists are thinkers who dismiss any connection between their constructions and the material interest of social classes and who claim that ideas are independent of the class base. Lenin expanded this concept of ideology by introducing the term "scientific ideology." For him, Marxism equaled the scientific analysis of capitalism, "the combination of a rigorous scientific principle and the revolutionary principle"[2] whose goal is to aid by means of program, strategy, tactics, and policy the oppressed masses in their struggle for survival. *The Great Soviet Encyclopedia* (third edition) defines socialist ideology as the theoretically elaborated consciousness of a class which opposes the reactionary ideology of the bourgeoisie. Ideology, it says, does not surface spontaneously from life's circumstances but is created by representatives of a class who arrive theoretically at the same conclusion that the class reaches in practice. Spreading through society and adapting itself to the level of mass consciousness, ideology acts on that consciousness and influences social psychology. Under socialism, the Marxist-Leninist scientific philosophy fulfills a "dominant role" and rallies the entire society around the working class and its party to consolidate and further develop socialism.[3] The authoritative *Soviet Political Dictionary* labels ideology as "the supreme revolutionary force directed toward the annihilation of capitalism and the building of communism,"[4] while the *Program of the Communist Party of the Soviet Union* (CPSU) terms communist ideology the "most humane ideology" whose objectives are to establish honest relations between individuals and nations, to ward off the threat of exterminating wars, to bring about world peace, and to establish freedom and happiness for all people.[5]

   These concepts of Soviet socialist ideology are still the foundation of Soviet politics, and they bear upon *glasnost'* and *perestroika*. Secretary General of the CPSU, Mikhail Gorbachev, has called the present period "the second world revolution since the birth of socialism." To Franz Josef Strauss, the late prime minister of Bavaria, Gorbachev said: "I am fighting on several fronts. I am fighting abroad for the credibility of my disarmament policy. I am fighting at home against the conservatives and reactionaries who do not want any change. I am fighting against the adventurers and the lunatics who believe that we are now going to throw the entire Marxist-Leninist system overboard."[6] During his visit to Poland in July 1988, Gorbachev remarked: "Lenin could serve as a model in this era of the second world revolution. . . . Lenin's life and struggle constitute a splendid example to be followed by the young."[7] It is in the context of these recent pronouncements that one should consider Zinov'ev's analysis of Soviet ideology.

Zinov'ev presents his basic ideas in the sociological work *The Reality of Communism* (*Kommunizm kak real' nost'*). He says: "Ideology is a definite teaching about the world, human society, mankind, and about vitally important features in people's lives." The task of ideology is to organize and standardize people's consciousness and to control them by forming a definite type of consciousness useful to the ruler. "People are programmed to think and act in a particular way." Ideology is disseminated and imposed upon the population from their infancy by "the ideological apparatus" consisting of both persons and institutions whose teaching is accepted "not because [the teachers] believe in its logical or empirical falsifiability but because of social circumstances and the pressure to accept."[8] Here Zinov'ev's ideas parallel those of Karl Mannheim,[9] who denied the cognitive value of ideology and regarded it as an aggregate of ideas aimed at maintaining structure supported by a particular social order.

Zinov'ev expressed his concept of Soviet ideology in his literary works as well. In the novel *The Radiant Future* (*Svetloe budushchee*, 1978), his views are voiced by Anton Zimin, a scientist and dissident thinker. Zimin makes a distinction between two Soviet ideologies— the official ideology of the privileged classes (the formal ideology) and the practical ideology of the lower classes (the real ideology). The official ideology, he maintains, is hypocritical and very convenient to those who profess it because it conceals the ignoble essence of Soviet reality. Practical ideology, on the other hand, is imposed upon the population by such factors as shortages of essential products, disinformation, fear of coming events, dreams of improvement, lack of protection from the authorities, and so on. He claims that Marxism is

nothing but "plagiarism accompanied by the destruction of the sources
which have been plundered and are still being plundered, while real
Communism, as a social structure, is a parasitical growth on the body
of Western civilization, a parasite which kills the being which has
given it birth and nourished it. . . ." [10]

SOVIET IDEOLOGY VS. LOGIC

In the same novel, Zinov'ev's alter ego states that there is no
concept in Marxism that satisfies the logical rules used in constructing
scientific notions, "nor is there a single Marxist statement that can be
verified by rules screening scientific statements." [11] Zinov'ev's line of
reasoning is threefold:

1. Lenin's definition of "matter" (*materiia*) as an objective reality
given in sensations wrongly assumes that "matter" is a common general concept; however, students of basic logic know that in rules that
identify concepts, the expression "objective reality" is more general
than "matter," and that expressions such as "objective reality" and
"given in sensations" are, from the point of view of the construction
of concepts, more primary than "matter." In addition, the term "matter" is by no means clearer than the term "objective reality."

2. The basic propositions of Marxism—such as that matter is primary and conscience secondary; that the world is knowable; that space
and time are objective; that the world is in constant change; that quan-
titative changes lead to qualitative; that society has an infrastructure
and superstructure; that there exist "productive forces" and "productive relations"—appear plausible at first sight. This is enough for ideology but not for science. To be scientific, a term must go beyond
plausibility. At close range, the correctness of Marxist propositions
and terminology turns out to be illusory. Zinov'ev's protagonist argues
as follows:

You say that the world is knowable. But is the unknowable knowable?
Where does that lead you? Either to tautology "the knowable is

knowable," or to hypothesis "everything is knowable," and the latter is extremely risky . . . the existence of insoluble problems has been proven. It is possible to prove that one cannot know the consequences of an event which might have taken place but did not. I can give you thousands of examples like it. . . . Everything is in flux, everything changes, you say, stealing this banality from the Greeks. But does everything? For example, the square, the root of minus one, the circular square, how do they change? . . . One of the vital laws of ideology is that one must never dig into its phraseology beyond the point of constituting a threat to its integrity and its grandeur.[12]

3. The Marxist obsession to create an earthly paradise ignores such aspects of society as the ever-present differentiation between social groups and their hierarchy, the continuous redivision of society into strata according to life conditions, and the diverse preferences and activities of the people. The result is that the well-known Soviet slogans "to everyone according to his labor" and "to everyone according to his needs" become mere propaganda and ultimately bring about a state of affairs that has nothing to do with their ostensible intention. In practice, a superior is evaluated higher than his subordinates, and the people's needs are determined by their social position.

That Marxism-Leninism defies logic can be deduced from consideration of the difference that exists between the Marxist premises and the communist reality, argues Zinov'ev. Here testimony is overwhelming: massive repressions, the low standard of living, the bondage to places of residence and work, huge differences in the standard of living between the higher and lower strata of society, the suppression of free thought, the absence of civil rights, bribery, the privilege system based on a variety of principles, economic chaos, wastefulness, and militarization of society.[13] The proponents of Soviet ideology refuse to acknowledge the connection between these empirical facts and the ideology they advocate, and they brand as slanderers those who postulate such a connection. Zinov'ev asserts that only western Marxists give credence to the belief that an ideal communist society can be established without the above-stated realities.

SOVIET IDEOLOGY VS. SCIENCE

The proponents of Soviet ideology insist that theirs is a "scientific" position. Zinov'ev argues that science and ideology cannot be yoked together. Science insists on precision of terminology, while ideology involves language that can be figurative in an unaccountable sort of way. Scientific assertions are statements that can be upheld and validated, while ideological propositions cannot be so validated. Scientific texts are read by a narrow circle of specialists, while ideological texts are directed to the population as a whole, irrespective of occupation or educational level. Hence, "the relationship between ideology and reality cannot be categorized in terms of truth or falsehood, but in terms of the extent to which a given ideology serves the purpose of conditioning people's consciousness."[14]

Paradoxically, however, the "scientific" pretensions of Marxism seem to be adequate for the needs of Soviet society. In his book *Without Illusions*, Zinov'ev says that the Marxist-Leninist ideology was developed as a "pretense to understand scientifically all things."[15] He pokes fun at Marx's knowledge of mathematics by pointing out Marx's inability to find solutions to simple mathematical problems. He ridicules the "scientist" in Engels who "invented" complicated forms of *materiia*, from mechanical transpositions to complex thought processes, arriving at so many nonsensical conclusions that "it would require the world academies of science to rectify his errors and absurdities." Zinov'ev criticizes Lenin's attempts to develop logic, citing that his only background in the subject was a high school textbook and "Hegel's crazy ideas." He ridicules present-day Marxist thinkers who maintain that because of Marxist influence, philosophy was upgraded to the level of science. The truth is quite the opposite, says Zinov'ev: "It was largely through Marxism that philosophy for the first time in history lost the quality of scholarly inquiry and became the nucleus or a component part of ideology."[16] Zinov'ev lists the complex historical and social causes Marxism has endorsed in its effort to claim a scientific basis. Marxism's alleged scientific grounding allows its proponents to present the Soviet society as a higher and natural product of objective historic laws, to consider the activity of the communist gov-

ernment in the light of the same objective laws, and to "depict the
interests and peculiarities of the [communist] leadership as intelligent
scientific foresight. . . ." [17] Zinov'ev emphasizes that Marxism expresses the yearning for an earthly paradise of an oppressed and hu-
miliated people, and he points out that this circumstance has nothing
to do with science. He concludes that Marxism may have started "its
historical career with intentions to scientifically explain the process of
social development"; in the end, however, it has rejected the scientific
approach to the society in which it has acquired "the position of the
ruling state ideology." [18]

SOVIET IDEOLOGY VS. RELIGION

Zinov'ev has some interesting things to say about the relationship between Marxist ideology and religion. He states that Soviet
ideology resembles religion in its quest for spiritual leadership, yet it
is quite different from religion in its principles. He says: "The psychological foundation of religion is faith . . . while the foundation of
ideology is acceptance . . . by reasoning, by conscious and subcon-
scious calculation. . . ." [19] Religion enters the "human soul" because
of an inner need, while "ideology is a behavioral and external phenomenon." The needs of the soul gave birth to the churches; as far as
ideology is concerned, it is "the other way around: it is the ideological
apparatus which imposes ideology on the people." [20] In his little-read
In the Antechamber of Paradise (*V preddverii raia*, 1979) Zinov'ev
notes that Soviet ideology came into existence as an antipode of Christianity, in that it also claimed the souls of the people; it inherited from
Christianity the concept of the spirit, which is contradictory to physical existence, or to—*materiia*; it borrowed from Christianity the problem of the relation between the spirit and *materiia*. [21]

Zinov'ev is not averse to invoking the concept of dialectics while
discussing Soviet ideology. On the one hand, he views the substance
of this ideology, dialectical and historical materialism, as an incoherent and illogical system that is senseless in theory and practice. Here,
he seems to concur with the findings of such rare Soviet scholars as

Iurii Tarnopol'skii, who concluded that "*diamat* is a militant, intolerant, and a destructive religion-like cult built on several inconsistent,
mostly unfinished, entirely polemic, and totally political texts which
in fact fail to develop a system."[22] Nevertheless, Zinov'ev also sees
Soviet ideology as a force that has freed millions of people from the
yoke of similarly absurd religious obscurantism. He invokes the virtually one hundred percent literacy in the USSR, the completion of the
secondary level of education by half of the population, and the access
to higher education of millions of Soviet citizens. He believes that
"traditional" religion is doomed in the USSR because both the spiritual
and the material life of the population are conducted in such a way as
to exclude religion from the people's perception. "Naturally, religion,
which is not encouraged and is at times even persecuted in communist
countries, cannot compete with ideology, which is imposed upon the
people from their birth by a powerful ideological apparatus."[23] In
Zinov'ev's opinion, the much-vaunted resurgence of religion in Russia
is merely a fashionable way of expressing restlessness, especially
among the intelligentsia.

Go to Golgotha (*Idi na Golgofu*, 1985)[24] is a fictional work recording the peregrinations of a God-seeking *homo sovieticus*. In it,
Zinov'ev is not concerned with the fact that Soviet ideology, having
succeeded in extirpating Christian values, has failed to bring about
positive substitutes. He remains emotionally detached and indifferent
to the idea that Soviet ideology has deprived people of "compassion"
and "mercy." He also remains indifferent to the ideologically motivated (as opposed to religiously motivated) behavior of such prominent *homines sovietici* as the late Georgii Malenkov, who used to
participate in the Russian Orthodox Church choirs and who asked for a
Christian funeral. In his apparent skepticism about the possibility of religious regeneration in Russia, Zinov'ev differs markedly from such recent Soviet authors as Chingiz Aitmatov, who seems to be particularly
disturbed by a lack of compassion in Soviet society,[25] or Daniil Granin,
who has written with similar concern about the lack of the quality of
mercy among his compatriots.[26] In contrast to them, Zinov'ev believes
in the ultimate victory of ideology over religion, at least in the USSR.
In his view, in communist countries ideology has an advantage over

religion because it makes the promise of upward social mobility to the people, and it spells out more clearly than religion the forms of behavior without which humanity cannot live in the type of society created by the Soviets.[27]

THE CONSEQUENCES OF SOVIET IDEOLOGY

I have been trying to demonstrate that Zinov'ev's analyses of Soviet ideology go beyond the usual western commentaries about it. While he seems to provide a devastating critique of it, he also proclaims his belief in its ultimate victory. He says that the dictatorship of ideology in the Soviet Union has been compromised and that everybody knows that "it stands for baseness, forgery, crime." [28] But in spite of that, he proclaims the triumph of ideology. In all his works, Zinov'ev presents the *homo sovieticus*, the ultimate product of Soviet ideology, as a psychologically flexible and adaptable *homo triplex* who thinks in one way, speaks in another, and acts in yet another way; a morally indifferent person, an "agent of the Soviet Union" (*agent Sovetskogo Soiuza*) who participates in the Soviet state power and in Soviet conquests; an intellectual and a primitive, who obeys the nomenklatura and spontaneously collaborates with the KGB; a spiritually dead secular materialist who exists *sub specie vanitatis*.[29]

There are those who claim that Marxists were originally guided by good intentions, but Zinov'ev retorts that "the road to hell is known to be paved by good intentions," and adds, "There were no intentions other than those of concrete people—members of the Marxist ideological army—who wanted to satisfy their own egotistical needs." [30] Yet he also says the following: "When the founders of Marxism promoted the idea of a communist society and an earthly paradise, they did not anticipate that the introduction of such high aspirations and ideals would bring about such awful abominations, and that these effects would be eventually self-evident and without doubt not accidental. Our deficiencies have followed our virtues." [31]

He asks: How could these effects take place while thousands of highly skilled specialists were busily at work interpreting and reinterpreting Marxism? Hardly anyone among them had noticed the "awful abominations" that Marxism put to practice. Is it possible that the specialists have erred? Or had the Marxist leadership been overcome with evil and for that reason done away with the high Leninist principles? Zinov'ev concludes that it was genuine socialism (or communism) that was established in the Soviet Union. It all happened in accordance with the known patterns of social development.

If socialism is to prevail in the West, Zinov'ev argues, it will be similar to that in the Soviet Union. "Of course, there will be some minor differences," he adds. "It is known that feudalism in France was kinder than feudalism in Russia. Communism [in the West] may be kinder if for no other reason than there is no Siberia." [32]

PERSPECTIVES OF SOVIET IDEOLOGY

Historically, any ideology has tended to weaken over time, owing to what Peter F. Drucker calls the inevitable loss of faith in the "salvation by the society." [33] David Brooks points out that the notion of the demise of ideology as such surfaces every five to ten years: Albert Camus wrote an end-of-ideology essay in 1946, Raymond Aron wrote one in 1955, Daniel Bell wrote *The End of Ideology* in 1960, and the periodical *The Public Interest* was founded in a flurry of such pronouncements in 1965. [34] One can read on an almost daily basis some western writer announcing the demise of Soviet ideology. In *Radical Principles*, Michael Waltzer says that no further enlightenment can be expected from Marxist theory, in either its original or its revisionist form. He points out that Marxism cannot explain, much less prevent, the outbursts of irrational savagery, the prolonged wars, the failure of the working-class parties to produce socialist societies, the birth and intensity of nationalist feelings, and the drift toward authoritarianism. [35] Even Robert Heilbroner, a long-time socialist scholar and one-time defender of Mao's Cultural Revolution, recently said that "less than seventy years after it officially began, the contest between capitalism and socialism is over: capitalism has won." [36] In 1989, Zbigniew Brzezinski published a book on the death of communism which accurately predicted the changes in Eastern Europe and the violence in China. [37] Even inside the USSR similar comments are beginning to surface. After a recent visit to the Soviet Union, Robert Conquest reported that his strongest impression of the people was their disgust and exhaustion with the "whole paraphernalia of falsehood and fallacious doctrine which had promised them, at the cost of endless sacrifice, a wonderful socialism, and which has in fact, as is now admitted, produced social and economic disaster." People are "simply sick of Marxism, fetishism of the party, the heroes of the revolutionary past." [38]

Zinov'ev differs greatly from all of these thinkers. He is skeptical about the demise of Soviet ideology. Perhaps because he has pondered its appeal more than others, or perhaps because of his low opinion of humanity in general, he believes that Marxism has proven to be an unbeatable ideological tool for the totalitarian regimes. It has produced not only a great deal of ideological texts, demagogic promises, and pseudo-scientific slogans, but also has offered a marvelous method of dealing with people and a rich phraseology that justifies the regime's deceptions. Marxism's vagueness and its senseless assertions are valuable tools for the society's ruling strata, he argues, especially when the right to interpret it is the prerogative of the party leadership and its ideological apparatus. Zinov'ev sees long-term strength in the Soviet ideology that may enable the party to survive the challenge from the inexperienced, confused, and divided opposition groups.

Zinov'ev sees the continuous disparity between the theory of Soviet ideology and its practice as a necessary dialectical unity of strategy and tactics. Already in 1979, he predicted the current Soviet liberal trends. In *The Antechamber of Paradise*, the protagonist is told by his superior:

Liberal trends are now emerging. We have to pretend for the sake of the West. We cannot do otherwise. We have difficulties to overcome, and we need contacts with the West. . . . This is temporary. We need to carry on the Party line elastically and cleverly. Patience and other things are important. This must not be interpreted as a retreat. On the contrary, we must keep [the final goals] in mind and be prepared. . . . A difficult task is given to you. Do not expect orders. Be creative. Learn to recognize the enemy not in the liberal windbags (they will be given what they look for: degrees, titles, apartments, etc., and will remain quiet), but in those who cannot be bribed and intimidated. We need to skillfully interfere with the important independent personalities who do not subject themselves to our control. Play it by ear! And be guided accordingly![39]

Zinov'ev regards radical changes in communist tactics as something to be expected. He would not be surprised to hear Aleksandr Iakovlev, the Politburo member responsible for Marxist-Leninist doctrine, proclaim that "the ideology of the owner is paramount" and that "instilling a sense of ownership is a good thing . . ." (*Pravda*, August 11, 1988).

Zinov'ev has this to say to those who live in freedom: "Speaking of power, I assure you that these [Marxists] parties will promise what they think you want. They will even refrain from the dictatorship of the proletariat, and they will scrap the primacy of the *materiia*."[40] He would not oppose Aleksandr Gel'man's claim in *Sovetskaia kultura* (April 9, 1988) that Soviet liberalization can be compared to "an unclenched fist . . . the hand remains the same and at a moment's notice it may again be clenched into a fist." Marxism-Leninism may have been discredited and the Soviet Union as a political product of ideology may not have surpassed economically any country on a per capita basis since 1917. Nevertheless, Zinov'ev maintains, in all that has been said about communism there has been little mention of the positive appeal it has to billions of people because of "its innate ability to generate ideas and means which organize the stream of life into a single meaningful whole."[41]

Zinov'ev does not deny that Soviet society continues to undergo an ideological crisis, a crisis that began during Khrushchev's time. He admits that "there has been a sharp increase in the number of highly educated people for whom the ideological teaching appears primitive and even idiotic."[42] He insists, however, that the crisis is not one of degradation but one of development.

CONCLUSION

In his political novels and essays, Aleksandr Zinov'ev has subjected Soviet ideology to a critique that cuts both ways. He pointed out that Marxism-Leninism is neither a science nor a religion. In contrast to any branch of science, Marxism-Leninism does not take the logical steps that lead to scientific notions. It stems from erroneous propositions; it lacks terminological precision and cannot be systematically verified. In contrast to religion, its psychological foundation is acceptance rather than faith, its source is an external circumstance rather than an inner need, and its outcome is not an organized church; it is itself a product of an organization. Its record stands for vileness, fraud, and crime. Its victim, the *homo sovieticus*, a fragmented, reified, alienated, exploited, and dehumanized creature, should be pitied and feared.

Zinov'ev distinguishes between the official Soviet ideology espoused by the privileged classes and the practical ideology shared by the lower classes. The former exists as a parasite nurtured by the West, and the latter is imposed upon the *homines sovietici* through disinformation and privation. Zinov'ev stresses that both ideologies form a dialectical unity and together make up a very convenient instrument for manipulating the masses.

Zinov'ev arrives at his conclusions as a confirmed dialectical materialist. If the Soviet state has not arrived at the ideal state of socialism (or communism), he claims, it is only because some of the objective social laws are still unknown. Consequently, in his opinion, the present crisis of the Soviet ideology does not represent a decline but a step in the process of enrichment and development of that ideology. In contrast to many western Sovietologists, he believes that Marxism-Leninism, although heavily flawed, will continue to fascinate the masses of the world by its simplicity, adaptability, and comprehensive responses to manifold needs. Zinov'ev has foreseen the liberal trend in Soviet ideology today, and he has touched the core of Soviet strength. But in his strength lies also his weakness. He has entirely ignored the controversy between the Russian nation and other nationalities in the USSR, a dilemma that even Mikhail Gorbachev admits is one of the most fundamental issues of our time.[43] Zinov'ev seems incapable of distinguishing those elements of Soviet ideology which have their roots in Russia's past from those which were imposed on the country by the Bolsheviks. He makes no room for nationalistic concerns, nor does he seem to be aware of them. Outside Russia, it would be difficult to find a writer who so consistently disregards the influence of Russian history and traditions on Soviet ideology, and the role of Russian and non-Russian nationalisms in weakening the Soviet ideology. While his analysis of this ideology is both enlightening and disturbing, the admiring reader may take some comfort in observing that factors other than religion or science or economics may play a role in weakening the Soviet ideology, and that its survivability, while greater than western commentators have generally believed, may not be as great as Zinov'ev seems to believe.

8   Russian Nationalism and

Soviet Intellectuals under

Gorbachev

The role of the intellectual in Russia has differed somewhat from that of nineteenth- and twentieth-century intellectuals in the West. In western countries cultural activity has been more specialized, and until recently the intellectuals have not been excessively active in politics. The situation has been different in Russia. Since the late eighteenth century, the Russian intellectual has been one of the central figures in the political life of the land. He or she has been a philosopher, historian, and politician, a sort of national guru whose job was not only to entertain and enlighten but also to lead toward certain political goals. Mikhail Gorbachev's reforms have widened the boundaries of the permissible as no Soviet regime has done since the early 1920s, and it is not surprising that various Russian intellectuals, including those who are influenced by nationalism, began to express their political views on the pages of the various Soviet periodicals.

This chapter will survey some recent expressions of political opinion and try to define their possible implications for the future of the Soviet Union.

It has to be borne in mind that the Soviet Union is the last multi-national empire of the world and that the problems Gorbachev faces have been smoldering ever since the provinces of the former Russian empire were reconquered by Moscow after the October Revolution. Yet the problems of nationalism under Stalin were not as serious as they are now. Stalin was like an oriental despot or an Egyptian pharaoh: he soared above all social groups and nationalities of the state. He professed neither social nor national affiliations, and everyone was equal in slavery in his eyes. This peculiar type of internationalism, internationalism in slavery so to speak, made Stalin's Russia, despite the officially sponsored Russian nationalism and persecution of some minorities at the end of his reign, distinctly different from that of Nazi Germany. Severe repression of any type of unsanctioned political activity also prevented the nationalist ideologies from spreading. While Russian nationalism played a role since the early 1930s, it was toned down by the official ideology of Marxism-Leninism-Stalinism. Since the end of the 1940s and especially since Leonid Brezhnev's ascension to power, however, Russian nationalism not only became openly supported by officialdom but spread among the various groups of intellectuals.

Russian nationalism under Gorbachev retains some of the features that characterized it in the period of Brezhnev: namely, it is strongly exclusive and it has messianic pretensions. Some of its adherents view Russians as leaders in the world community. At the same time, growing economic and international problems (e.g., the humiliating defeat in Afghanistan), as well as the growing influence of the national republics where the native bureaucracy has started to push aside ethnic Russians, led to the development of new characteristics. Those who still believe in Russia's leading role in the world community point out that Russians should be open to the West and include in their ranks all who are ready to share Russia's culture and values. Other Russian nationalists have a different view. Their philosophy has isolationist undertones and repudiates the Soviet Union's goals of industrial development.

Dmitrii S. Likhachev (1906–), academician and one of Russia's leading specialists in Old Russian literature, is an example of the first category of westernized liberal nationalists. In his view, Russian Christian humanism made Russia the leader of the world, while the Christian foundation of Russian culture simultaneously permits a certain openness toward the West. According to Likhachev, "love," "meekness," and "spirituality" are culturally inborn in Russians, while being at the same time at the core of Christian values. Sounding surprisingly similar to nineteenth-century Russian ideologue N.Ia. Danilevskii, Likhachev pointed out in his famous essay on "Russia" that these characteristics are also present in the old wholesome paganism in which the Russians had partaken, and this was the reason why Christianity was accepted in Russia with such ease. Christianity has become the cornerstone of Russian culture: "there was no place in the world where there was such a love of the shining gold cupolas and tops of churches seen from afar. The golden flame of the church and the golden flame of the candle—these are the symbols of spirituality."[1]

According to Likhachev, Christian love manifested itself in the Russian preference for collectivism; it was this concern for others that made Russia, more than any other European nation, Christian in its very essence:

When one compares Sergei Radonezhskii [the Russian political and religious leader of the fourteenth century] and Francis of Assisi, one sees significant differences in both big and small matters. Francis regarded poverty as the greatest virtue of the monk, and so did Sergei; but while Francis preached poverty and wandering to the monk, Sergei forbade him to leave the monastery and beg. The monk should work and earn his daily bread. Sergei himself worked in the fields and Pafnutii Borovskii [a follower of Sergei's] managed the monastery's estate from his death bed. Abbot Filipp Solovetskii introduced many improvements into the Solovetsk Monastery, and he regarded this as the main achievement of his tenure as abbot. Iul'iana Osorgina reached great heights of piety while managing her estate, and she explicitly compared her managerial feats to the feats of piety. One could find many examples of such an approach to labor among the Russian saints. In Russia, Christian ideals acquired an important characteristic: the love of work and concern for the well-being of the entire collective, whether it be a monastery, principality, state in its totality, or ordinary landlord's family with its servants.[2]

Likhachev further maintains that Christianity in Russia led to universalism and tolerance; this is proven by the fact that, unlike any other nation, Russia has been able to absorb foreign nations and their cultures. To him this absorption is not a conquest or subjugation but rather a peaceful incorporation of various individual cultures into one universal culture. The best part of every culture is Christian humanistic spirituality with its concern for humanity as a whole as well as for the particular individual; since this spirituality is best represented in Russian culture, other cultures, without knowing of it, partake of Russian culture insofar as they partake of this Christian spirituality. Thus, their absorption in Russian culture is not an act of violence but rather a natural development.

Having elaborated on the idea of Russian tolerance of other nations and Russian vision of statehood as cooperation (as opposed to the western idea of conquest), Likhachev maintains that these Russian traits became visible at the very beginning of Russian history. Here he recalls the famous Varangian theory of the founding of the Russian state. The theory is based on the story in the Russian *Primary Chronicle* that attributes the founding of the Russian state to the Vikings, who were invited by the indigenous people of Kiev to come and rule over them. This theory has often been discussed from the point of view of Russian nationalist interests, and the results have been inconclusive.

The factual element of the story, i.e., the question whether the Varangians were indeed the founders of the Russian state, does not concern Likhachev at all. It is the spirit of the nation that really matters. "In the very essence of the legend about the invitation of the three Varangian brothers, one can see what I have tried to demonstrate for a long time, namely, the idea of a brotherhood of tribes whose princes descended from these ancestor-brothers," says Likhachev. Similar features can be seen in other legends incorporated into the *Primary Chronicle*. For example, Oleg, one of the first Russian princes, while campaigning against the Byzantine empire, led an army which included not only early Russians but also Belorussians, Ukrainians, and those tribes that were the ancestors of present-day Yugoslavs, as well as Scandinavians and representatives of the Finno-Ugric tribes. All were treated equally and looked to Oleg as a national leader. In later history, the story of various ethnic and religious groups peacefully coexisting in Russia has been repeated.

Thus, Russian culture is characterized by a spirit of tolerance, which gives it its universalist tendency and enables it to absorb other cultures. But while Russian culture provided others with a moral backbone, it was itself ameliorated by them. Likhachev implies that Russian culture can exist only as a worldwide culture because its Christian and ecumenical spirit requires this. Russian culture cannot withstand loneliness and self-sufficiency. This is why Russia has striven with passion to learn from the cultures of the past: from Greece, from the countries of the Balkan peninsula, and especially from Bulgaria and Italy. Russia has drawn from them in the areas of architecture, music, painting, and literature. In the nineteenth century, Russian culture borrowed from France, Germany, England, and Spain.

And here Likhachev begins to develop the idea that had been articulated by Dostoevsky a century before, that the West has created a great cultural treasury during a thousand years of its history, but the West abandoned its heritage, and it was the Russians for whom the sacred stories of the great European past became dear. Modern Europe has little to offer from a cultural and social point of view. Thus, while calling on the younger generation to study old Europe's cultural heritage, Likhachev passes over in silence modern European culture. He regards this culture as being at the service of consumerism and is quite contemptuous of it.[3]

Russia becomes a center that "gathers together" world cultures, and the Russian intellectual becomes a universal person, a cosmopolitan in the best sense of the word, a person for whom "the stones of Europe" are still sacred. This assures him or her a prominent place in the world community. It is in this light that one should view Likhachev's suggestion that since the great works of art belong to all humanity, some international organization should be created to take care of them.

Likhachev is definitely familiar with the facts in ancient as well as contemporary Russian history that hardly fit his model of a "meek" and "cultural" nation. His own tragic experience (he was an inmate in one of the first Soviet concentration camps created on the Solovki Islands in the White Sea) hardly fits the idealized image of Russia that he promotes. He does not try to explain the less attractive facts of Russian history by blaming them on foreign influence, a not uncommon way of "solving" the problem among the Russian nationalists. (According to them, after Peter the Great, Russia was nothing but a German "suburb" and the October Revolution was organized by minorities.) Likhachev does not advance such a simplistic and discredited view. Instead, he seems to assume that the Christian wholesomeness of Russian culture would be impossible without these black spots on the Russian past and present, which allow Russians to be self-critical and humble. Russia created the violence, so to speak, to torture itself and to suffer. Without this violence Russia's imitation of Christ would have been impossible.

In this process of imitating Christ, the Russian state plays the role of the villain. With few exceptions, society and state, as well as culture and state, are polar opposites. It is Russian society and not the Russian state that is the carrier of Russian culture. "In Russia, the state is opposed [to Russian society] not only intellectually and politically but also spiritually."[4] And it is not accidental that it was the Old Believers who epitomized the Russian soul and Russian culture: they stood in strong opposition to the state. Thus, rather arbitrarily, "the Russian state" is excluded from participation in "Russianness." Likhachev does not explain how this squares with his earlier idea of the Russian state having been created nonviolently.

One can find a similar approach to Russia's destiny in the works of Arsenii Gulyga, the noted Russian specialist in the history of European philosophy. He acknowledges that one can find in Russian history examples of a loss of a sense of individualism and a surrender to totalitarian rulers. In an article entitled "About the Russian Soul,"[5] Gulyga asserts that the Russians should not blame their problems on Stalin and his henchmen (they all belonged to minority groups), but should rather blame themselves. Then Gulyga asserts that love of a totalitarian leader is not truly a Russian characteristic but rather an aberration, and that the essence of the Russian soul can be found in writers such as Dostoevsky. For Dostoevsky, the individual was the most important element of Russian culture. According to Gulyga, this demonstrates that Russians are not Orientals with no sense of individualism but have a cultural link with the West. But they also have surpassed the West in that the individual and the collective coexist harmoniously in Russian culture rather than being opposed to each other. In Russia, individuals do not separate their own existence from the good of the collective and from the idea of helping others. These are essentially Christian characteristics. According to Gulyga, Dostoevsky was right in asserting that the Russian national character has its foundation in Christianity. Elaborating on the wholesomeness of Russian nationalism, Gulyga writes: "Today once again we need a national renaissance. I believe in it, for the Russian spiritual forces are not sapped. The qualities which are the essential elements of [the Russian soul] such as kindness, hospitality, and responsiveness are extremely important to mankind, which is under a threat of self-destruction. Dostoevsky said that 'universal responsiveness' is an essential trait of the Russian national character. [Russians] are ready to help not only other Russians but anyone who needs it; they are able to take on others' problems as their own." And then we hear again the story we heard from Likhachev: that the Russian national character transcends national boundaries in the sense that any human being who cares about another becomes a Russian. "To be a Russian is not a question of origin but of behavior, not of blood but of culture. Russian culture is open to everybody. One could become Russian by accepting [Russian] national values."

For Likhachev and Gulyga, Russia, while maintaining its cultural and spiritual leadership, is not separable from the West. But a Russian writer, Valentin G. Rasputin (1937–), disagrees. Pointing to Russia's Christian essence, Rasputin states that Russia has no bellicose propensities and its conquests were a result not of military strength but of certain mysterious acts, the sacrifices Russians endured with Christian patience. As an example, Rasputin offers the Russian conquest of Siberia, which he suggests was not really a conquest but a martyrdom. The Russians were "freezing to death in flimsy shelters without salt or bread." They "faced hunger and wild beasts" and "fell under arrows of the natives."[6]

Rasputin's view of Russian nationalism as being imbued with the Christian values of love and sacrifice (both for fellow Russians and for people of other nationalities) is quite similar to Likhachev's and Gulyga's. However, as mentioned before, Rasputin's view of Russia's relationship to other countries is different from that of the other two nationalists. Rasputin states that Russian culture is for the Russians only. It cannot transcend ethnic and territorial boundaries. Only ethnic Russians can possess the real Russian soul. It is impossible, or at least quite difficult, to be a real Russian spiritually unless you are Russian ethnically. It is also impossible to be a real Russian if you live outside Russian territory. Furthermore, no cultural or ethnic groups can enrich one another. Each should live in its own cultural heritage and be proud of its ancestral roots. "An Armenian should be proud that he is Armenian, an Estonian, that he is Estonian, a Jew, that he is a Jew." One should be proud of one's cultural heritage and understand that one is a member of a particular national group. One should not spend time studying the cultures of other nations but rather study in depth one's own culture and history. In this connection, Rasputin praised the decision to republish the works of the Russian historians of the nineteenth and early twentieth centuries. He regarded their writings as indispensable to the rise of national consciousness among Russians. "As told by Karamzin, Kliuchevskii and Solov'ev, Russian history will be popular and will be the great discovery of Russia. At first, it will be thousands who will venture to meet their past, and they will be followed by millions and millions; and they, having recovered their sight and having been taught by the fate of the nation, will understand what patriotism is all about."

Rasputin's is a "parochial" nationalism that apparently has no claim to world domination or to the leadership of humanity. Rasputin states explicitly that Russia does not need an empire. He sees as useless for Russia the country's wars with the Poles, Lithuanians, and Turks. Russians should not attempt to lead the world either. They should not play a messiah to the utopian dream of having a state in which all nations of the earth will live happily as one big family. Russia is to live separately from other nations, have occasional contacts with them, but be spiritually self-sufficient.

Though Rasputin's view of the West is generally not favorable, it would be unfair to consider him to be violently antiwestern. According to him, some nations (including some western nations) are ahead of Russia in developing moral and cultural values, and this manifests itself in their attitudes toward ecological problems. Rasputin also does not blame the West for all of Russia's problems. Yet, in his opinion the West is guilty of two impositions on Russia: that of technology and that of moral degeneration.

To explain Rasputin's view, a digression is necessary. The idea that civilization is responsible for moral degeneration has often appeared in European cultures. Russian "Slavophiles" of the nineteenth century provide an example. They blamed the "westernized" urban culture for being the source of moral degeneration. In that connection they blamed Peter I for linking Russia to the West. Yet, the Slavophiles never attacked Peter for introducing Russia to western technology. Both the first and second generations of Slavophiles were in agreement that Russia, while retaining its political and cultural features, should be eager to accept western technology. The Soviet ideologists accepted the Slavophile view and went further. They regarded technological development as the most important criterion of social progress. And Russian mystical philosopher Nikolai F. Fedorov (1828–1903) maintained that modern technology would lead to humanity's final victory over nature and that at this point the resurrection of the dead would be possible. The Slavophile and Soviet ideology merged with Fedorov's in a movement of Russian emigrés who called themselves the Eurasians. They looked at Soviet industrialization from a Fedorovist point of view and praised it, hoping that it would lead to the fulfillment of the Slavophile dream.

Rasputin stands in opposition to these views. According to him, technological progress leads the peoples of the world (and Russia of course) to destruction. It has created the possibility of a nuclear holocaust and the reality of industrial pollution. Industrial development is responsible for the destruction of nature, and it will finally destroy human life, which is a part of nature. Rasputin understands that western countries have embarked on a nature conservation program far in excess of any efforts in this direction undertaken by the Russians. Yet, in his view it is western culture with its urbanization and consumerism that is responsible for the deterioration of nature in Russia. The negative influence of western civilization on Russian culture is taken by Rasputin to be a matter of course.

Rasputin views the October Revolution as detrimental to Russia's development, and he considers collectivization and the great purges to be the necessary corollaries of it. The terror of the Revolution originated in the intellectual developments of the late nineteenth century when religion, with its respect for the individual, was under attack by radical intellectuals. The glorification of "vulgar materialism" in the writings of some prerevolutionary intellectuals was a prelude to what happened in 1917. In Rasputin's words, moral degeneration started "not yesterday, not in the 1930s, but much earlier, more than one hundred years earlier. . . ." Early in the twentieth century, morality in its Kantian and Christian meaning disappeared from public consciousness. The relativity of moral norms was thus related to urban civilization brought about by the influence of western culture.

This antireligious approach to life eradicated patriotism and its moral foundation. Already in the 1920s "patriotism as the consciousness of the nation was branded and trampled in the mud. The word 'patriot' became a synonym of 'member of the White Guard,' and the word 'memory' became associated with savagery and ignorance." Some regeneration of patriotism and, implicitly, of religious feeling took place during the Great Patriotic War [World War II].[7] After the war, the process of moral erosion continued and it was connected with western mass culture and consumerism. Rasputin adamantly opposes rock music as a bearer of dangerous western influences.[8] He feels that emphasizing economic performance and developing consumerism should be avoided in Russia. Russia neither can nor needs to reach the economic level of western countries. Instead, the Russian people should concentrate on spiritual development in its nationalistic form.[9] While one should know foreign classics, one should concentrate mainly on one's own national roots: "Going back to the roots, that is the most important task now: everything else will follow." Rasputin praises the

nationalistic organizations in present-day Russia while condemning
the supporters of western-type ideology: "We have reached the point
where such words as *motherland, patriot, memory,* or *history* are
branded as nationalistic stuff. Mass culture, rock music, the entertain-
ment industry are not only permitted but are implanted in our midst
and propagandized. It seems that somebody would like to turn openness into anarchy to pave the way for foreign values and to suppress
patriotic activity." [10]

Other prominent Russian writers and the general public have expressed similar ideas. [11] In November 1987, a reader's letter published
in *Sovetskaia kul'tura* said that Soviet intellectuals lost self-respect in
their admiration of the West: "I am surprised that we try so hard to
glorify [things western] and thus lose self-respect. Are we not making
a contribution to world culture? They [westerners] do not pay attention
to us, do not show our movies, yet we get out of our skin to heap
praise on them." [12] Shortly afterward, a *Sovetskaia kul'tura* editor
sympathetically bemoaned "the avalanche of urbanization and industrialization" that devours the centers of Russian culture. [13]

The right wing of the Russian nationalist movement generally
blames the West for the world's and Russia's problems. Among them
is the well-known painter Il'ia S. Glazunov (1930–), who occupies
the interesting position of belonging to the opposition and the establishment at the same time. His antiwestern feelings express themselves
in his view on world history and on Russia's history in particular. He
disseminates his views widely through popular newspapers and other
publications. [14] According to Glazunov, moral values are central to human society. They hold it together and inspire the great works of art.
In the European context, it was Christianity that provided these values
to the people. This religion, and therefore the humanistic foundation
of European civilization, were preserved until the middle of the nineteenth century. Then the religious and moral foundation of western
culture began to give way to Marxism, which preached relativity of
moral values and was a form of Satan's intervention in human history
meant to destroy human beings by using them as instruments. This
western invention led to Leninism and to the revolutionary movement
in Russia. Russia and the West could have avoided the catastrophe if

the Russian minister of the interior, Petr A. Stolypin (1862–1911), had not been assassinated. "I love Stolypin . . . he was a great man! . . . If his reforms had succeeded, there would have been no revolution in Russia."

Glazunov condemns abstract art because it implies that reality, and therefore moral standards, are relative. He believes that space and human features should not be changed at the whim of the painter. "Avant-gardism" necessitates "permissiveness." The philosophy of permissiveness has created a perfect ideological setting for the leftist terrorist regimes, and it is not surprising that most of the avant-gardists (many of them Jews) were either direct participants in, or sympathizers with, the Bolshevik Revolution. "All of this [avant-garde] culture is communist culture." Both Casimir Malevich and Pablo Picasso were communists. Chagall was a gun-carrying commissar. Such people "destroyed our culture and departed for the West, where they became idols of so-called modern art. . . ." Avant-gardism "for Europe and America is nothing else than an expansion of the Comintern." Jews and other minorities played an important role in the vicissitudes of Soviet society and are largely responsible for collectivization and the purges. Glazunov states that Trotsky was Stalin's precursor, especially in regard to the forced collectivization, which [as is now officially acknowledged in the Soviet press] cost at least several million lives. Reviewing the present political and intellectual scene, the painter again points to "avant-gardism" in art as representative of western cynicism and consumerism, and he states that it could bring further disasters to Russia.

Aggressive Russian nationalism and anti-Semitism are apparent in Glazunov's political comments. Yet, he is not consistent and tends to avoid extremist statements, probably because he wants to remain part of the establishment in which aggressive nationalism and racism are still not permitted. He has asserted, for instance, that the Society for the Support of Young Painters, which he sponsors, is open not only to the Russian Soviets but also to others. Yet, his views and those of Rasputin are very much in tune with the tenets of the chauvinistic and anti-Semitic organization *Pamiat'* (Memory), of which he says he is not a member.

Pamiat' came to being in 1985 shortly after Gorbachev took power. The roots of this organization, however, go back to the times of Brezhnev and earlier. The Society for the Preservation of the Monuments of Russia's Past, which was formed during Brezhnev's reign, was the godfather of *Pamiat'*. Ideologically, *Pamiat'* has its roots in Russian nationalism and in extreme anti-Israeli, anti-Zionist, and anti-Semitic propaganda. According to one of its leaders, a certain Aleksandr interviewed by an emigré publication, *Pamiat'* is "a flexible organization with no rigid structure and no political leadership; it does not espouse any kind of [political] stance."[15] But other knowledgeable persons disagree and say that *Pamiat'* not only collects membership dues but also enforces discipline among its members, which they claim number several hundred thousand.[16] Apparently, *Pamiat'* is not a homogeneous organization and has several layers. Some of its members, and that includes many intellectuals, loathe to be openly anti-Semitic and espouse views similar to those of the nationalistic Russian writers discussed earlier in this chapter. The rank-and-file, however, are explicitly anti-Semitic.

Aleksandr's views are similar to those of Rasputin and Glazunov. He, too, believes that the problems Russia faces are of global dimensions. He is bothered by technological progress and its source, western civilization. Aleksandr does not deny that technology, and computers in particular, have made life easier. Yet, their disadvantages overshadow their advantages. Here Aleksandr points to the ecological damage technology has caused. He maintains that technological progress is inseparable from westernization and thus from immorality. Aleksandr points to the increasing use of sexually explicit scenes in Soviet movies and attributes this to western influence. The recent movie *The Little Vera*, whose female star posed for *Playboy*, exemplifies this trend. Second, Aleksandr points out that there has occurred a general degradation of human life and its reduction to the most primitive form. He points to the "ugly rock" music which, together with pornography, has been a western import. Third, Aleksandr charges that westernization leads to a decline in interpersonal relationships. All of these processes, he says, affect not only Russia but the entire world, and they are a result of the process of westernization, which is occurring everywhere.

Having exposed the dangers of westernization, Alexandr presents the alternatives for the Russian society and the entire world. It is not economic development *per se* and the raising of living standards but religious spirituality embedded in national tradition that should be the pivotal center of human life. Aleksandr does not preach the idea of going back to nature, that is, consciously abandoning technology, and he does not want Russia to go back to "feudal darkness." However, he says that economic and political progress should be subordinated to the moral and spiritual well-being of the society. If this well-being is in danger, then not only technological progress but also political freedom should be cast aside.

Aleksandr does not claim that Russian Orthodoxy is the best choice for everybody. He claims no messianism of any sort, and points out that each nation should retain its own cultural tradition. He believes that *Pamiat'* has among its members not only Russians but also Moslems, Jews, and representatives of other religions. *Pamiat'* appears sympathetic to all foreign groups that espouse similar ideals. In short, "the people who respect their own history and culture and tradition— such people have a strong bond all over the world."

Aleksandr's views represent the most civilized layer of *Pamiat'* membership. Ideologically, they coincide with the ideas espoused by many intellectuals, including Solzhenitsyn (whose popularity among *Pamiat'* members has been acknowledged[17]). But underneath this surface runs a strong current of irrational chauvinistic Russian views and virulent anti-Semitism. While the ideas of the "civilized" layers of *Pamiat'* members have been nourished by the writers of so-called village prose (one of whose representatives is Rasputin), the tradition of pre-1917 anti-Semitism nourishes the grassroots layer of *Pamiat'*.

Anti-Semitism has a long history in Russia. It had been the official philosophy of the tsarist government. After the Bolshevik Revolution, anti-Semitism and chauvinism in general were officially regarded as major crimes. However, already by the late 1920s, anti-Semitism was subtly supported by the ruling party elite. It was used to fight the left opposition, many of whose members were Jewish, starting with Trotsky. After the short intermission during the "Great Patriotic War" (the official name for World War II) when the government used Jewish and other nationalisms in the struggle against Nazi Germany, anti-

Semitic feeling came to the fore once again. Anti-Semitism became particularly virulent by the late 1940s, when preparations were started to deport most of the Jews to Siberia. After Stalin's death in 1953, anti-Semitism was toned down somewhat. Yet, once again it became a focal point of Soviet propaganda after the 1967 Six-Day War, and especially after the beginning of the mass emigration of Jews from the Soviet Union. The new campaign differed from previous ones by the presentation of Zionist Jews as vicious, brutal, and powerful (in Soviet cartoons parallels were drawn between the German fascists in their treatment of conquered peoples and Zionists in their treatment of the Arabs). At the same time, it was implied that the Zionists controlled the American government. It was further implied that Jews have been organized in the network of Masonry, with Zionism as one of its branches (earlier, it was suggested that Zionism was only a branch of bourgeois nationalism). Jews were presented as a devilish people, and, since Russia was the most Christian country, it was not surprising that it became Satan's prime target.

In this context, Marxism is viewed as a Jewish-western concoction meant to destroy tsarist Russia's harmonious social relationships. The Black Hundreds political movement of prerevolutionary Russia (responsible for many a Jewish pogrom) began to be viewed as quite harmless.[18] The brutality of the Bolshevik Revolution is attributed to the participation of Jews in it. At the same time, Lenin is presented as an embodiment of wholesome Russian nationalism and is said to have had nothing to do with revolutionary terror or even with Marxism.[19] Stalin is presented in the same fashion and virtually cleansed of responsibility for the collectivization and the purges. Trotsky is presented as the prime force behind collectivization, and Lazar Kaganovich, also a Jew, is regarded as responsible for the purges and the destruction of the ancient monuments in Moscow. Here he was motivated not by Marxist ideology but by his Jewishness and concomitant hatred of everything Russian. At the same time, the late 1940s campaign against "cosmopolitans" is considered meritorious, and only some writers are upset—not by the persecution of Jews but by the fact that because of the similarity of some Russian names to Jewish ones, certain ethnic Russians became victims of persecution.[20]

It is characteristic of present-day Russian anti-Semitism that Jews are viewed not as a religion but as a race.[21] An assimilation of Jews into Russian life is viewed as impossible. In a recent issue of *Komsomol'skaia pravda*, P. Gorelov, a member of the Gor'kii Institute of World Literature in Moscow, pointed out that poet Iosif Brodskii (a Jew) has no love for Russia or any other country and is a rootless cosmopolitan. In the same issue, a letter to the editor quoted a critical evaluation of Brodskii published in the strongly nationalistic emigré journal *Chasovoi*.[22]

While viewing Jews (and to some extent other minorities and the West as well) as Russia's enemies, the extremists from *Pamiat'* have no visible imperial or messianic ambitions, and their political program is based on isolationist principles: Jews and others, mostly westernized liberals, are to be pressured, purged from jobs, and forced to emigrate.[23] At the same time, Russia should keep itself aloof from international involvement. The recent demonstration in Moscow against Soviet-Israeli rapprochement is evidence of such attitudes. While hatred toward Israel was one of the reasons behind the demonstration, there were other considerations. Russia should not become involved in the Middle East, but rather be concerned with its own problems, such as defending ethnic Russians against the Zionists.[24]

The ideology of nationalism embraced by many Russian intellectuals has some similarities with the traditional Slavophilism of the nineteenth century. Like their present-day followers, the Slavophiles emphasized Russia's attachment to Christian virtues such as unselfishness, spirituality, and concern for others, while regarding the West as materialistic, depraved, and aggressive. At the same time, there are differences. Unlike their predecessors, the modern Russophiles often fulminate against technological progress. One could hardly find in present-day Slavophilism any imperial ambitions, and in most cases it is free of messianic ambitions as well. In fact, it is often distinctly parochial. This is why even the most extreme *Pamiat'* members are different from the German Nazis, with their desire not only to purge Jews from Germany but also to lead the world struggle against the Jews. *Pamiat'* limits its goal to cleansing Russia of Jews and other undesirable minorities, and it has no interest in the world implications of Zionism.

These changes in the self-perception of modern Russian nationalism can be explained by the peculiarities of Soviet political and economic development. While nineteenth-century Slavophilism (as well as the blend of Slavophilism and Marxism present in Stalinist times) was an ideology of the rising empire, Russophilism of the present time is an ideology of the empire in decline.

Gorbachev's revelations about the problems of the USSR shook the very foundations of Russia's national pride. It is now officially acknowledged that Soviet culture and science often fall behind the West. Moral degradation is appalling, with cynicism and promiscuity widespread. It is officially acknowledged in the Soviet press that "hard currency prostitution" (i.e., for foreigners only) has become one of the most desirable professions, and that Moscow prostitutes solicit foreigners much more aggressively than do their counterparts in many western capitals. In this situation Russia could hardly claim to be "the city on the hill," or the example of morality and righteousness as the nineteenth-century Slavophiles viewed it. The defeat in Afghanistan and the rise of the movements for independence among the empire's minorities shake the myth about Russia's military might and about its peaceful ways of incorporating other nations into the empire. "The Third Rome," whose golden eagle and invincible legions held sway over an enormous empire, is no longer an option. The revelations about the pathetic conditions of the Soviet economy have struck the final blow against the national pride of Russians. From now on Russian nationalism could not support the Eurasian vision presenting Russia as being on its way toward the fulfillment of Fedorov's dream: the victory over nature and death.

In this situation Russian nationalism had no choice but to abandon its messianic and imperial fantasies and opt for parochial isolationism. This trend in the Russian national consciousness parallels a new attitude toward Soviet minorities and toward the Eastern European countries. It seems likely that Moscow, having lost the support of a considerable part of the Russian population for an imperial policy, will make some concessions to the minority nationalities and to the satellite states in Eastern Europe. Even abandoning some parts of the empire should not be excluded. At the same time, it would be a mistake to see the future of the USSR as a process of automatic and progressive disintegration; the political process is more complicated. However, the threat of disintegration (involving a physical threat to Russians and other ethnic groups in the various republics) and *Pamiat's* popularity among the population and the conservative part of the party apparatus[25] add up to an explosive situation. As a *Literaturnaia gazeta* writer put it, "tension in the country is extreme."[26] In this situation, the blending of *Pamiat'*-style nationalism and neo-Stalinism might lead to the creation of a new authoritarian regime of the fascist type, either with Gorbachev or without him. In this situation Russian imperial ideology might reemerge. The future will show what tendencies will prevail and what kind of political and ideological combination will emerge.

9   Fyodor Dostoevsky as Bearer

of a Nationalist Outlook

The extreme nationalist outlook of Dostoevsky casts a shadow on his reputation as a spiritual teacher and prophet, though it did no harm to his creative genius. In fact, it served as an inspiration and motivation. (It is with good reason that André Gide said that high literature can hardly be compatible with starry-eyed idealism.)

Dostoevsky's transition to a true nationalist position took place soon after his release from penal servitude and was its unexpected consequence. Before penal servitude, like Aleksandr Solzhenitsyn before the Gulag, he was, one might say, merely an honest Russian patriot. At that time Dostoevsky "dreamed" of necessary reforms and, above all, of the abolition of serfdom.

What then distinguishes lawful patriotism from a pernicious bias toward nationalism? Nationalism is based on the idea of national superiority and national exclusivity, as well as on the view that the nation constitutes the highest form of moral-religious and political community. This fact often gives rise to the temptation of interfering in the lives and fates of other nations, of transforming them according to one's own image and likeness, either by acting "lovingly" by means of peaceful persuasion and irresistible influence or, in extreme cases, by the use of violence, as Dostoevsky argues in the name of Christ's "doctrine of the sword." [1]

I am inclined to say that it is precisely this transformation of Dostoevsky from a Russian patriot into a Russian nationalist that provides the most reliable key to understanding Dostoevsky's own declaration concerning his "regenerated convictions." [2]

Intimations of this process can already be felt in a little-known poem written by Dostoevsky in May 1854: [3] "Concerning European Events in 1854" ("Na evropeiskie sobytiia v 1854 godu"). [4] Here the patriotic sentiment, "the absurdity of frightening a Russian with a Frenchman" (*Smeshno frantsuzom russkogo pugat'*), already takes on a strong nationalistic tone:

> The past stands as answer to you,
> And your alliance has long not frightened us.
> We will escape in this hour of peril,
> Our salvation the cross and church, faith and throne!
> Within our souls this law has formed,
> As sign of victory and deliverance!
> We did not lose our faith simple-heartedly
> (When some western nation came to us).

The theme of "victory and deliverance" in the name of and thanks to faith later develops into an assertion about the special mission of Russia, regarding not only the "Golden-horned Porte," that is, Constantinople, for which the French vainly feel "great pity," but also "deep Asia":

> It is not yours to fathom Russia's fate!
> Is not her destiny clear to you?
> The East is hers! To her millions
> Of generations tirelessly stretch their hands.
> And ruling over deep Asia, [5]
> She imparts youthful life to all,
> And the regeneration of ancient East
> (So God commanded!) by Russia is near,
> This again is *Rus'*, this subject to the tsar,
> The splendid dawn of the future!

"Albion," which has "corrupted its peoples" with opium, is severely condemned. The "Jew, who has crucified Christ today,/ Who
has once again sold Eternal Love," is stigmatized. And all the betray-
ers of Christ are damned wholesale:

> He commanded that they be called the body of Christ,
> He himself—the Head of the Orthodox Faith!
> With infidel to fight for the Church
> Is a deed benighted, sinful and inglorious!
> A Christian for a Turk and against Christ!
> A Christian—defender of Mohammed!
> May shame be yours, apostates of the Cross!
> Extinguishers of Divine Light!
> But God is with us! Hurrah! Holy is our deed,
> And who would not gladly lay down his life for Christ!

To those who may perhaps object that Dostoevsky composed this
poem with mercenary intentions reluctantly and against his conscience, one might respond, first, that it was written with genuine
fervor and inspiration; second, that all of the themes touched on here,
already revealing an integrated world-view, strikingly coincide with
later pronouncements made by the author until the very end of his life;
and, third, that Dostoevsky himself, not without some degree of pride,
and, it would seem, not without some foundation, liked to assert:
"You won't be able to produce the tiniest shred of proof about the
person of Fyodor Dostoevsky that he had lied for the sake of gain, for
honor or from false pride." [6]

Dostoevsky's poem was presented by the commander of the Seventh
Siberian line battalion, Lieutenant Colonel Belikhov, to the chief-
of-staff and, naturally, did not become known in the literature of
that time.

On the other hand, two years later, in a letter from Semipalatinsk
dated January 18, 1856, Dostoevsky entrusted his new manner of
thinking to Apollon Nikolaevich Maikov, with whom he carried on a
friendship in the 1840s. Yes, he, Dostoevsky, had been fascinated by
"French ideas" before his penal servitude, but "only in their scientific
aspect." However, this happened to many: "The whole matter was
one of exclusivity and truth." Apollon Maikov himself did not escape

at that time a fate common to all those who "reason, feel and try to understand." In addition, "it may well be that those who were most devoted to the ideas of exclusivity were always Russian. And so it turns out that in its very nature all feelings of exclusivity evoke their opposite." Such a transition is made easier by the fact that "we haven't changed as people. I am answerable for myself." For, continues Dostoevsky, "Ideas change, the heart remains the same. . . . Russia, duty, honor?—yes! I was always genuinely Russian—I tell you this in all sincerity." "It is possible to be mistaken about an idea, but it is not possible to be mistaken with one's heart and to become dishonest by mistake, that is, to act against one's convictions." And so, the former "idea" is effaced without any internal conflict with one's "conscience." In the transition from "exclusivity" to its "opposite," a kind of harmonious, genetic connection is perceived. "I always followed that which seemed better and straightforward and I didn't act against my conscience; whatever I gave myself up to, I did so with passion." What took place was not a revolution but a reevaluation. Thus, the former aspirations directed toward "French ideas" now are rechanneled in the direction of "great Russia's" mission: "I fully share with you the patriotic feeling of a *moral* liberation of the Slavs. That is Russia's role, of great, noble Russia, our holy mother. . . . I also share with you the idea that Europe and its mission will be brought to a conclusion by Russia. For me this has *long* [emphasis mine] been clear." The spiritual displacement is noted by a single adjective: love for Russia is replaced by love for a *great* Russia.

It was precisely the recognition and realization of this latent Russianness within himself that helped him not only to endure penal servitude but also to draw a lesson from it for the rest of his life. In the same letter to Maikov, Dostoevsky writes:

I assure you that I am close to all that is Russian to such a degree that, for example, even the convicts did not frighten me. They were Russians, my brothers in misfortune, and more than once I had the good fortune of finding nobility in the heart of a brigand because, strictly speaking, I could understand him; because I was Russian myself. Misfortune made it possible for me to learn much in a practical manner. It is possible that this practice had a great influence on me, but I also learned in a practical way that I had always been a Russian in my heart.

The rest of the writer's life until his death was dedicated to a deepening of this Russianness with a constant intensification of its nationalist coloration. The first public culmination of this new cycle of thought appeared in September 1860 in a programmatic announcement of the journal *Vremia*, which was placed in and distributed by the major newspapers. The short program outlined at the end of the announcement forms a part of Dostoevsky's large programmatic article that constitutes a manifesto of *pochvennichestvo*, as Dostoevsky termed the chief philosophy of *Vremia*. The main points of the declaration are as follows:

> The reform of Peter the Great cost us dearly: it separated us from the people. . . . After the reform there was only one instance of a reunification between them and us, the educated class—eighteen-twelve, and we saw what the people were made of. . . . We finally became convinced that we too are a distinct nationality, original to the highest degree and that our task was to create a new form for ourselves, our own and native, taken from our soil, taken from the national spirit and national sources. . . . It is possible that the Russian idea will consist in a synthesis of all those ideas which are being developed so tenaciously and courageously in Europe by its separate nationalities. . . .

The "Russian idea" was to win a resounding triumph when it was put to a test in western Europe, where Dostoevsky went for the first time in the beginning of June 1862. The highlights of his travels included visits to Paris, London, and Cologne, a trip down the Rhine, and tours of Switzerland and Italy. Summing up the results of his observations in "Winter Notes on Summer Impressions, a Feuilleton for the Summer" (*Vremia*, 1863, nos. 2 and 3), Dostoevsky relates how he was struck by the "bourgeoisity" of the western Europeans ("to amass money, they acquire as many things as possible"), and not without caustic irony he expresses his distress at the fact that "freedom, equality, and brotherhood" are only empty slogans there. In the only letter that has reached us from that period (to N.N. Strakhov, Paris, June 26–July 8, 1862), Dostoevsky places what was for him an already characteristic boundary between "excellent things," which are worth looking at, and everyday reality, which can only evoke "boredom" and even "nausea." The French, who because of his education were closer to him than other Europeans, are strongly taken to task, especially in contrast to the Russians:

> You mentioned self-satisfied, impudent, and insignificant people who rage in our spas. . . . Our people are simply rascally voluptuaries, for the most part intelligent, and here they are fully convinced of the justice of their behavior. The Frenchman is calm, quiet, honest and polite, but he is false and money means everything to him. He has no ideals. Don't ask him for convictions, he doesn't even entertain the thought. The general level of education is woefully low (I am speaking of officially schooled people, but then there are not many of those and, after all, is schooling education in the sense that we are used to understanding the word?).

Dostoevsky's second trip to Europe in August–October 1863 was connected with his unsuccessful romance with A.P. Suslova and with gambling on ·the roulette wheel. The highlights were Wiesbaden, Paris, Baden-Baden (meeting with Turgenev), and Italy (Rome, Livorno, Turin, Naples). The correspondence of these months is naggingly personal, and material and financial problems predominate. He lacks the peace of mind to "even give vent to any of the sensations experienced by travelers" (to Strakhov from Rome, September 18–30). Nevertheless, here and there one comes across judgments of countries he visited. As before, one encounters a dichotomy of impressions relating to Europe's past and present. He has come to "loathe Paris" and "Turin is most boring" (to M.M. Dostoevsky from Turin, September 8–20). On the other hand, "The Louvre is a great thing, and the whole embankment, all the way to Notre Dame, is something amazing" (to N.M. Dostoevsky from Paris, August 28). And also, "yesterday morning I visited St. Peter's. A powerful impression . . . with shivers down my back. Today I visited the *Forum* and all its ruins. Then the *Coliseum!* Well, what can I tell you . . ." (to Strakhov from Rome, September 18–30). Apparently Dostoevsky had already formed a lasting opinion about western Europeans: "for a tourist like myself, simply looking at the customs, Frenchmen are repulsive. . . . Indeed, the best things here are fruit and wine: that doesn't get boring" (to V.D. Konstant from Paris, September 1). In such a context one notes the fact that during this second visit abroad the basic ideas for *The Gambler* and *Notes from the Underground* were conceived. After all, the common denominator for both works is the open struggle with the West, with its typology of characters and, most important, with its ideology of "Russianness."

Nevertheless, Dostoevsky's final shift in the direction of unbridled nationalism took place during his "second exile," occasioned by his fear of creditors and his illness (April 23, 1867, to the end of 1871), which, in moments of especially strong homesickness, seemed more difficult to bear than penal servitude in Siberia. There at least he was among his own people. In the letters of this period, which finishes a cycle and reaches its apogee in *The Possessed* (written in the course of 1870 and 1871 and appearing in print a year later, the novel led directly to the first installment of *Diary of a Writer* in Vladimir Meshcherskii's *Grazhdanin*, Dostoevsky, according to an apt observation by Dolinin, "is angered and irritated by trifles; he despises and hates. His thoughts are only on Russia, on Russian social and political life, on Russian literature and journalism." [7]

His nationalistic outlook receives its final coordinates and is inscribed into a kind of magic square: the Russian people, a Russian Christ, a Russian state, and Russian messianism. Simultaneously these four aspects reflect one and the same essence, comprehended intuitively, which is focused in the center of the square and which can be called Dostoevsky's "fundamental idea." Dostoevsky's five "novel-tragedies" are illuminated from the inside by this, the fundamental idea.

The main resting places in these wandering years were Dresden, Geneva, Vevey, Milan, Florence, and again Dresden. But any of these cities means no more to Dostoevsky than simply an accidental place of residence. "Why am I in Dresden? Precisely in Dresden and in no other place? And precisely why was it worth dropping everything in one place and coming to another?"—he appears to be deliberating out loud in a a letter to Maikov from Geneva (August 16–28, 1867). As

Dolinin correctly points out, " 'The great spiritual strivings of European civilization,' the fruits of these strivings in the past, in an established culture, he was still able to perceive and to find comprehensible, at least in the field of art. But the present, created every second, was absolutely alien to him, repelled him to the point of disgust by the utter distinctiveness of its 'fleshiness,' of its powerfully established forms within the bounds of national history and experience." [8]

Sharply distancing himself from the westernizers, "a group that had totally renounced Russia," [9] Dostoevsky simultaneously disassociated himself from the Slavophiles, who rejected the contours of the present in Russia since, in their opinion, these contours did not correspond to the deep essence that connected the past to the future of the Russian nation. For Dostoevsky the reverse was true, "Russia is *contemporary*; that which is taking place in it at the moment is being elevated into a kind of ideal that illuminates its past and future." [10] In the letters from this period elements of "coarse empiricism" are combined with curious dialectical shifts. Higher than the Russian nation stand values implanted in it. Higher than God himself stands the Russian God, in essence a Russian Christ, "the living idea" of the divine, which has disappeared in the West. At the same time, higher than the Russian Church stands Russian Orthodoxy. Higher than the tsar stands the monarchy, that is, the Russian type of statehood ("Our constitution consists in mutual love of the Monarch for the people and the people for the Monarch").[11] Higher than Russia itself stands its mission of renewing all humanity. "*Political dominance*, the preeminence of the Great Russian [*velikorusskii*] people—this is what constitutes the driving force of its present-day world view." [12] In a letter to A. N. Maikov, written February 18, 1868, Dostoevsky expressed himself precisely in these terms:

Our essence . . . is infinitely higher than that of Europe. And in general all moral conceptions and aims of Russians are higher than those of the European world. We have a more direct and noble belief in goodness which is expressed in Christianity and not in a bourgeois resolution of the problems of comfort.

The world awaits a great renewal through the Russian idea (which is tightly welded to Orthodoxy . . .) and this will take place in about a century. This is my passionate belief. But that this great deed may come to pass, it is necessary that the *political right* and the preeminence of the Great Russian people over the entire Slavic world be established finally and unquestionably. (And our paltry little liberals preach the disintegration of Russia into united states! Oh, morons!)

This fundamental complex of ideas and views will find a further conceptual development in regular issues of *The Diary of a Writer*, which is a kind of a bible of Russian nationalism. In her profoundly reasoned book *Understanding Russia: The Holy Fool in Russian Culture*, Ewa M. Thompson observes:

> In *Diary of a Writer* Dostoevsky argued that the Russian peasant, coarse and foolish and crafty though he may appear, is ultimately closer to the moral ideal than the western burgher, who outwardly observes all the proprieties of the moral code but is not possessed of the spirit of truth. The Russian peasant is wiser and more moral than his western counterpart, even though outwardly he may not so appear. His "inner attitude" is right, whereas the inner attitude of western peasants is wrong. From the vantage point of the late twentieth century, one can say that such reinforcements of uncritical nationalism have not served Russian citizens well. . . . In their political writings, Kireevskii, Danilevskii, Aksakov and Dostoevsky prepared the ground for the Soviet dialecticians. . . . All the soldiers who fell in Russia's foreign wars and all the Sobakeviches residing in Russian country manors could not convince a Russophile ideologue that the Russian myth was flawed and that it might bear bitter fruit.[13]

Bypassing the delicate question about the deep-rooted nationalism of the mature Dostoevsky, which at times blended into zealous chauvinism, scholars usually balk as if facing a stone wall. Some are prone to assertions that the works of Dostoevsky—who is, after all, one of the great literary geniuses—captivate readers by their artistic merit and not by the consistency or cogency of the political doctrine expressed by him. Others feel that Dostoevsky's "ideology" should in general be separated from, on the one hand, his "true" artistic works, and, on the other hand, from his "false," or at any rate "controversial," journalistic works. This kind of distinction allegedly helps to separate the wheat from the chaff.

It is difficult to agree with such approaches of both western and Soviet specialists. After all, their direct consequence is to remove from Dostoevsky's poetics its moral center. Dostoevsky's nationalism not only thoroughly suffuses his five novel-tragedies, but it also imparts to them a unique and intense pathos. Long ago N. N. Strakhov called Raskol'nikov a nihilist, but an "unhappy" nihilist. To this Dostoevsky replied, "You alone have understood me." [14] Paraphrasing Strakhov's judgment, one can characterize Dostoevsky as an "unhappy nationalist." The whole pathos of his large novels (for at the same time Dostoevsky was able to define in a significant manner the pathogenesis of some of the most serious contemporary illnesses, such as, for example, fascism and totalitarianism) stems from a fatal, yet, in its own way, a logical displacement of planes. Not feeling under his feet sufficiently firm soil (and this from a *pochvennik!*), Dostoevsky the artist was forced, or, one should say, was condemned to endless proofs by rule of the contraries.

Dedicating *The Possessed,* at Pobedonostsev's instigation, to the heir to the throne, A. A. Romanov (the future Alexander III), Dostoevsky, in a letter of February 1873, in which he expresses "without flattery" his innermost convictions, sheds a clear light on the essential tragedy of his art: "In the delight we experience from our own self-degradation, we have forgotten history's immutable law, which consists in the fact that without *arrogance* about our significance in the world as a nation, we can never be a great nation nor can we leave after ourselves something even a trifle original for the benefit of mankind."

Psychologically, proofs "from contrary points of view" bring with them two inevitable consequences. First, any defensive position is disadvantageous for the artist, especially if the latter feels that "these days to think in this manner in our country and to espouse such thoughts means to condemn oneself to the role of a pariah." [15] Second, as a result of this extremely negative position (regardless of any motifs indicating an offensive posture, or individual "positive" scenes tied mainly to his understanding of a Russian Christ), Dostoevsky as an artist-thinker was sometimes inclined to become dependent to a certain degree on the very thing he consciously damned. His damaging nationalism fluctuates between utopia and antiutopia. Basic features of this antiutopia appear throughout his entire novelistic output, from the epilogue in *Crime and Punishment* (in Raskol'nikov's dream) to the "Legend of the Grand Inquisitor" (where Christ, invested with Russian qualities,[16] appears to be helpless before "the head of this multitude 'thirsting for power merely to attain filthy pleasures' "). But they are worked out in the preparatory materials for *The Possessed:*

"If Orthodoxy is *all,* then Russia is *all.* If not, then better to burn it down."

"And so all of this is a fantasmogoria," exclaims Shatov in despair, "and it should be burnt down."

"It should be burned," laughs the prince. "Or you could go into a decline for some five or ten centuries, turn into savages and start a new civilization—a slow burning."

. . . There are only two ways of initiating action: either faith, or to burn. Nechaev took the second,—he is strong and calm.[17]

An even more mysterious light is shed on the last remark about Nechaev by the fact that in the entire account devoted to him, Dostoevsky remarks as if in passing, "A man of exceptional intellect . . . he viewed Russia intelligently." [18]

In his pauses between utopia and antiutopia Dostoevsky did not stop being a Russian nationalist. An understanding of "Russianness" equally contained within itself two opposite paths toward one and the same final goal, toward apocatastasis: "Listen, figure it out yourselves: the beast is wounded, a third of the grasses has perished, the Eastern whore, the pregnant wife, all are Russia. 'The groom and bride shall have no voice.' If only for a joke, don't you really find a similarity?" [19]

Serving to unite Dostoevsky the artist with Dostoevsky the publicist, these pauses of a Russian nationalist form an explosive beginning of his dread and dangerous genius.

Translated by Jerzy Kolodziej, Indiana University

10   Pushkin: Ideologist of

Post-Petrine Russia or

European Humanist?

In his speech delivered on June 18, 1880, at the Pushkin Memorial ceremony in Moscow, Ivan Turgenev quoted Pushkin's fellow-
author and literary executor, E.A. Baratynskii, as having written to a
friend: "Can you imagine what amazed me more than anything in all
these poems? The abundance of thoughts! Pushkin a thinker! Could
this have been expected?" [1]

In the same speech, Turgenev called on his listeners to recall Peter
the Great, "whose nature was somewhat akin to the nature of Pushkin
himself." [2] The idea of a parallelism between the roles of Peter and of
Pushkin may be traced back to Belinskii, [3] the conception of Pushkin
as a "national" poet to Gogol'. [4] The notion of Pushkin as a political
thinker or ideologist, however, has, with a few notable exceptions,
been less well received by scholars, perhaps out of respect for one
supreme as a creative artist, perhaps because Pushkin himself ad-

vanced no claim to be so regarded. Exceptions are S.L. Frank, whose essays "Pushkin as a Political Thinker" (1937) and "Pushkin on Relations between Russia and Europe" (1949)[5] succinctly summarize the case for seeing Pushkin as a major political thinker; Wacław Lednicki, who has analyzed Pushkin's attitude toward Peter the Great in his monograph *The Bronze Horseman*;[6] and Leonard Schapiro in his *Rationalism and Nationalism in Russian Nineteenth-Century Political Thought*.[7]

Frank and Schapiro agree broadly in applying to Pushkin the description of him by P.A. Viazemskii as a "liberal conservative"[8] ("liberal monarchist" might be equally applicable). How does this definition bear on the question in the title of this chapter—the alternatives of which, it should at once be made clear, are not mutually exclusive? An answer will be sought through examining briefly in turn Pushkin's attitudes toward Peter and his successors, toward the Decembrist conspiracy, toward Napoleon and the French Revolution, toward the Greek and Polish national uprisings (which occurred during the period of his adulthood), and toward the European "idea."

The most positive statement of Pushkin's admiration for Peter is to be found in his "Stanzas" ("Stansy," 1826), especially the third and fourth verses:

> With autocratic arm
> He boldly sowed enlightenment,
> But did not despise his native country:
> He knew its destiny.

> Now academician, now hero,
> Now sailor, now carpenter,
> With his all-embracing mind
> He was the eternal workman on the throne.[9]

In *Poltava* he patriotically links with "the genius of Peter" the progress of Russia to adulthood. *The Bronze Horseman*, above all, glorifies Peter's most symbolical achievement but not without reservation, as Lednicki pointed out: "Himself a decided European, a pupil of the French writers of the eighteenth century, and a great reformer of Russian poetry, Pushkin enthusiastically accepted Peter the Great as a reformer, an enlightener of Russia, and, finally, as the creator of a great empire. However, this did not exhaust the poet's attitude toward the Russian tsar. This attitude was ambiguous. . . ." [10]

The ambivalence of the poet's attitude is especially apparent in "My Genealogy" ("Moia rodoslovnaia"), with its ironical tone and specific allusion to the execution in Peter's reign of a member of the Pushkin clan. By contrast, the "Postscript" to this poem provides the key to the emotional link in virtue of adoption and promotion of the poet's maternal ancestor Abram Gannibal. It is not psychologically far-fetched—indeed, it might be considered a cliché of explanation—to see in Pushkin's dramatically mixed ancestry the basis for his own temperamental juxtaposition of rebelliousness and craving for law and order.

In Pushkin's attitudes toward Peter's successors on the throne of Russia there is no simple pattern. Catherine II aroused in him mixed emotions—respect for her foreign policy successes ("Sweden humbled and Poland annihilated—these are Catherine's great claims to the Russian people's gratitude"), revulsion toward her personal example ("The debauched sovereign also debauched her state"). [11] For Alexander I, Pushkin had little or nothing good to say despite his patriotic pride in the defeat of Napoleon—credit for which, however, if we may judge by his poems "Before the Sacred Tomb" ("Pered grobnitseiu sviatoi") and "The Commander" ("Polkovodets"), he gave to the Russian generals rather than to the emperor. It is clear that during the last decade of Alexander's reign the influence of Chaadaev, of the Turgenev brothers, and of future Decembrists of his acquaintance, together with the ideas current in the "Arzamas" and "Green Lamp" societies, confirmed in Pushkin both patriotic fervor and youthful iconoclasm and love of freedom in every sense. It was not for Pushkin alone that the last years of Alexander were claustrophobic: many could have echoed his words (from a letter to his brother Lev of early 1824): "Holy Russia is becoming unbearable to me. *Ubi bene, ibi patria.* . . ." [12] But the episode of his reference in a letter to "taking lessons in pure atheism" [13] and his subsequent discharge from state service and exile to Mikhailovskoe was the last straw. Finally, we have, by contrast, the intriguing "special relationship" between the

poet and the young new emperor Nicholas: this requires no comment
other than the speculative suggestion that Pushkin was initially dis-
posed to look for Petrine virtues in Nicholas, who, however, came to
display "beaucoup de praporchique" and only "un peu de Pierre le
Grand."[14]

December 1825 marks a watershed in Pushkin's life but not neces-
sarily in his ideas. As for the facts, the account given in his letters to
friends in the first months of 1826 of his relationship with the conspirators and attitude toward the conspiracy rings true: "I do not belong to the conspiracy, and had no political ties with the rebels . . .
[although] I had connections with the greater part of the present conspirators" (to V.A. Zhukovskii, January 1826).[15] "I of course could
not bear good will toward the late Tsar. . . . But I never preached
rebellion or revolution—on the contrary" (to A.A. Del'vig, February
1826).[16] Notwithstanding what he may have said to the contrary to
Nicholas at their September 1826 meeting,[17] it is inherently implau-
sible that Pushkin would have been a participant in the events of December 14, even had he been in Petersburg at the time. He had earlier
commended Chaadaev's intention to go abroad (Chaadaev likewise
"missed" the Decembrist action), and there is evidence that the conspirators thought it prudent to leave him in ignorance of their plans—
for example: "As for news from Petersburg, I know nothing of what
is going on there" (to P.A. Osipova, August 8, 1925).[18] "What's going
on where you are, in Petersburg? I don't know a thing, and everybody
has ceased writing to me" (to P.A. Pletnev, January 1826).[19]

Did the shock of the December debacle "cure" Pushkin of the "political radicalism" that, according to Frank, characterized the poet in
his Kishinev-Odessa period? Did it mark, as Adam Mickiewicz suggested in his lectures on Slavonic literatures at the Collège de France,
"a loss of courage and nerve, the beginning of a decline"?[20] Did Pushkin already possess a conscious, formed ideology which was oriented
against autocracy and which could be shaken and discarded in favor
of servile support for the status quo? Was his reiterated claim (letter
to P.A. Viazemskii of July 10, 1826)[21] that "I have never liked revolt
and revolution" sincere? I believe that it was; and, if so, it appears to
follow that the significant change was that of the person of the sover-

eign, not of Pushkin's attitudes or ideas. First, if we consider the most critical or freedom-affirming of his pre-1825 poems, we see that they attack not autocratic monarchy as such but arbitrary, extralegal abuse of monarchical power: in "Freedom" ("Vol'nost' "), he criticizes "unjust use of power," [22] in "To Chaadaev" ("K Chaadaevu"), "self-willed power" (*samovlastie*),[23] while in "The Countryside" ("Derevnia"), he expresses the hope that he will live to see "the people freed from oppression and slavery, fallen by the will of the tsar. . . ." [24]

Second, in those brilliant long poems "Prisoner of the Caucasus" and "The Gypsies," in which he "settled accounts" with the spirit of Romanticism, Pushkin savagely demolishes extremism in the pursuit of freedom and self-assertion and, conversely, asserts acceptance of law and social order (albeit, in the former poem), with a gratuitous streak of connivance at Russian imperialism: "Submit, Caucasus: Ermolov is coming!" [25]

Third, not later than 1822—the date of his *Notes on the History of the Eighteenth Century*—Pushkin had begun, with Karamzin as mentor, the serious study of history that was to become a major pursuit in his later years. Is it unreasonable to attribute his commitment to the aim of a law-based society resting on monarchy and civil liberty at least in part to the fact that the two periods of history that he selected for special study, the Time of Troubles and the Pugachev rebellion, demonstrated most graphically the woes resulting from failure to achieve this aim? It is entirely logical that Pushkin should have proposed to contemplate the Decembrist tragedy "through Shakespeare's eyes" [26] and set himself to write a Shakespearean tragedy on the life and death of Boris Godunov.

It is not inconceivable that, in the fullness of time, Pushkin might have been impelled to attempt a dramatic treatment of the life of Napoleon. For, in his poem on the death of this arch-enemy of Russia, there is a calm and dignified magnanimity worthy of Shakespeare, while the repetition in it of the word "the die" (*zhrebii*) seems in some measure to exonerate Napoleon of responsibility for his deeds. This attitude toward the dead emperor contrasts interestingly, as S.L. Frank pointed out, with Tolstoy's attempt to ridicule and belittle his memory.[27]

No less striking, and consistent with the ideal of liberty restrained by law, is Pushkin's indirect judgment on the French Revolution in his poem "André Chénier" in which he has the French poet explore the contradictions that may result from over-zealous implementation of revolutionary slogans:

> . . . the law,
> On freedom relying, proclaimed equality:
> And we cried: bliss!
> O woe! O foolish dream!
> Where are freedom and the law? Over us
> The axe alone holds sway.
> We have overthrown the tsars. But a murderer with his hangmen
> Have we elected tsar. O horror! O disgrace![28]

This poem, written in the first half of 1825, suggests clearly and forcefully how Pushkin, though sympathetic to the Decembrists' aims—at least, those of the Northern Society—could not have condoned the methods to which the more extreme among them were prepared to resort to achieve them.

In addition to the Decembrist rising, two other events in the 1820–30 decade might be said to have provided a test of the ideological stance of a Russian "liberal"—the Greek war of independence, associated with the Phil-Hellenism exemplified most famously by Byron, and the Polish Rising of November 1830.

Pushkin, living in Kishinev in the years 1820–23 and for the following year in Odessa—principal base of the Greek community in Russia and seat of the Philiki Hetairia[29]—was uniquely qualified to observe, assess and, had it aroused his sympathy, propagate support for the Greek independence movement. Indeed, in a letter from Kishinev of March 1821,[30] drafted but, significantly, unsent, he describes, seemingly with enthusiastic approval, the inception of the movement and the preparations of Ypsilanti and his Romanian ally, Tudor Vladimirescu, and poses the question: "What is Russia going to do?" It appears that at one point a rumor reached his friend, the historian Mikhail Pogodin, that Pushkin himself "had slipped away to join the Greeks";[31] but by 1824 direct contact with them in Odessa had cooled the poet's ardor for their cause. While still maintaining (in a draft letter

probably intended for the Decemberist M.F. Orlov)[32] that "nothing
has been so *narodno* [in agreement with the spirit of the people] as
the cause of the Greeks . . . ," he argues in writing to Viazemskii
(June 1824) that "it is unforgivable puerility that all enlightened European peoples should be raving about Greece. The Jesuits have talked
our heads off about Themistocles and Pericles, and we have come to
imagine that a nasty people, made up of bandits and shopkeepers, are
their legitimate descendants and heirs of their school-fame. You will
say that I have changed my opinion. If you would come to us in
Odessa to look at the fellow countrymen of Miltiades, you would
agree with me."[33]

Pushkin's reaction to the Polish Rising of 1830–31 in the form of
his celebrated poems "To the Slanderers of Russia" and "The Anniversary of Borodino" has been cited as evidence of a surrender of
liberalism to patriotism of a peculiarly ugly and chauvinistic type; and
this accusation has been reinforced by the angry lines in Mickiewicz's
"To My Muscovite Friends" ("Do przyjaciół Moskali," 1832) which,
without naming him, appear certainly to refer to Pushkin:

Some have been dealt perhaps by Fate a sterner punishment;
But one of you perhaps, recipient of shame-bearing honors, has
Betrayed for ever his free spirit to the Tsar's favor
And now at the palace threshold makes obeisance.[34]

It is sufficiently clear from the original title of the poem, "To the
Slanderers of Russia: Commentary on the speech delivered by General
La Fayette," and from the internal evidence of the poem, together with
the historical references in "The Anniversary of Borodino" and "Before the Sacred Tomb," that uppermost in the poet's mind was a genuine fear of the French, on the pretext of aiding Poland, seeking revenge for the humiliation of 1812. The fact remains, as V.A. Frantsev
pointed out in his *Pushkin and the Polish Rising of 1830–1831*,[35] that
anti-Polish sentiments were not new in Pushkin and can be traced back
at least to his 1824 poem "To Count O." ("Grafu O."), addressed to
the Polish count Gustaw Olizar (who had sought in vain to court the
daughter of Pushkin's patron, General Raevskii). There is in fact an
actual verbal echo of the earlier poem in the latter:

TO COUNT O.

O singer! Since times of old
among themselves
Our peoples have been warring,
Now our side groans,
Now yours perishes before the storm.[36]

TO THE SLANDERERS OF RUSSIA

For long among themselves
These peoples have been warring:
Before the storm more than once has bowed
Now their side, now ours.[37]

It would appear that the outburst in the 1831 poem did not spring solely or purely spontaneously from immediate events.

The tenor of Pushkin's correspondence in 1830–31 about the Polish events, in particular his letters to Viazemskii and to General Kutuzov's daughter Elizaveta Khitrovo, is one of sorrow rather than of hatred for the Poles. Nevertheless, "The Slanderers of Russia" provoked, even among his close associates, very varied reactions, ranging from A.I. Turgenev's comment, "Pushkin is a barbarian in relation to Poland," [38] to Chaadaev's unexpectedly wholehearted expression of approval in a letter of September 18, 1831: "I have just seen your two poems. My friend, you have never given me so much pleasure. At last, you have arrived as a national bard; you have at last divined your mission." [39]

Paradoxically, the most explicit statement of Pushkin's own political credo is to be found in his celebrated letter of October 19, 1836, to Chaadaev containing a critique of the latter's "First Philosophical Letter." Here Pushkin asserts his patriotism unequivocally: "for nothing in the world would I have wished to change my country, or to have a different history than that of our ancestors, just as God has given us it." [40]

And he affirms his belief in the positive aspects of Russian history, above all in the great debt owed by western nations to Russia for, as he sees it, saving European civilization from the Mongols. For this very reason Pushkin was, as he puts it in this letter, "embittered" by the absence in Russia of certain features of Europeanism that he admired, for example, "public opinion," which his own namesake in *Boris Godunov* had seen as the key to success and political health;[41] and, conversely, by the persistence of "indifference toward all duty, justice and truth," and "the cynical disdain for human thought and dignity."

In his speech at the Pushkin Memorial ceremony quoted at the beginning of this chapter, Dostoevsky hailed the "universality" (*vsechelovechnost'*) of Pushkin's artistic genius.[42] Universality is, unfortunately, an infinitely flexible concept, such that "Pushkinism" has, as John Bayley puts it, become a "claustrophobic phenomenon . . . the sense of a body of literature ingested and absorbed by its admirers to the point where the original seems merely the starting-point of their ideas."[43]

As a thinker, Pushkin was certainly not the ideologist of post-Petrine Russia, as his contemporary, Minister of Education S.S. Uvarov (variously described by Pushkin as a "clown" or a "scoundrel")[44] perhaps was; but, leaving aside occasional lapses from toleration or charity (as in his uncompleted poetic farewell to Mickiewicz, "He Dwelt Among Us . . ."),[45] he was a consistent advocate of an ideology of balance—balance between patriotism and Europeanism, between the monarchical principle and the popular will, between freedom and law, between public opinion and the influence of such "masters of the mind" as Byron or Napoleon—a balance which, it must be said, largely eluded him in his own life. Finally, in a narrower political sense, Pushkin may be seen as an advocate of that "state based on the rule of law" for which today the Russians hanker but which remains in Russia a will-o'-the-wisp.

11   Soviet Russian Writers and

the Soviet Invasion of Poland

in September 1939

The Molotov-Ribbentrop Pact signed in Moscow on August
23, 1939, initiated two years of Soviet-Nazi friendship. These years
were the most successful, in terms of the annexations and nationalities
policies, of the entire seventy-two years of Soviet history. During this
time, five new republics were formed, and the territory of two others
was significantly enlarged. Conventional wisdom has it that ideological concerns and Stalin's personality dominated Soviet politics during
this period, whereas later, when Hitler attacked, Russian nationalism
was dusted off and employed as an ideological weapon in the fight
against the Nazis. Further, that between 1941 and 1945 Stalin appealed for help to Russian national sentiments and to the Russian Orthodox Church, and Russian nationalism was given a green light while
socialist internationalism was toned down.

My study of the Soviet press of this period indicates that in many ways these commonly accepted interpretations are not correct. It was during the years of Soviet-Nazi friendship that Russian nationalism had its heyday, whereas later, during the war with Hitler, toleration and even encouragement of other nationalisms were in evidence. Nationalist ideologies loomed large in the USSR during the years of friendship with Hitler *and* during the Soviet-German war. The recent manifestations of nationalism in the Soviet Union testify to misstatements in this regard perpetuated by Soviet scholars and to some extent by those western scholars who rely somewhat uncritically on Soviet sources. In this chapter I shall concentrate on a small portion of these developments: the campaign to denigrate Poland launched by the Soviet Russian writers after the Soviet invasion and occupation of eastern Poland in September–October 1939.

Why did the Soviets spend so much effort promoting enmity toward another Slavic nation? The reasons, it seems to me, were both ideological and pragmatic. Poland was a mostly Catholic nation, and both the tsars and the commissars regarded Catholicism as a fundamental enemy. They saw Poles as ineffectual rivals—but rivals, nevertheless—in the competition for leadership among the Slavs. Second, what was needed by the Soviets at that time was a Russian-Ukrainian-Belorussian rapprochement, and this could be best achieved at the expense of Poles. One way to win the Ukrainians and Belorussians was to emphasize what they had in common with the Russians while deemphasizing their kinship with the Poles. Thus, the annexation of western Belorussia and western Ukraine, which belonged to Poland before 1939, was presented in the press as a "unification" of Belorussia and Ukraine—never mind that Soviet control was in many ways harsher than Polish.

This campaign of nationalist hostilities was launched at a meeting of the Moscow chapter of the Union of Soviet Writers held on the day of the invasion and reported the next day in *Pravda*. The meeting was chaired by Fedor Gladkov. More than two hundred writers attended. Predictably, they decided to support the invasion and sent a letter to Stalin to that effect. The letter said: "The Polish state, created through the suppression, exploitation of national minorities, built on the forceful polonization of the Ukrainian and Belorussian population, bent on the total annihilation of their culture . . . has fallen apart at the first serious trial. . . . We salute the beloved Red Army, defender of the oppressed, glory and pride of the Soviet nation . . . all free, equal and happy nations of the Soviet Union . . . support the government and the Party of Lenin and Stalin."[1] Among the signatories were Margarita Aliger, Aleksandr Bogdanov, Fedor Gladkov, Il'ia Selvinskii, and the Ukrainian writer Mikola Cherniavskii, who later perished in Stalin's Gulag.

Thus started the period of vilification of things Polish and of presenting Poland as a place where a few Polish nobles (*pany*) oppressed a great number of Ukrainians, Belorussians, and Jews. Articles were printed under titles such as "Holy Hatred" ("Sviataia nenavist' ") to whip up emotions and encourage pogroms against Poles.[2]

On September 18, 1939, *Pravda* carried Nikolai Aseev's poem entitled "Fully Erect" ("Vo ves' rost"), which ridicules Poles and declares that "Only crumbs remained of Poland" (*Ot Pol'shi ostalas' samaia malost'* . . .). "They [the Poles] did not like our habits; they turned up their noble noses at us . . ." (*Oni ne liubili povadok nashikh; vel' mozhnyi krivili rot* . . .). Now they got what they deserved.

On September 19, 1939, in *Pravda*, Margarita Aliger published a passionate poem entitled "September 17, 1939."[3] The poem stands out even among the other Pole-baiting works of the time, and its commitment to the invasion is remarkably strong. This is not another ode to Stalin written by someone desperately trying to hold onto life but an expression of a deeply held conviction that Poland must perish. The invasion is presented in the poem as the fulfillment of Justice, who, incidentally, turns out to be a fluent speaker of Russian. It is significant that in the poem the adjective "great" is reserved for things Russian rather than Soviet. Later in the poem, the expression "Soviet boys" is used, but no aggrandizing adjective accompanies it. In the conditions of aggressive war waged by the Soviets, Aliger's praise of the Russian language was not unlike the Nazi writers' praise of the greatness of German culture during the Nazi invasion of Europe.

On September 19, 1939, as many as thirty-nine articles, poems, stories, and testimonials about the Soviet invasion of Poland appeared in *Pravda*. It seems clear that *Pravda* was launching a massive campaign to erase any doubts among the Russian-speaking segment of the population as to the appropriateness of the invasion.

On October 10, 1939, *Literaturnaia gazeta* published a letter in verse by a group of people identified as the "Komsomol poets." The letter is addressed to the workers of western Ukraine and western Belorussia. It speaks of two cities in eastern Poland, Vilnius [Wilno] and Przemyśl, implying that they were, respectively, Belorussian and Ukrainian. (Vilnius became the capital of Lithuania after World War II, whereas Przemyśl remained with Poland.) The letter also speaks of the sufferings of Belorussians and Ukrainians under Polish occupation, and expresses joy that the Red Army invaded Poland.

On November 15, 1939, *Literaturnaia gazeta* made it known that the military invasion of Poland was followed by a cultural one. Soon after the Red Army moved in, said *Literaturnaia gazeta*, writers and journalists followed "to conduct meetings with the population, to distribute leaflets and articles to newspapers, and to participate in the local government." This meant, among other things, that Russian writers and journalists took over the editorial offices of Polish publications. The fate of Polish journalists was not reported at that time. We know today that those Polish writers and journalists whom the Soviets replaced were dismissed, executed, or sent off to the Gulag.[4]

On September 30, 1939, *Pravda* published two poems, one by Samuil Marshak and the other by Viktor Gusev. Marshak's "In Those Days" ("V eti dni") describes the entrance of the Red Army into the town of Molodechno in western Ukraine. Here, "Ukrainians and Belorussians, young and old," greet the Soviets "in a friendly fashion." The soldiers lift up little children and promise them a great future. Gusev's poem "Happiness" ("Schast'e") begins with a description of how a coat-of-arms of a Polish nobleman was trampled. A Belorussian peasant tells the Soviet Russian soldier "how terrible it was to live in gentlemen's Poland" and how happy he was to see his Soviet "brothers."

In the same issue of *Pravda*, Valentin Kataev's "Travel Notes" ("Putevye zametki") paints a horrible picture of life in the Second Polish Republic and describes the happy peasants welcoming Soviet soldiers. Kataev devoted much of the months of September and October to the writing of eulogies of the invasion. In addition to the one mentioned above, he published them in *Pravda* on September 26, October 6, 18, 22, and 29. He also contributed to the promotion of ethnic animosities by the use of the lie: for example, he claims in *Pravda* on October 18, 1939, that Jews had no right to vote in "gentlemen's Poland." In reality, in the Second Polish Republic Jews not only voted but maintained their own political parties. The various Jewish parties consistently managed to elect representatives to the Seym [the Lower House], and there was a scattering of persons of Jewish background in other parties and groups.[5] A few weeks later, Kataev wrote an article in which he described in detail the bittersweet joy of the wife of a "communist who was shot by Poles" and who now found herself to be a citizen of the Soviet Union.[6]

In *Literaturnaia gazeta* on November 26, 1939, there appeared Evgenii Dolmatovskii's poem "Midnight" ("Polnoch") describing an old family mansion previously owned by a Polish nobleman and now occupied by Ukrainian Cossacks. While describing the act of expropriation of a Polish family who obviously lived in that area for a long time, Dolmatovskii speaks longingly of Moscow. In the context of what happens in the poem, the evocations of Moscow, its streets and boulevards, its girls and passersby, suggest that Russians are friends of Ukrainians whereas Poles are their enemies.

Similar sentiments are expressed in P. Kornienko's article in the same issue of *Literaturnaia gazeta*. "The End of a Long-lasting Tragedy" ("Konets mnogovekovoi tragedii") alleges that Russians and Ukrainians belong to the same nation while the "Polish landowners" are enemies of both. The article contains quotations from an anonymous *History of Poland, Lithuania and Ruthenia* said to have been published in Lviv in 1879. This book allegedly divided all Slavs into "ancient Poles, Poles, and princes" (*liakhy, poliaki i vladyki*). Kornienko's article is a good example of the use of verbal provocation to promote ethnic animosities.

In September and October of 1939, there appeared in the Soviet Russian press an inordinate number of articles praising things Russian and reminding Russians of the Polish-Russian wars of the sixteenth and seventeenth centuries. A movie about Minin and Pozharskii was widely reviewed at that time, and so was Mikhail Glinka's opera *Life under the Tsar*, referring to the period in Russian history known as the Time of Troubles when the Polish crown prince Władysław Vasa claimed the Moscow throne. In articles, poems, and stories, suggestions were made that Russia, Ukraine and Belorussia shared the same nationhood. On October 10, 1939, in *Literaturnaia gazeta*, V. Pertsov speaks of the "glorious military past of the Russian nation." In *Literaturnaia gazeta* on September 26, there appeared a poem by Belorussian author Piatro Glebka, translated by Mikhail Isakovskii and Petr Semynin. The poem suggests that Belorussia and Russia were separated by the wicked "Polish gentlemen" (*pany*): "We were born in the same country/ But our fate was different/ The entire world admired our growth/ Whereas you suffered oppression all the time." (*Nas kraina odna porodila/ Da neravnoe schast'e dala/ My rosli vsemu svetu na divo/ Vas nevolia vezde steregla.*)

Mikhail Zhivov's article "The Testimony of Polish Literature"[7] paints a heart-rending picture of life of the working masses in "gentlemen's Poland." Zhivov's article implies that in Poland a small class of "Polish gentlemen" (*pol'skie pany*) oppressed a huge mass of non-Polish urban and rural proletariat. However, a year later, the Soviet scholarly monthly *Sovetskaia iustitsiia* admits that it was necessary to find Polish-Russian translators in the courts located in cities and towns of western Belorussia because the local population spoke only Polish.[8]

Maksim Ryl'skii published anti-Polish poems in *Pravda* on March 24, 1940, and in *Izvestiia* on September 17, 1940. In one of them, he reminisces about the year of Soviet rule over the Ukraine, calling it "great." "The traces of [Polish] nobility are disappearing"; the "pans" who "wielded the whip" are no more, he declares. When the winds of history changed, however, Ryl'skii changed his tone as well, and he published a pro-Polish article on August 13, 1941, in *Izvestiia*. At that time Stalin, frightened by Hitler's attack, allowed those deported Poles who were still alive in the Gulag to reenlist in the Polish army. Now Ryl'skii addresses "the nation of Mickiewicz, Słowacki, Chopin and Copernicus" in friendly words, and calls upon Poles to "erase the shame" of the Nazi occupation by fighting bravely against it.

Meetings of the "intelligentsia" were organized in the conquered towns and villages of eastern Poland. Invariably, the intelligentsia declared itself in favor of the Soviets. This happened at the end of September in Minsk and Białystok (*Pravda*, October 1), Vilnius (*Pravda*, October 2), and Slonim (*Pravda*, September 26). On October 9, *Pravda* reported that 6,500 members of the intelligentsia who in "gentlemen's Poland" were unemployed now received jobs in the "Belorussian" city of Vilnius. "Gentlemen's Poland strangulated Belorussian culture," alleges the article.

Similar sentiments are expressed in *Pravda* on September 27, 1939, in Mikhail Isakovskii's poem "Sunrise" ("Na voskhode solntsa"). Like Margarita Aliger and Valentin Kataev, Isakovskii was exceptionally active in vilifying things Polish at that time. He contributed to *Pravda* other anti-Polish poems on October 6 and November 5. On October 15, 1939, *Literaturnaia gazeta* published his review of *Brothers* (*Brat'ia*), a Detizdat collection of what seems to have been anti-Polish poems for children. I was unable to obtain that book, but the promptness with which it was published and reviewed indicates that at least some of the material must have been prepared in advance of the Soviet invasion, then four weeks old. According to the reviewer, the book starts with a description of the Red Army soldiers destroying the boundary markers on the Polish-Soviet border.

Isakovskii was also intent on confusing things Russian with things Ukrainian and Belorussian. In the poem "In Those Days" ("V te dni"), published in *Pravda*, he speaks of fighting the Poles unto death and remarks that the inhabitants of Ukraine and Belorussia are "simple Russian boys" (*prostye russkie rebiata*) who love their Russian homeland (*rodina*). In the poem, a Belorussian peasant addresses the Red Army thus: "You have fought a life-and-death battle with the Polish nobility/But you have not fouled our wells/And did not even pick up one apple in our orchards/Nor have you trampled upon a single flower bed. . . ."[9] Alas, these words go beyond the limits of poetic licence. For reports about the state of affairs in the villages and towns subjected to the invasion, J.T. Gross's recent book must again be invoked.[10]

In a poem published in *Pravda* on October 10, 1939, Semen Kirsanov charges that in "gentlemen's Poland . . . the nobleman, the priest and the policeman made everyone work until they were totally exhausted." Kirsanov contributed similar views to *Pravda* on November 15, 1939. On July 23, 1940, he published in *Pravda* a poem that describes how the three Baltic countries, Latvia, Lithuania, and Estonia, asked to join the Soviet Union, a country the poet compared to a magnet (*strana-magnit*). But the greatest magnet of all, says Kirsanov, is Stalin himself, and various countries are irresistibly drawn to him. "The old world is getting a bit smaller, while we are accepting Soviet Estonia, Lithuania and Latvia," he says.

Aleksandr Tvardovskii, who in the 1960s became one of the leading figures in the anti-Stalinist movement, wrote quite differently in the years of the Stalin-Hitler Pact. On October 10, 1939, he published in *Pravda* a poem about the glorious Red Army attacking Poland: "the Poles are fleeing from Red Army soldiers, from the song of free men, from the greath truth." On October 21, 1939, he published another poem in *Pravda* entitled "Song about the Soil" ("Slovo o zemle") in which the collective speaker expresses his hatred of the *pans* and calls the Polish rule "illegal and accursed" (*nepravaia i prokliataia vlast'*). Tvardovskii charged that "we worked for the accursed Polish noblemen,/ and then had to beg them for a piece of bread." The word *pan* and its derivatives are used seven times in this short poem, and always in opposition to the "we" or the *narod*, who by implication included Russians, Ukrainians, and Belorussians. Likewise, the word "soil" (*zemlia*) used in the title refers to the Russian, Ukrainian, and Belorussian soil—but not to the Polish soil even though Poles, too, lived and labored in that area. As is well known, the word "soil" carries rich and positive connotations in Russian: *matushka-zemlia, rodnaia zemlia*, and so forth. Thus, when the speaker says, "We did an honest thing . . . we reached for our own soil" (*na chestnoe delo my shli . . . Gde vidano, dobrye liudi/Svoei chuzhat'sia zemli*), he reinforces in his readers the conviction that in waging an aggressive war, the Russians were in the right.

The list of writers who praised the Soviet invasion in articles, poems, and statements also includes M. Bronkov (*Literaturnaia gazeta*, September 26, 1939), Aleksandr Korneichuk (*Pravda*, Septem-

ber 26, 1939), Ianka Kupala (*Pravda*, October 6, 1939), Vasilii
Lebedev-Kumach, P. Lidov (*Pravda*, October 2 and October 10,
1939), Sergei Mikhalkov (*Pravda*, October 8, 1939), P. Ponomarenko
(*Pravda*, June 3, 1940), K. Potapov (*Pravda*, October 2, 1939), Aleksandr Prokof'ev (*Leningradskaia pravda*, September 22, 1939), Il'ia
Sel'vinskii (*Pravda*, September 18, 1939), A. Sitkovskii (*Literaturnaia gazeta*, September 17, 1939), E. Stepanov (*Pravda*, October 4,
1939), Nikolai Tikhonov (*Pravda*, November 29, 1939), Stepan Tru-
dov, Vanda Vasilevskaia (*Pravda*, October 27, 1939 and November 7,
1939), Viktor Vinnikov (*Pravda*, November 6, 1939), and Iosif Utkin
(*Literaturnaia gazeta*, October 15, 1939).

This survey is by no means exhaustive, but it does document
some major manifestations of anti-Polish feelings among the Russian-
speaking writers and journalists in the Soviet Union. As such, it is
indicative of several things. First, it appears that in the 1930s, writers
were easily "persuaded" to advance in their writings not only a
Marxist-Leninist vision of Soviet reality but also Soviet Russian imperialism. A number of well-known Soviet Russian writers eulogized
the invasion of Poland and presented it as a "liberation from the Polish
yoke." Many of them supported the invasion and, by implication, the
Soviet-Nazi Pact. This fact should perhaps be given more prominence
in the evaluations of Soviet literature of the 1930s and '40s. Not
infrequently, the writers of that period are discussed as if they were
"normal" writers forced to write according to the canons of "socialist
realism," rather than the people whose conceptual world was deeply
mired in the duplicity engendered by the Soviet system. Obviously,
people like Aleksandr Tvardovskii, who said that the Soviets did an
honest thing in invading Poland, or Margarita Aliger, who described
the Soviet destruction of Poland as an event opening up a new epoch
of history, had a long way to go before their words could regain a
measure of truthfulness. Writers such as these were not just servile to
the regime; they contributed to the dragging of the Russian literary
language to a level of mendacity from which it could not easily recover. The impact of these developments on Russian literature and on
the concepts and ideas that prevail in Soviet literary discussions today
deserve more attention than they have received so far.

12 Soviet Russian Musicological

Reevaluations of Stravinsky's

Neoclassical Phase

The Soviet musicological literature devoted to an interpretation of the neoclassical trend in twentieth-century Soviet and European music has contributed some pertinent reevaluations of this stylistic form. According to the prevailing criticism in Soviet musicological literature during the late 1930s and '40s, the major drawback of neoclassicism was its estrangement from the national spirit. Therefore, neoclassicism was declared to be stilted, artificial, and lacking in the essential national denomination and identity. In the 1960s and later, several Soviet music historians studied the neoclassical phase of Igor Stravinsky's compositions.[1] In particular, the musicologist M.S. Druskin devoted a number of his studies to Stravinsky.[2] His favorable appraisal broke away from the tradition of harsh criticism of Stravinsky in the 1930s, '40s, and '50s. This chapter gives a detailed account of these interpretive changes and their relation to the changes in the perception of Russian national identity.

Before the official acceptance of the doctrine of socialist realism, party leaders, writers, and artists discussed the values a work of art should embody. Lenin's principle of acceptance of the party ideology (*partiinost'*) was fundamental, as well as his interpretation of the art work as emanating from the national spirit in content and in form (*narodnost'*). Furthermore, an art work should truthfully reproduce typical characteristics and typical circumstances (*tipichnost'*), a requirement derived from Engels' explanations of inherent qualities of an art work. Andrei Zhdanov asserted that the arts should play an educational and propagandistic role, thus reinterpreting as typical "the reality in its revolutionary development." In addition, the attitude of an art work should be uplifting and therefore promote optimism and a positive outlook.[3]

These discussions in the political and literary fields concerning the role of the arts were reflected in the changes of the ideological policies of various influential music organizations. The Russian Association of Proletarian Musicians and the Association of Proletarian Writers were liquidated in April 1932 following the resolution of the Central Committee "On the Reorganization of Literary-Artistic Organizations." The ideological policy of these associations was perceived as consisting of "nihilistic and formalistic distortions."[4]

In addition, a decisive break was announced with the alien ideological influences, such as formalism and reactionary bourgeois tendencies. The influence of "modernistic music" was declared to be "defective" and "vulgarizing" for Soviet music. The classical heritage was debased by modernistic trends. Implementation of so-called "theories" that were "excusing the confusion and cacophony in music" was severely criticized.[5]

Another revision of the ideological and creative postulates for the arts occurred when changes were officially proclaimed in the resolution of the Central Committee in February 1948. The resolution was declared the "decisive blow to formalism" in terms of creative approach and artistic attitudes. Similarly, it was stated that party guidance in ideological matters helped the musicologists to "eliminate their mistakes in order to find the right road in solving the most important problems."[6]

Shortly after the principle of socialist realism was introduced in 1934 at the First Congress of the Union of Soviet Writers, Stravinsky lost his place in the pantheon of Russian composers. B.V. Asaf'ev's *A Book about Stravinsky (Kniga o Stravinskom)*, published in Leningrad in 1929, was one of the last works in which Stravinsky was objectively evaluated.[7] As late as 1935, the ballet *Petrushka* was performed in Leningrad. The program notes for this performance were provided by Druskin, who was Asaf'ev's former student.[8] Subsequently Druskin's comments appeared revised in a booklet entitled *"Petrushka" Igoria Stravinskogo*, published in Leningrad in 1935.[9] After 1935, Stravinsky's neoclassical tendencies were severely criticized. It was alleged that the compositions Stravinsky created during his neoclassical period relinquished the Russian folk music idiom and did not fulfill the other requirements postulated by socialist realism. His abandonment of Russian folk music was particularly criticized. His polytonal harmonies and "constructional manner of arbitrary melodic and rhythmic configurations" marked him "as one of the leading representatives of modernism in music." [10]

Except for sporadic visits to the Ustilug estate near Kiev before World War I, Stravinsky did not return to his homeland after emigrating to Switzerland in 1912 until some fifty years later, in autumn of 1962. He alienated himself from the Soviet government, although his alienation from Russia itself was only superficial. Even when he appeared to embrace different cultural experiences elsewhere, he remained anchored to the Russian musical spirit instilled during his formative years. At one point, Stravinsky said that "during my whole life I talked Russian, thought in Russian and had a Russian style. . . . Perhaps it is not immediately evident in my music, but it is ingrained in it, in its hidden nature." [11]

Stravinsky's creative and personal identity was shaped by his apprenticeship in the compositional class of his mentor, Rimskii-Korsakov. After the death of Stravinsky's father, his mentor became a paternal figure for him.[12] In his monograph on Stravinsky, Mikhail Druskin stated that it was Rimskii-Korsakov who introduced Stravinsky to Russian peasant culture and the folk rituals accompanied by ceremonial songs. These discoveries found their reflection in the compositions of the 1910s: *The Rite of Spring, Le Renard, Saucer Songs, Les Noces*, and others.[13] In addition, Druskin emphasized the significance of Musorgskii's operatic scores, which provided Stravinsky with musical projections of the chant of the Orthodox Church, the well-loved "bell sonorities," and the archaic songs of the Old Believers. Tschaikovsky's music, with the "power of melody," exercised another lasting and even stronger impact on Stravinsky.[14] Druskin pointed out that the Russian influences on Stravinsky's music, in particular in their seemingly "hidden form," appeared primarily in the works of his first creative period. This period encompassed some fifteen years, starting with *Fireworks*, the ballet music *Firebird*, the comic opera *Mavra*, and the choreographic cantata *Les Noces*. According to Druskin, the consequent evolution of Stravinsky's creative path brought new musical works that have been only superficially discussed, and these discussions stressed their apparent antinational characteristics.[15] The situation needed correction. With the change of cultural policies following the death of Stalin in March of 1953, that became possible.

In the late 1950s, Soviet musicologists were preoccupied mainly with the problems of Russian music, with barely any interest in foreign music. Boris Schwarz explained this lack of research on foreign music as resulting from a scarcity of primary sources on western music in Soviet libraries.[16] Yet even the Russian and Soviet topics were at times severely censored. In a collection of musicological studies published in 1986 in Moscow, J.I. Nest'ev traced the prevailing attitude in official circles toward Prokof'ev's works. Even after his return to the Soviet Union in 1932, Prokof'ev had been sporadically a target of criticism because of his "cosmopolitan" or "western" tendencies.

Igor Stravinsky suffered the same treatment. In the 1956 edition of the *Great Soviet Encyclopedia*, Stravinsky's early compositions *Fireworks* (1908), *The Firebird* (1910), and *Petrushka* (1911) were described as positive achievements "characterized by their splendor of orchestral color . . . that with some other of Stravinsky's compositions entered into the repertoire of the symphony orchestras around the world." However, already *Petrushka*, and in particular *The Rite of Spring*, showed decisive "elements of aestheticism, acute stylization, and violent polytonal harmonies." His later compositions, like the vocal miniatures and pantomimes *Renard* and *Les Noces*, showed "primitivism with decadent deformations." Compositions created after emigration to America "reflected the American bourgeois culture." Stravinsky composed without discrimination as if guided only by current demands: "He fulfilled most different demands—from the Catholic mass to 'Circus polka' (1942) and 'Ebony Concerto' for clarinet and jazz orchestra (1945)." [17]

Interestingly enough, some twenty years later, traces of similar evaluations of avant-garde tendencies were still present in articles written for the 1976 edition of the *Great Soviet Encyclopedia*. In this edition avant-gardism was declared to be an expression of "the mood of petit bourgeois individualism, anarchism or political indifference." In contrast to such deviations in the musical art of the West, the Soviet and other socialist musical cultures were defined as displaying "a consistently democratic, popular character . . . [that] distinguishes socialist musical culture from other musical cultures." In addition, the well-established criteria of socialist realism were still the basis of accepted artistic values: "partiinost' " interpreted as party spirit and "narodnost' " as closeness to the people. The doctrine of socialist realism was declared to be "the method" that, together with narodnost' and partiinost', constituted the "artistic foundation of Soviet music." [18]

While similar evaluations reflected the ideologically sanctioned yet retrogressive agenda of Soviet musicology, a number of musicological studies of the 1960s brought a remarkable change. The stereotyped formulas previously used in the interpretation of musical works gave way to a new and more balanced outlook. In pursuit of a fresh and truthful evaluation of creative men and women and their work, Soviet Russian musicologists have apparently besieged the worn-out postulates of socialist realism. These efforts were directed toward abandoning the imposed isolation that led to parochialism and stagnation. Therefore, this period could be linked to the spirit of Pushkin's verses describing the founding of St. Petersburg as a symbolic "hacking a window through to Europe" (*v Evropu prorubit' okno*). [19] It was in the same city, today's Leningrad, that musicologists introduced new topics and methods of research more than a hundred years later. At the heart of these investigations is the musicological output of Mikhail Seme-

novich Druskin, written during the 1960s, which helped establish the
new directions in Soviet musicology.

In 1929 Boris Vladimirovich Asaf'ev had published an inspired
study on Stravinsky. In this book Asaf'ev was among the first to point
out Stravinsky's innovative attitude toward the folk music idiom. According to Asaf'ev, Stravinsky did not use a stylized approach in compositions of his first creative period. He treated the folk melodies not
as an archaic layer, as something to be stylized, but rather as a living
language. Stravinsky once said that he intended "to rework the art . . .
created by the common people's genius" (*pererabotat' iskusstvo . . .
sozdannoe geniem naroda*).[20] His intention came to fruition later on,
in the radical adaptation of various compositional models used in the
creation of his neoclassical works. Asaf'ev pointed out that the *Serenade for Piano*, composed in 1925, is an example of the neoclassical
method of model adaptation. Stravinsky embodied in this work all the
lyrical elements associated with the form of the serenade and succeeded in projecting a universal and broad range of meanings. He
managed to depict the enchanting inflections of lute and guitar music
and all the lyricism underlying the exalted, romantic mood, yet he
translated all this into a concise, even laconic, contemporary piano
style. Similarly, he combined in the *Royal March* from the *Soldier's
Story* a typical military march, with all the rhythmical and intonational
features of this genre, with a contemporary idiom of which he was a
master.[21]

Druskin availed himself of Asaf'ev's analytical judgments in further
analyses of Stravinsky's music. In the process of clarification of
Stravinsky's compositional style, he explained in the following way
his understanding of the term "adaptation" of a model: "All that
fascinated him . . . or for some reasons interested him, he studied
and adapted, changing it after his liking and suitability. In adapting
the creative models, Stravinsky preserved their structure—melodic,
rhythmic, textual, compositional."[22] The breadth of Druskin's observations and the validity of his statements, notably concerning the contribution of Stravinsky, drew appreciation in Russia and abroad. His
studies on Stravinsky published in Soviet musicological journals during the 1960s led to the publication of the monograph *Igor' Stravinskii*

that appeared in Leningrad in 1974 and went through several editions. In due course Druskin was honored by his colleagues as one of the leading Soviet Russian musicologists. In a special volume published in 1981 under the title *History and Contemporaneity* (*Istoriia i sovremennost'*), dedicated to the fiftieth anniversary of Druskin's professional activities, composer A. P. Petrov stated with pride that Leningrad had given to the Soviet culture exceptional representatives of musical thought: B.V. Asaf'ev, A.V. Ossovskii, I.I. Sollertinskii, M.S. Druskin.[23]

In his introductory statement, Petrov described the 1960s as years that resulted in an enhancement of international contacts in the cultural field as Soviet composers acquired opportunities to gain information about the musical achievements in western Europe. It was the period during which new compositional techniques were introduced that did not correspond to the ideological requirements of Soviet art. Druskin's musicological work followed the general development of music created outside Soviet boundaries in the twentieth century. His research corresponded to the as yet unmet Soviet need for orientation and comprehension of intricate qualities of contemporary music. Many composers and musicologists felt that a new appraisal of Stravinsky's musical legacy was imperative. Druskin's evaluations stirred the imagination and encouraged new interpretations.

Andrei Petrov, himself a practicing composer, felt that Druskin's work helped composers clarify their own compositional task within the framework of contemporaneity.[24] He praised Druskin's monograph on Stravinsky, considering it to be Druskin's highest achievement. The progressive musicologist's book discussed issues that were on the mind of each and every composer, such as the development of music in general, the evolution of the musical language, the influence of music on the public, and the professional goals of the composer.

The spiritual world of Stravinsky, as conveyed through his music, exerted a considerable influence on contemporary compositional issues. Stravinsky's creative imagination, captured in his compositional work, coincided at times with the artistic attitudes of many of his colleagues abroad, be they Soviet, French, Polish, or American composers. He was a person through whom the Soviet composers could rejoin the European and world musical community. That is why Druskin's book, in its sophisticated understanding of the cultural climate of the twentieth century, was so helpful in the impending Soviet Russian discussions about the artist and his time.

It was Druskin who elucidated Stravinsky's role in the formation of the neoclassical style. He argued that Stravinsky succeeded in adapting certain ancient musical models to modern musical means, and creatively reintroduced them into the contemporary musical idiom. This re-creation did not consist of a "stylized" approach but went much deeper, being directed to the radical adaptation of models while using new musical means. Although other ideas were abundant at the time, Stravinsky remained a neoclassicist for a longer period and with greater consistency than any other leading artist of his day.

In the 1960s, the neoclassical developments in European music were also reexamined by the new generation of Soviet musicologists.[25] Another scholar from Leningrad, Lev Raaben, observed that the emergence of neoclassicism played an important role in the "revolution" of the musical language of the twentieth century.[26] The harmonic innovations of Aleksandr Scriabin's *Prometheus* and the polytonal and polymodal harmonies of Darius Millhaud, Arthur Honneger, Francis Poulenc, and others evolved even earlier as a response to an urgent need for radical change. Further enrichment came from the inclusion of modal idioms contained in folk music, as utilized in the compositions of Zoltán Kodály and Béla Bártok. Bártok's compositions revealed an intricate relationship of atonal and modal means underlying the expressionistic qualities of his musical language. Another source of inspiration was the music of non-European nations, in particular India, as seen in the compositional work of Albert Roussel, André Jolivet, and Olivier Messiaen. Raaben believed that the emergence of neoclassicism and other innovations were together responsible for the development of contemporary musical language.

It is well known that Pierre Boulez attributed the radical change and the emergence of the "new music" of the first half of the twentieth century mainly to Arnold Schoenberg and Igor Stravinsky. Raaben thought it unjust to underline only the technical aspects of these changes, and thought that this was a biased and tendentious judgment. Furthermore, Raaben disagreed with Boulez's interpretation of Stravinsky's contribution because Boulez declared Stravinsky's compositional inventions to be limited to the domain of rhythm while still preserving the classical tonal relations of the tonic, dominant and subdominant. Boulez considered Stravinsky's retention of harmonic progressions established by the composers of the classical era to be inadequate, not to say faulty.

Raaben declared Boulez's opinions about Stravinsky's contribution to be one-sided, because they reduced Stravinsky's contribution to one compositional aspect, namely, rhythmic configurations, even though they presented them as the most important element of his music. Raaben stated with a degree of indignation that, the "apostles" of the New Viennese school were too concerned with their own importance and their own contribution, while denying the historical role of innovators to other contemporary movements and of Stravinsky in particular.[27]

On the other hand, Raaben acknowledged both Schoenberg and Stravinsky as creators of compositional systems of importance to the subsequent development of music. He allowed the possibility of not accepting their individual compositional systems because of different aesthetic principles or acquired taste, but maintained that it would not be possible to deny their artistic importance.

While pleading for a more truthful recognition of Stravinsky's contribution, Raaben clearly adopted a defensive posture. He was obviously concerned with identifying Stravinsky's work as part of the national treasure of Russian artistic achievement, contrasting the unjust (in his view) promotion of Schoenberg's innovations with the inadequate treatment of Stravinsky's. But Raaben's acknowledgment of the possibility of diverse artistic criteria in evaluating Stravinsky's neoclassical phase attested also to his knowledge of such possibilities—something that could not happen in Soviet musicology in Stalin's time. In his attempt to give justice to different views, he acknowledged the reality and creative impact of both Stravinsky's and Schoenberg's compositional systems. In stressing that Stravinsky's contribution was unjustly slighted by the proponents of the New Viennese school, he exemplified the Russian concern that their contribution to music be fully recognized.

In order to emphasize the validity of Stravinsky's compositional credo, Raaben described Schoenberg's dodecaphony, championed by his followers, as incapable of overshadowing the innovations of Stravinsky. Raaben noted that Stravinsky developed his compositional system slowly, until it eventually crystallized in his works of the neoclassical period. His system was based on a special creative method rooted in the manifold modifications of varied genres and stylistic models contained in musical compositions of different epochs and national cultures. This method replenished and enriched in a fundamental way the musical resources of the twentieth century, resulting in a distinct esthetic and stylistic formation known as neoclassicism.

Raaben's conclusions should be considered in the context of the musicological exploration that followed the rigid guidelines of socialist realism in the 1930s, '40s, and '50s. The studies and essays on music at that time reflected the postulates of socialist realism. Hence, musicology evaluated the neoclassical style as being artificial and severing all ties with the national musical traditions. The compositions showing an inclination toward neoclassicism were proclaimed "decadent" or artificially constructed. Often it was stated that neoclassical compositions projected values of the bourgeois class, serving its imperialistic goals. Arnold Al'shvang was among the first to introduce such an evaluation of Stravinsky in his essay "The Ideological Path of Igor Stravinsky," published in the journal *Sovetskaia muzyka* in 1933. Al'shvang stated in the opening sentence: "Stravinsky is an important and almost complete artistic ideologist of the imperialist bourgeoisie." [28]

The musicological research conducted in the late 1950s, '60s, and thereafter brought the necessary corrections to the socialist realist view. Neoclassicism became recognized as one of the leading stylistic trends between the two world wars, and it began to be studied. Since the principle of "national roots" (*narodnost'*) was considered one of the validating features of an art work, Soviet musicologists brought this overlooked aspect into their discussion of neoclassicism. Druskin and Raaben were among the first to trace the influence of various national musical idioms in the compositions of Stravinsky and other major Soviet Russian composers who belonged to the neoclassical stylistic orientation.

As recently as 1974, the evaluation of neoclassicism in the *Great Soviet Encyclopedia* asserted that neoclassicism projected a dichotomy of both positive and negative qualities. On the one hand, it fostered clarity and orderliness in the organization of ancient musical styles; on the other, it often led to "cold, formal imitation and artistic recreation of obsolete methods." [29] However, notwithstanding this view, which is clearly a relic of the past, a number of Soviet musicologists, Druskin and Raaben foremost among them, pointed to the positive properties of neoclassicism. In their separate appraisals, they established that major composers of this neoclassical trend found their source of inspiration in the tradition of national music. The stylistic models from their national past had provided, in the time of social unrest, the feeling of stability and affirmation of the continuity of existence. Thus, a more progressive view of neoclassicism corresponded in Soviet musicology to an increased affirmation of the values of Russian national music.

Raaben further stated that the feeling of political and economic instability that permeated the period between the two world wars created a need for the classical requirements of clarity and balance. Many composers found reassurance in the projection of orderliness and formal control typical of the compositions from the preclassical and classical eras. This helped incorporate neoclassicism into the compositional schools of many countries. Neoclassicism consequently became the dominant stylistic trend in the interwar period. Although it was strongly grounded in the respective national traditions, neoclassicism also reflected some universal traits, such as avoidance of the exaggerated emotionalism of late romanticism. Moreover, neoclassicism hastened the renewal of European music after the possibilities of late romanticism had been exhausted. [30]

Raaben repeatedly stressed that, contrary to prevalent opinion, the neoclassical style often became strongly identified with the national tradition. This happened not only in Russian music but also in French. Darius Millhaud's *First Sonata for Viola and Piano*, for instance, was based on the themes of French songs of the seventeenth century, and it was also reminiscent of another well-known form of French music: the suites of Couperin and Rameau. In 1928 and 1933, respectively, Poulenc composed in the style of the celebrated French harpsichord miniatures his *Three Pieces: Pastorale, Toccata and Hymn*, and the *Album Leaf* comprising *Arietta, Phantasy*, and *Gigue*. Similarly, Poulenc's *Suite for Two Oboes, Two Bassoons, Two Trumpets, Two Trombones, Percussions and Harpsichord* presented in a stylized manner such French dances of the sixteenth century as pavane, branle, and others. In order to further enhance his *Suite*, Poulenc used the old instrumental setting of the wind ensemble and employed modal harmonies. As a result, his *Suite* is one of his most accomplished and original neoclassical works. Likewise, some compositions of Albert Roussel showed both impressionistic and neoclassical characteristics, in particular his *Suite en Fa*. Similar features were expressed in the music for *Bacchus et Ariadne* and in *Aeneas*, composed in the 1930s.[31]

Raaben agreed with Druskin's statement that neoclassicism became truly universal only in the compositions of Stravinsky. According to Raaben, Stravinsky's neoclassical compositions showed his deep musical erudition and revealed his comprehension of many stylistic epochs and national styles. Because of the strength of his compositional capacity Stravinsky included in his neoclassical idiom not only the national and cultural traditions of the Russians but also the traditions of many other countries.[32] Thus, during his residence in France in the 1930s, Stravinsky was influenced by the Greco-Roman themes of the French composers, who had a predilection for themes going back to ancient mythology. While in France, Stravinsky composed *Apollon Musagete, Persephone*, and *Serenade for Piano*, in which this French preference—*le gout français*, as it was called—was obviously reflected.

Furthermore, Raaben acknowledged that Druskin spoke justly of the importance of the baroque era as another source of inspiration for Stravinsky. This tradition, going back to the works of Bach and Handel, was reflected in a number of Stravinsky's compositions, among them *Concerto for Piano, The Symphony of Psalms, Oedipus Rex*, and *The Dumbarton Oaks Concerto*. The last was dubbed as the seventh *Brandenburg Concerto* because of its similarity to the baroque model. Stravinsky's *Concerto for Violin* showed Vivaldi's influence. The spirit of classicism was present in the *Symphony in D-major*, which had overtones going back to Haydn, while the *Symphony in Three Movements* showed the influence of Beethoven. Other influences were also present in Stravinsky's work, according to Raaben. The closeness to the models of romanticism was noticeable in *Capriccio for Piano and Orchestra* and in the ballet *Le Baiser de la fee*.[33]

In his discussion of neoclassical tendencies in Stravinsky, Raaben assumed that social turmoil, if it happened in the artist's time, was reflected in his work. He pointed out that the expressionists of the New Viennese school have reflected the chaotic social reality by means of a deformation of form-building musical components. The rational dodecaphonic constructivism of their compositions did not evoke a feeling of stability but rather its opposite. In contrast, the musical art of past centuries seemed to provide the needed stability, with its balance of form and content, tonal centricity, and avoidance of excessive sentimentality and pathos. Most important, Raaben stated that neoclassicism did not present a flight to the proverbial ivory tower, as was sometimes declared, but rather introduced means for active participation in the struggle for salvaging ethical and moral values in times of general turmoil.

With this line of reasoning Raaben tried to discredit earlier postulates of Soviet musicologists about the isolationism and decadence of composers displaying neoclassical tendencies. He succeeded in presenting a new and positive aspect of neoclassicism previously overlooked in Soviet musicology. In that time of economic crises and political upheavals, the composers were relentlessly searching for renewed order and stability as well as trying to uphold the serenity and dignity of their creative endeavors. The neoclassical idiom served both goals well.

Raaben further asserted that neoclassicism did not cease to exert its propitious influence after World War II. Neoclassicism was not just a domain of bourgeois society; it also played a role in the new Soviet society. As proof, Raaben pointed to the multitude of partitas, toccatas, cycles of preludes and fugues, suites and concertos written by Soviet composers, Shostakovich being a prominent example. His cycles of preludes and fugues, chorales, toccatas, partitas, symphonies, and chamber ensembles testified to the possibilities of using neoclassical modes in a socialist setting. However, Raaben was careful to point out that Shostakovich's ideological and semantic attitudes were remote from neoclassicist aesthetics. Finally, Raaben claimed that neoclassicism gave birth to a new phenomenon, dubbed by him "polystylistics," in which the neoclassicist composers incorporated models from different styles and epochs into their work. In other words, this style enabled composers to superimpose the past upon the present, or vice versa. Thus, the past was made to serve the present.

In her book on the problems of musical aesthetics as discussed in the theoretical works of Stravinsky, Hindemith, and Schoenberg, Nelli Grigor'evna Shakhnazarova, another noted Soviet musicologist, posited that neoclassicism was characterized by the domination of the intellect in the compositional process. The strict organization, the orchestrational restraint, and the absence of open emotionalism all pointed to a definite rationalistic tendency in neoclassicism. In her opinion, dodecaphony also expressed this rationalistic tendency, but was more one-sided about it than neoclassicism. Shakhnazarova claimed that this tendency reflected the composers' assumption that order can be introduced into the existing chaos of sounds by adopting a rational approach. She felt that the theoretical works of these composers had been inadequately presented in Soviet musicology and for that reason that the neoclassical tendencies in their musical works had been misunderstood. This was a pity, because they articulated some of the most important postulates of contemporary music. In her concluding chapter, Shakhnazarova pointed to the important role that Hindemith in particular had played in the appearance of neoclassicism as a phenomenon of contemporary music. However, in her opinion, Stravinsky's best compositions, notably *The Rite of Spring*, represented best the artistic consciousness of humankind.[34]

The attention to Stravinsky's heritage during the 1960s and later brought about the reprinting of Asaf'ev's *Book about Stravinsky*. This second edition was published in 1977, almost fifty years after the first.[35] This long break exemplified the stagnation in Soviet musicology during the Stalin years and beyond.

The introduction to the second edition by B. Iarustovskii deserves special attention because of the author's candid evaluation of the change in the ideological postulates of musicology in the 1970s. Like everything else, musicology was gradually freed from the shackles of socialist realism and the necessity to address only a limited range of subjects. The fact that Iarustovskii was at the height of his musicological career and fame might have contributed to his frank discussion of the banishment of Astaf'ev's book and its favorable presentation of Stravinsky's compositional achievements.

All these musicological and sociological works testify to the profound influence of the composer of *Petrushka* and *The Rite of Spring* on his Soviet Russian compatriots. His visit to the Soviet Union in the early 1960s further stimulated the growing interest in his compositional legacy. As a consequence of Stravinsky's influence and resulting musicological studies dealing with his work, Asaf'ev's book was again "remembered" and prepared for reprinting. According to Iarustovskii, Asaf'ev's monograph had been maligned by the adherents of the Russian Association of Proletarian Musicians, and then repeatedly in the late 1930s and 1940s by the heirs of these ideologists.

Iarustovskii reminded the reader that Asaf'ev correctly stated that the final and crucial acceptance of Stravinsky's work and a true comprehension of his artistic nature remained a goal to be pursued by Soviet composers. He concluded that the published works of M. Druskin, I. Vershinina, V. Smirnov, Iu. Kholopov, V. Kholopova, A. Shnitke, L. D'iachkova, S. Savenko, G. Alfeevskaia, and others have created a solid foundation of Stravinskyian research in the Soviet Union.

Iarustovskii also spoke of one common denominator in all these works by Soviet musicologists dedicated to the preservation of Stravinsky's heritage. They approached Stravinsky as one of the great figures of the contemporary scene, but they also referred to "his primeval [*stikhiinoi*] Russian nature," thus confirming Asaf'ev's earlier pronouncement. Iarustovskii concluded that Stravinsky was indeed accepted by his compatriots and that this acceptance spurred the dedicated preservation and renewed research into his heritage.

It should be added that Iarustovskii's introduction to Asaf'ev's book was testimony of an informed contemporary. Born in 1911, Iarustovskii witnessed the emergence of the Proletkult ideology and of socialist realism. Unfortunately, his introduction was one of the last works he wrote. He died in 1978.

Iarustovskii himself was obviously strongly aware of the richness that Stravinsky's compositions could bestow on the musically-minded members of Soviet society. By trying to elucidate Stravinsky's unique vision, he helped stimulate both research and an appreciation of Stravinsky in his country. The process of the acceptance of Stravinsky's heritage was one of the turning points of the new ideological path taken by the Soviet musical scholars. *The Message of Igor Stravinsky*, to uphold the title of Theodore Stravinsky's book on his father, was perpetuating his Russian artistic bequest. Stravinsky's work, in its magnificent versatility, will remain as a monument to the perseverance and patriotism of a Russian artist living abroad yet continuing to "think in Russian." It is appropriate to conclude with Horace's poem made famous in Russia through Pushkin's translation:

Unto myself I reared a monument;
A path trod thereto by people shall never overgrow with grass.

About the Authors

LOUIS ALLAIN is chair of the oldest French Department of Slavic Languages (created in 1892) at the Charles de Gaulle University in Lille and author of *Dostoievski et Dieu: La morsure du divin* (1982), *Dostoievski et l'Autre* (1984), and *Etiudy o russkoi literature* (1989). He is now preparing a Leningrad edition of Russian emigré literature of the 1930s.

LIBOR BROM is Professor of Foreign Languages and Literatures and Director of Russian Area Studies at the University of Denver. After obtaining degrees in business, economics, and law in Europe, he received his doctorate in Slavic Languages and Literatures from the University of Colorado. He is the author of eight books dealing with Slavic cultures and Soviet affairs.

JELENA MILOJKOVIC-DJURIC is a Research Fellow at the Mosher Institute, Texas A&M University. She received her Ph.D. in musicology from the University of Belgrade and has published papers on folklore and musicology in *Byzantinoslavica, Southern Folklore Quarterly, Musikforschung, Cross Currents,* and other periodicals.

HERMAN ERMOLAEV is Professor of Russian Literature at Princeton University. He specializes in the Soviet period and is the author of *Soviet Literary Theories 1917–1934: The Genesis of Socialist Realism* (1963) and *Mikhail Sholokhov and His Art* (1982). He is also editor and translator of Maksim Gor'kii's *Untimely Thoughts: Essays on Revolution, Culture and the Bolsheviks, 1917–1918* (1968).

JOHN G. GARRARD is Professor of Russian Literature at the University of Arizona. A graduate of Oxford and Columbia, he has chaired the departments of Slavic Languages and Literatures at the University of Arizona and the University of Virginia. He is the author, with Carol E. Garrard, of *Inside the Soviet Writers' Union* (1990). Among his other books are *Mikhail Lermontov* (1982), *The Russian Novel from Pushkin to Pasternak*, editor (1983), and *The Eighteenth Century in Russia*, editor (1973).

GEORGE GIBIAN is Goldwyn Smith Professor of Comparative and Russian Literature at Cornell University. He is the author of *The Interval of Freedom: Soviet Russian Literature during the Thaw* (1960) and *The Man in the Black Coat: Russia's Literature of the Absurd* (1989). He has translated and edited various Russian and Czech literary classics.

YURI GLAZOV is Professor of Russian Literature at Dalhousie University in Halifax, Canada. A graduate of Moscow State University, he is the author of books and articles in English and Russian, among them *The Russian Mind since Stalin's Death* (1985) and *Tesnye vrata* (1973).

JERZY KOLODZIEJ is Assistant Professor of Slavic Languages and Literatures and Director of the Summer Workshop in Soviet and East European languages at Indiana University. He has translated numerous works of Russian literature for Ardis Publishers.

SIDNEY MONAS is the author of *The Third Section: Police and Society in Russia under Nicholas I* (1961) and numerous articles and reviews on Russian literature and history. He has translated authors as diverse as Zoshchenko, Dostoevsky, and Mandelshtam. He is currently editor of *The Slavic Review.*

DMITRY V. SHLAPENTOKH is a Fellow at the Russian Research Center at Harvard University. A graduate of Moscow State University and the University of Chicago, he has taught at Old Dominion University, Monterey Institute of International Studies, State University of New York at Oswego, Michigan State University, and Institute for Youth Leaders Abroad in Jerusalem. He is coauthor of *Ideologies in the Period of Glasnost* (1988) and has published articles on Soviet topics in literary and cultural journals.

EWA M. THOMPSON is Professor and Chair of the Department of German and Slavic Studies at Rice University. She is the author of *Russian Formalism and Anglo-American New Criticism* (1971), *Witold Gombrowicz* (1979), and *Understanding Russia: The Holy Fool in Russian Culture* (1987).

HARRY WALSH is Director of the Program in Russian Studies at the University of Houston. His research interests are in modern Russian literature and language policy in the USSR, and he has published on these subjects in *Slavic and East European Journal, Slavonic and East European Review, Canadian-American Slavonic Studies, Comparative Literature,* and other journals.

MARCUS WHEELER is Professor of Slavonic Studies at the Queen's University of Belfast, Northern Ireland. He is author of *The Oxford Russian-English Dictionary* (1972, 2nd ed. 1984) and of journal articles on Russian lexicology and on Russian and Slavonic intellectual history and culture.

Notes

CHAPTER I

1. Quoted in Caryl Emerson, *Boris Godunov: Transpositions of a Russian Theme* (Bloomington, IN: Indiana University Press, 1986), p. 30.
2. Wolfgang Schlott in *Osteuropa.*
3. *О Русь, взмахни крылбями: поэты вселенского круга* (Moscow, 1986).
4. "Bol' otechestva," Ogonyok, No. 34 (August 1988).
5. The correspondence circulated widely in typescript form. It was printed in *Sintaksis*, No. 17 (1987), 80–89.
6. *Literaturnaia gazeta*, May 17, 1989, p. 7.
7. See also P'etsukh on "Romantic Materialism" in *Volga*, May-June 1989:
8. Вы тоже пострадавшие
   А значит обрусевшие
   Мои без вести павшие
   Твои безвинно севшие. *Веселые времена*, p. 106.
9. *Novyi mir*, No. 3, 1989.
10. Ibid., p. 15.
11. Ibid., p. 29.
12. Ibid., p. 49.
13. From Esenin's poem "Пришествие:" *Из прозревшей Руссии/Он несет свой крест.*
14. In his review article "The Future of Eastern Europe" (*Problems of*

Communism, March-April 1989, 121–26), John A. Armstrong describes the central and later east European cult of life in the country, as opposed to the city, contrasting it with the Mediterranean positive valuation of urban life. This view was connected with a perception in eastern Europe of cities as foreign and nonnative, without a similar pejorative view in the Mediterranean. Of particular importance to our subject is Roman Szporluk, *Communism and Nationalism: Karl Marx versus Friedrich List* (Oxford University Press, 1988). See also Szporluk's article, "Dilemmas of Russian Nationalism" (*Problems of Communism*, July-August 1989, 15–35).

15. See the passages quoted and commented upon in 1924 by Georgii Gorbachev. Георгий Горбачев, *Очерки современной русской литературы* (Leningrad, 1924), pp. 62–67.

16. *Orbis* (University of Pennsylvania, Summer 1988), pp. 440–42, and Professor Aron Katsenelingoigen's reply, pp. 442–44.

CHAPTER 2

1. See Stalin's letter to Bednyi dated December 12, 1930, in V. I. Stalin, *Sochineniia*, Vol. 13 (Moscow: Politizdat, 1951), pp. 23–27.

2. Cf. *Tikhii Don* (Moscow: Khudozhestvennaia Literatura, 1941), p. 169, and *Tikhii Don* (Leningrad: Khudozhestvennaia Literatura, 1945), p. 171.

3. Konstantin Simonov, "Glazami cheloveka moego pokoleniia (Razmyshleniia o V. I. Staline)," *Znamia*, No. 3 (1988), 61.

4. Anatolii Anan'ev's interview, *Nedelia*, No. 34, August 21–27 (1989), 13.

5. Ibid.

6. Iraklii Abashidze, Chabua Amiredzhibi, and Otar Chiladze, "Pis'mo v redaktsiiu," *Nash sovremennik*, No. 7 (1986), 188–89.

7. *Nash sovremennik*, no. 5 (1986), 133.

8. "Perepiska iz dvukh uglov," *Vremya i my*, No. 93 (1986), 194–95.

9. See V. Iukht's letter in *Ogonyok*, No. 13 (March 25–April 1, 1989), 23.

10. M. F. Antonov, V. M. Klykov, and I. R. Shafarevich, "Pis'mo v sekretariat pravleniia Soiuza pisatelei RSFSR," *Literaturnaia Rossiia* (August 4, 1989), 4. *Oktiabr'* is the organ of the Writers' Union of the Russian Republic.

11. See *Nedelia*, No. 34 (August 21–27, 1989), 13, and "O slavianofilakh, rusofobakh i liubvi k Rossii . . . ," *Knizhnoe obozrenie*, No. 35 (September 1, 1989), 3.

CHAPTER 3

1. John B. Dunlop, *The Faces of Contemporary Russian Nationalism* (Princeton, NJ: Princeton University Press, 1983), pp. 218–27, 312–18.

2. Vsevolod Surganov, "Nazvanie obrazyvaet," *Literaturnaia gazeta*, 1971, No. 42.

3. Sergei Lykoshin, *Za beloi stenoi: rasskazy, literaturnye zametki* (Moscow: Sovremennik, 1984), p. 161.

4. *Puti narodnosti i realizma* (Leningrad: Sovetskii pisatel', 1980), 66.

5. Philippa Lewis, "Peasant Nostalgia in Contemporary Russian Literature," *Soviet Studies*, 33, No. 4 (Oct. 1976), 556.

6. "The Search for Russian Identity in Contemporary Soviet Russian Literature," *Ethnic Russia in the USSR: The Dilemma of Dominance*, edited by Edward Allworth (New York: Pergamon, 1979), p. 90.

7. "Kuda stremitsia 'edinyi potok'?" *Sovetskaia kul'tura*, March 17, 1987, 6.

8. "Meli v eksterritorial'nom potoke," *Nash sovremennik*, No. 9, 1987, 173–79.

9. "K kakomu khramu ishchem my dorogu?" *Nash sovremennik*, No. 3, 1988, 155.

10. Mozhaev, "Chto zhe meniaetsia v derevne," *Pravda*, February 25, 1989, 3.

11. Mozhaev, "Vozrodit' khoziaina," *Pravda*, July 31, 1989, 4.

12. "God velikogo pereloma. Khronika deviati mesiatsev," *Novyi mir*, No. 3, 1989, 51.

13. Arsenii Larionov, *Lidina gar'*. Kniga pervaia (Moscow: Sovremennik, 1986), p. 240.

14. "The Origin of Pamyat," *Survey*, 30, No. 3 (March 1989), 86.

15. *Gibel' volkhva* (Moscow: Sovremennik, 1987).

16. *Nash sovremennik*, No. 3, 1985, 19.

17. Ibid., 35.

18. *Kramola*. Pervaia kniga: Stolpotvorenie, *Nash sovremennik*, Nos. 1–4, 1989.

19. Iurii Surovtsev, *Neobkhodimost' dialektiki* (Moscow: Khudozhestvennia Literatura, 1982), p. 185.

20. Sergei Lykoshin, *Za beloi stenoi*, pp. 121ff.

21. Mikhail Lobanov, *Ostrovskii* (Moscow: Molodaia gvardiia, 1979), pp. 128–34.

22. "I Prize Decency in People," *Soviet Literature*, No. 8 (486), 1988, 139.

23. Belov, *God velikogo pereloma. Khronika deviati mesiatsev*, p. 6.

24. "Poslanie drugu, ili pis'ma o literature," *Nash Sovremennik*, No. 4, 1989, 7–8.

25. L. Vil'chek, " 'Vniz po techeniiu derevenskoi prozy," *Voprosy literatury*, No. 6, 1985

26. "Kakaia ulitsa vedet k khramu," *Novyi mir*, No. 11, 1987, 150–88.

27. "Знать не желают арбатские души,
Как умирают в Нарыме от стужи
Русский священник и нищий кулак.
Счастливо длится арбатское детство,
Где-то на Волге идет людоедство.
На Соловках расцветает ГУЛаг."
Андрей Василевский, "Страдание памяти,"
Октябрь, No. 4, 1989, 185.

28. "Pozhar," *Nash sovremennik*, No. 5, 1985, 15.

29. Ibid., 7.

30. Viktor Astaf'ev, "To Live Your Life," *Soviet Literature*, No. 1 (478), 1988, 42.

31. "Pozhar," 11.

32. Ibid., 33.

33. Iaroslav Shipov, "Uezdnyi chudotvorets," *Nash sovremennik*, No. 4, 1989, 122.

34. "Environmentalism in the USSR: The Opposition to the River Diversion Project," *Soviet Economy*, Vol. 4, No. 3 (1988), 223–52.

35. *Nash sovremennik*, No. 12, 1986, 96.

CHAPTER 4

1. *Zhizn' i sud'ba* first appeared in *Oktiabr'*, Nos. 1–4, 1988; later in 1988 it was published as a separate book, in 200,000 copies, by the "Knizhnaya palata" publishing house in Moscow. *Vse techet . . .* was published in *Oktiabr'*, No. 6, 1989. The manuscripts of both works had previously been smuggled out of the Soviet Union and published in the West: *Vse techet . . .* (Frankfurt/Main: Possev-Verlag, 1970), with a second edition, 1974; *Zhizn' i sud'ba* (Lausanne: L'Age d'Homme, 1980).

2. Even the party's official daily paper published a highly favorable review of *Life and Fate*: Anatolii Karpov, "Narod bessmerten. O romane V. Grossmana 'Zhizn' i sud'ba'," *Pravda*, July 4, 1988.

3. Some western scholars have attempted to divide the Russian nationalist-conservatives into groups, fine-tuning them according to their public statements and manifestoes. See, for example, the informative article by John B. Dunlop, "Russian Nationalists Reach Out to the Masses," *Working Papers in International Studies*, I-90-1 (The Hoover Institution, January 1990).

It is perfectly true that some groups are more pro-Soviet than others, some more interested in the Russian Orthodox Church than others, some more neo-Stalinist, some more interested in environmental issues, some more receptive to economic reform. However, what unites nearly all these groups is their often extreme Russian nationalism, and their desire to retain or even increase Russian hegemony over the Soviet multinational empire. That is why the twelve Russian nationalist associations have formed a united front to support like-minded candidates in Republic elections scheduled for the spring of 1990—see Paul Goble, "Platform of the Russian Patriotic Bloc," *Report on the USSR*, Vol. 2, No. 2 (January 12, 1990). The great majority of members in these various associations fear the breakup of the present Soviet state. See Gregory Gleason, "Strong Center or Strong Republics? The 'New Federalism' in the USSR," *Working Papers in International Studies*, I-90-4 (The Hoover Institution, January 1990).

The hidden (sometimes open) agenda throughout their statements is that Russians are not responsible for the terrible destruction of life and property in the Soviet period; it is always somebody else who is to blame, usually non-Russian Soviet nationalities, and in particular Jews, who are perceived as aliens in the Russian environment, if they are not western dupes or unregenerate spies. A special exception is made for Stalin, a Georgian, simply because he was always an anti-Semite and became a Russian nationalist.

4. Valentin Kiparsky, *English and American Characters in Russian Fiction* (Berlin, 1964), p. 11. Quoted in Ronald Hingley's judicious and witty book, *The Russian Mind* (London: Bodley Head, 1977), p. 123. By "Caucasian" Kiparsky meant someone from the Caucasus.

5. Andrey Sinyavsky, "Russian Nationalism," in *Russian Nationalism Today*, a Radio Liberty Research Bulletin (December 19, 1988), 29.

6. Most notably Hugh Trevor-Roper, who remarked of Hitler's Germany and Stalin's Russia: "They admired, studied, and envied each other's methods: their common hatred was directed against the liberal nineteenth-century west-

ern civilization which both openly wished to destroy." Quoted by Alan Clark, *Barbarossa: The Russian-German Conflict, 1941–45* (New York: William Morrow, 1965), p. 396.

7. See the section "Everything for the Nation!" in *The Best of Signal: Hitler's Wartime Picture Magazine* (Greenwich, CT: Bison Books, 1984). This collection of photographs, unpaginated, is reprinted from the English-language editions of *Signal*, which provides fascinating examples of German wartime propaganda.

8. See Martin Gilbert, *The Holocaust: A History of the Jews of Europe during the Second World War* (New York: Holt, Rinehart and Winston, 1985), pp. 47–48.

9. The two numbers given in the text refer to the Russian original (Lausanne, 1980) and the English translation by Raymond Chandler, *Life and Fate* (New York: Harper & Row, 1986). I have quoted Chandler's translation, making changes only where necessary, chiefly for reasons of style.

10. Americans have enjoyed religious liberty so long that most are unaware that the question of whether or not the government should support or ostracize individual sects was ever even an issue. It was George Washington, the country's first president, who set the government on a path of not only toleration but true equality for all faiths, including Judaism. When he became president, there were fewer than 3,000 Jews in the newly created United States, but Washington was determined to preserve their liberty to worship as Jews. In response to the letter they wrote thanking him, Washington said: "It is now no more that toleration is spoken of, as if it was by the indulgence of one class of people, that enjoyed the exercise of their inherent natural rights. For happily the Government of the United States, which gives to bigotry no sanction, to persecution no assistance, requires only that they who live under its protection should demean themselves as good citizens, in giving it on all occasions their effectual support." *Washington: A Profile* (New York, 1969), p. 183. Quoted in Paul F. Boller, Jr., "George Washington and Religious Liberty," *William and Mary Quarterly*, Series 3, 17 (1960).

11. The Russians have adopted the word "Fascist" rather than "Nazi" chiefly, it seems, because it fits more readily into their language as a declinable noun.

12. That this is true for other Jews as well is stated in *The Journey Back from Hell* (New York: William Morrow, 1988), p. 14: "Saul Friedlander says that the 'Nazi persecutions were the first encounter for assimilated Jews like my family actually with Judaism—it was Hitler who made them Jews again, if you wish.'"

13. *Chernaia kniga*, comp. Vasilii Grossman and Il'ia Erenburg (Jerusalem: Tarbut Publishers, 1980).

14. "Staryi uchitel'," in Vas. Grossman, *Gody voiny* (Moscow, 1946), pp. 155–56. Grossman has the Danes at the top of his staircase, followed by the Dutch, French, Greeks, Serbs, Poles, Ukrainians, and Russians. Hence the Russians are only a step above the Jews.

15. See his eloquent *Barbarossa: The Russian-German Conflict, 1941–45* (New York: William Morrow, 1965), p. 207. Clark quotes German statistics as recording 1,981,000 Russian deaths in prisoner-of-war camps and compounds. Under the heading of "Exterminations; Not accounted for; Deaths and disappearances in transit," the German records list 1,308,000. Clark also points out that these horrifying figures should be "augmented by the very large (but unverifiable) totals of men who were simply done to death on the spot where they surrendered."

16. *The Road to Berlin* (Boulder, CO: Westview Press, 1983), pp. 94–95.

17. A recent book, Desmond Seward's *Napoleon & Hitler: A Comparative Biography* (New York: Viking, 1989), makes a similar point: "Hitler seems to have thought that Marxist socialism had destroyed Russian nationalism. It was his most costly mistake."

18. During a personal interview in Moscow in August 1989, Vitalii Korotich, chief editor of the weekly *Ogonyok*, received a telephone call informing him of the campaign, initiated by Igor' Shafarevich, to seek Anan'ev's removal. Shafarevich, a close friend of Solzhenitsyn and a corresponding member of the Soviet Academy of Sciences, is a fierce Russian nationalist who likes to trace the source of all Russia's problems to Jews and other alien elements. Korotich predicted, correctly, a long hard-fought battle to protect Anan'ev against the Russian chauvinist onslaught. As of December 1989, the battle continued. See "I snova o zhurnale "Oktiabr'," *Literaturnaia gazeta*, December 20, 1989.

19. On the controversy over Grossman in the emigré journal *Kontinent*, see Shimon Markish, "Liubil li Rossiiu Vasilii Grossman?" *Russkaia mysl'*. February 21, 1986, 12.

20. Bill Keller, "Russian nationalists: Yearning for an Iron Hand," *The New York Times Magazine*, January 28, 1990, 48.

21. See "Literatura—edinaia sovetskaia ili national'naia?—a dialogue between Anatolii Bocharov and Mikhail Lobanov in *Literaturnaia gazeta*, September 27, 1989. This was one of several dialogues initiated at the beginning of 1989.

22. For an astonishing range of chauvinistic and anti-Semitic statements by

Russian nationalists, see the partial transcript of the VI Plenum of the Board of RSFSR Writers Organization, held November 13–14, 1989: "Vsyo zaedino," *Ogonyok*, No. 48 (December 1989), 6–8, 31. The sometimes incoherent ranting of some speakers recalls Nazi rallies in the thirties.

23. "Dobro vam! (Iz putevykh zametok)," *Znamia*, No. II, 1988, 4–62. This is the first publication of the complete text that Grossman had hoped to publish in *Novyi mir*. When Alcksandr Tvaidovskii insisted on cutting certain passages, Grossman was furious and withdrew the work, even though he very much needed the money. After the "arrest" of his manuscript of *Life and Fate*, Grossman found it impossible to have his works published or republished anywhere. It was published after his death, in abridged form, in a one-volume collection of his works and in *Literaturnaia Armenia* (Nos. 6–7, 1967). The title is translated from a standard Armenian greeting.

24. "Dobro vam!," p. 11.

CHAPTER 5

1. E.R. Curtius, *European Literature and the Latin Middle Ages* (Princeton, NJ: Princeton University Press, 1953).

2. Yuri Lotman, Boris Uspensky, L. Ginzburg, *The Semiotics of Russian Cultural History* (Ithaca, NY: Cornell University Press, 1985).

3. Fredric Jameson, *The Political Unconscious* (Ithaca, NY: Cornell University Press, 1981).

4. Annabel Patterson, *Censorship and Interpretation* (Madison, WI: University of Wisconsin Press, 1984).

5. Gregory Freeze, "The Soslovie (Estate) Paradigm and Russian Social History," *American Historical Review*, Vol. 91, No. 1 (February 1986), 11–36.

6. N. V. Gogol, *Dead Souls* (New York: Holt, Rinehart & Winston, 1965), 155; *Sobranie sochinenii*, 6 vols. (Moscow, 1949), Vol. 5, p. 135.

7. I.S. Turgenev, *The Hunting Sketches* (New York: Signet Books, 1962); "Zapiski okhotnika," in *Polnoe sobranie sochinenii*, 12 vols., (St. Petersburg: Izdanie Marksa, 1898), Vol. 1. In Turgenev's novella, "Spring Freshets" ("Veshnye vody"), the weak but well-intended and good-looking hero, Sanin, is engaged to marry a beautiful Italian girl, Gemma. Her position as an "exile" (they meet in Frankfurt) and her strong family ties and sense of family honor are part of the attraction he feels for her. But she is almost completely a stereotype of the heroine-victim. (Not quite, since she ends by

going to America and marrying happily.) Not so with Maria, the woman who lures Sanin away from Gemma. She is powerful, capricious, self-willed, and tyrannical, even her appearance, though not quite as beautiful as Gemma's, is far more interesting. She is Russian, and of peasant origin. Demonic in her pursuit of a kind of absolute freedom, and utterly indifferent to the victims she leaves in her path, she has a reality and an attraction that Gemma lacks. She is an extraordinary expression not only of Turgenev's ambivalence to the type of the strong woman, but of his almost equally deep ambivalence as well to the self-emancipating peasant!

I should add that the *improvisatore* of Pushkin's unfinished story, "Egyptian Nights," is convincing enough as an itinerant Italian poet who depends on his audience's generosity for his living, yet he remains a *secondary* character, fundamentally a foil for Pushkin's narrator, a Russian and a nobleman.

8. L.N. Tolstoy, *Collected Works*, 22 vols. (Oxford: Oxford University Press, 1932), Vol. 5; "Polikushka," in *Sobranie sochinenii*, 20 Vols. (Moscow, 1961), Vol. 3, pp. 324–81.

9. L.N. Tolstoy, *War and Peace* (New York: Norton, 1966), 1073; *Sobranie sochinenii*, Vol. 7, p. 53.

10. L.N. Tolstoy, "How Much Land Does a Man Need?" *Master and Man* (London: Dent, 1973), 65–83; "Mnogo-li cheloveku zemli nuzhno," in *Sobranie sochinenii*, Vol. 10, pp. 384–96.

11. N.S. Gumilev, *Selected Works* (Albany, NY: SUNY Press, 1972), 49; "Iz logova zmieva," *Stikhotvoreniia i poemy*, (Leningrad, 1988), 168.

12. Susan Layton, "The Creation of an Imaginative Caucasian Geography," *Slavic Review*, Vol. 45, No. 3 (Fall 1986), 470–85.

13. L.N. Tolstoy, *The Cossacks* (London: Penguin, 1961); "Kazaki," *Sobranie sochinenii*, Vol. 3, pp. 162–323.

14. L.N. Tolstoy, "Hadji Murad," *Great Short Works* (New York: Harper, 1967); "Khadzhi Murad," *Sobranie sochinenii*, Vol.14, pp. 23–148.

15. A.S. Pushkin, "The Queen of Spades," in *Complete Prose Tales* (New York: Norton, 1968); "Pikovaia dama," in *Polnoe sobranie sochinenii*, 10 vols. (Moscow, 1957), Vol. 6, pp. 317–56.

16. I.A. Goncharov, *Oblomov* (London: Penguin, 1978); *Oblomov* (Moscow: Gosizdat, 1958). See E. Krasnoshchekova, *Oblomov Goncharova* (Moscow: Khudozhestvennaia Literatura, 1970).

17. F.M. Dostoevsky, *The Brothers Karamazov* (New York: Random House, 1933), 441–56; *Brat'ia Karamazovy*, in *Polnoe sobranie sochinenii*, 30 vols. (Leningrad: Nauka, 1976), Vol. 14, pp. 376–89.

18. F.M. Dostoevsky, *Crime and Punishment* (New York: Signet, 1968), 492; *Prestuplenie i nakazanie*, in *Polnoe sobranie sochinenii*, Vol. 6, p. 394.

19. I.A. Turgenev, *Smoke* (London: Heinemann, 1901); *Dym*, in *Polnoe sobranie sochinenii*, Vol. 3.

20. P. Ia. Chaadaev, *The Major Works*, translation and commentary by R. McNally (South Bend, IN: University of Notre Dame Press, 1969), p. 28.

21. Abram Tertz, *On Socialist Realism*, translated by George Denny (New York: Pantheon, 1960).

22. Andrzej Walicki, *The Slavophile Controversy* (Oxford: Clarendon Press, 1975).

23. P. Ia. Chaadaev, pp. 199–218.

24. Joseph Frank, *Dostoevsky: The Stir of Liberation, 1860–1865* (Princeton, NJ: Princeton University Press, 1986), p. 38.

25. A.I. Gertsen, *Sobranie sochinenii*, 30 vols. (Moscow: Nauka, 1956), Vol. 7, especially pp. 101–133 and 271–306.

26. F.M. Dostoevsky, *The Possessed* (New York: Signet, 1962); *Besy*, in *Polnoe sobranie sochinenii*, Vols. 10 and 11.

27. A. A. Blok, "Vozmezdie," *Sobranie sochinenii*, 6 vols. (Moscow, 1971), Vol. 3; see also the essays in Vol. 5 and the diary in Vol. 6.

28. V. G. Rasputin, *Farewell to Matyora* (New York: MacMillan, 1979); "Proshchanie s Materoi" in *Izbrannye proizvedeniia*, 2 vols. (Moscow: Molodaia Gvardiia, 1984), Vol. 2.

CHAPTER 6

1. B. Farnsworth, *William Bullitt and the Soviet Union* (Bloomington, IN: Indiana University Press, 1967), p. 3; Alex de Jonge, *Stalin and the Shaping of the Soviet Union* (London: Collins, 1986), p. 2.

2. Oleg Moroz, "Poslednii diagnoz," *Literaturnaia gazeta*, September 28, 1968.

3. S. Allilueva, *Tol'ko odin god* (New York: Harper & Row, 1969), p. 337; Milovan Djilas, *Razgovory so Stalinym* (Frankfurt: Possev Verlag, 1970), p. 148.

4. W.W. Kulski, *The Soviet Regime: Communism in Practice* (Syracuse, NJ: Syracuse University Press, 1954), p. 125.

5. V.I. Lenin, "On the National Pride of the Great Russians," *Collected Works*, Vol. 21 (London: Lawrence and Wishart), pp. 103–104.

6. N. Riasanovsky, *Nicholas I and Official Nationality in Russia, 1825–1855* (Berkeley, CA: University of California Press, 1959), pp. 74–75.

7. Mikhail Geller, *Mashina i vintiki* (London: Overseas Publications, 1985), pp. 241–42.

8. Ibid., p. 245.

9. N.S. Khrushchev, "Vospominaniia," *Ogonyok*, No. 28 (July 1989), 31.

10. A.V. Antonov-Ovseenko, "Stalin i ego vremia," *Voprosy istorii*, No. 3 (1989), 110.

11. Mariia Ioffe, "Odna noch'," *Khronika* (New York, 1978), pp. 33–34.

12. Ibid., p. 34.

13. Konstantin Simonov, "Glazami cheloveka moego pokoleniia: razmyshleniia o Staline," *Znamia*, No. 3 (1988), 3–66; No. 4 (1988), 48–121; No. 5 (1988), 69–96.

14. Aleksandr Avdeenko, "Otluchenie," *Znamia*, No. 3 (1989), 5–73; No. 4 (1989), 78–133.

15. Avdeenko, *Znamia*, No. 3 (1989), 51.

16. Simonov, *Znamia*, No. 4 (1988), 66.

17. Avdeenko, *Znamia*, No. 4 (1989), 104.

18. Simonov, *Znamia*, No. 4 (1988), 54–55.

19. Ibid., 98.

20. Avdeenko, *Znamia*, No. 4 (1989), 129.

21. Ibid., 132–33.

22. Ibid., 133.

23. Simonov, *Znamia*, No. 4 (1988), 119.

24. Simonov, *Znamia*, No. 3 (1988), 9; No. 4 (1989), 120–21.

25. Mark Popovskii, *Zhizn' i zhitie Voino-Yasenetskogo* (Paris: YMCA Press, 1979), p. 371.

CHAPTER 7

1. K. Marx and F. Engels. *Sochineniia*, 2nd ed., Vol. 3 (Moscow: Gosudarstvennoe Izdatelstvo Politicheskoi Literatury, 1955), p. 12, footnote.

2. V.I. Lenin. *Polnoe sobranie sochinenii*, 5th ed., Vol. 1 (Moscow: Izdatelstvo Politicheskoi Literatury, 1960), p. 340, footnote.

3. *The Great Soviet Encyclopedia*, 3rd ed., Vol. 10 (New York: Macmillan, 1976), p. 121.

4. *Soviet Political Dictionary* (Moscow, 1940), p. 204.

5. *Program of the Communist Party of the Soviet Union* (1961).

6. Franz Josef Strauss, "Current Aspects of World Politics," *Democracy International* (December 1988), 18.

7. *The Denver Post*, July 12, 1988.

8. Alexander Zinoviev, *The Reality of Communism*, trans. by Charles Janson (New York: Schocken Books), p. 218.

9. K. Mannheim, *Ideology and Utopia* (New York: Harcourt, 1936).

10. Alexander Zinoviev, *The Radiant Future*, trans. by Gordon Clough (New York: Random House, 1980), p. 249.

11. Ibid., p. 30.

12. Ibid., pp. 79–81.

13. Ibid., p. 31.

14. Ibid., p. 226.

15. Aleksandr Zinov'ev, *Bez illiuzii* (Lausanne: L'Age d'Homme, 1979), pp. 27–33.

16. Ibid., p. 28.

17. Ibid., p. 29.

18. Ibid., p. 31.

19. *The Reality of Communism*, p. 22.

20. Ibid., p. 223.

21. Aleksandr Zinov'ev, *V preddverii raia* (Lausanne: L'Age d'Homme, 1979), p. 317.

22. Yuri Tarnopolsky, "Science, Philosophy, and Human Behavior in the Soviet Union, by Loren R. Graham." *Academic Questions* (Winter 1988–89), 80.

23. *V preddverii raia*, p. 215.

24. Aleksandr Zinov'ev, *Idi na Golgofu.* (Lausanne: L'Age d'Homme, 1985).

25. *Pravda*, February 14, 1987.

26. *Literaturnaia gazeta*, March 18, 1988.

27. *Bez illiuzii*, p. 32.

28. Ibid., p. 32.

29. Libor Brom, "Dialectical Identity and Destiny: A General Introduction to Alexander Zinoviev's Theory of the Soviet Man," *Rocky Mountain Review*, Vol. 42 (1988), 15–27.

30. *Bez illiuzii*, p. 32.

31. Ibid., p. 47.

32. Ibid.

33. Peter F. Drucker, *The New Realities: In Government and Politics/In Economics and Business/In Society and World View* (New York: Harper & Row, 1989).

34. David Brooks, "Voyage to the End of Ideology," *The Wall Street Journal*, July 26, 1989.

35. Michael Waltzer, *Radical Principles* (New York: Basic Books, 1980).

36. Arnold Beichman, "The Returns Are In and Socialism is Out," *The Wall Street Journal*, September 6, 1989.

37. Zbigniew Brzezinski, *The Grand Failure: The Birth and Death of Communism in the Twentieth Century* (New York: Scribner's, 1989).

38. Robert Conquest, "Back to the USSR," *National Review*, August 18, 1989, 24.

39. Aleksandr Zinov'ev, *V preddverii raia*, p. 330.

40. Aleksandr Zinov'ev, "Za chto borolis', na to i naporodilis'," (Address to the Society of Intellectuals SIEL, Paris, December 1978); *Bez illiuzii*, p. 48.

41. Aleksandr Zinov'ev, *V preddverii raia*, p. 576.

42. Aleksandr Zinov'ev, *Ni svobody, ni ravenstva, ni bratstva* (Lausanne: L'Age d'Homme, 1983), pp. 90, 91.

43. William Safire, *The New York Times*, April 24, 1989.

CHAPTER 8

1. *Literaturnaia gazeta*, October 12, 1988.
2. Ibid.
3. *Pravda*, May 13, 1988.
4. *Literaturnaia gazeta*, October 12, 1988.
5. *Moskovskie novosti*, November 29, 1987.
6. *Literaturnaia gazeta*, January 1, 1988.
7. *Pravda*, June 24, 1988.
8. *Pravda*, November 9, 1987.
9. *Literaturnaia gazeta*, April 26, 1989.
10. *Literaturnaia gazeta*, January 1988.
11. *Pravda*, October 22, 1988.
12. *Sovetskaia kul'tura*, November 12, 1987.
13. *Sovetskaia kul'tura*, February 1, 1988.
14. *Sovetskaia kul'tura*, July 23, 1988; Izvestiia, November 4, 1988.
15. *Novoe russkoe slovo*, January 7, 1988.

16. *Novoe russkoe slovo*, November 12, 1988.

17. Ibid.

18. *Izvestiia*, August 14, 1988.

19. *Sovetskaia kul'tura*, May 31, 1988.

20. *Literaturnaia gazeta*, October 12, 1988.

21. *Izvestiia*, August 14, 1988; *Literaturnaia gazeta*, September 21, 1988. The idea of race and biological heritage is gaining popularity in the Soviet Union. It is used not only to support the view that Jews are a nationality rather than a religion but also to propagate the concept of genetic determinism and the idea of consciously breeding a human intellectual elite.

22. *Komsomol'skaia pravda*, March 19, 1988.

23. On November 6, 1988, in *Moskovskie vedomosti*, Grigorii Baklanov, editor of the liberal magazine *Znamia*, complained that members of the *Pamiat'* group physically threatened him. On the threats made by the members of *Pamiat'* to liberal and Jewish intellectuals, see *Izvestiia*, August 14, 1988.

24. *Izvestiia*, 1989

25. *Novoe russkoe slovo*, November 12, 1987, January 13, 1988; *Sovetskaia kul'tura*, May 31, June 11, 1988; *Komsomol'skaia pravda*, January 21, July 23, 1988.

26. *Literaturnaia gazeta*, January 1, 1988.

Note: The author was unable to recover some quotation sources for this article.

CHAPTER 9

1. ". . . sam Khristos propovedoval svoe uchenie tol'ko kak ideal, sam predrek, chto do kontsa mira budet bor'ba i razvitie (uchenie o meche), ibo eto zakon prirody . . . ," *Neizdannyi Dostoevsky, Zapisnaia knizhka 1863–64* (*Literaturnoe nasledstvo*, Vol. 83), p. 174.

2. "Odna iz sovremennykh fal'shei," *Dnevnik pisatelia za 1873 god.*

3. After completing a four-year term of penal servitude (on about February 15, 1854), Dostoevsky became a private in the Seventh Siberian line battalion stationed in Semipalatinsk.

4. This poem, written in Semipalatinsk, was first published in *Grazhdanin* in 1883, that is, after the writer's death.

5. A direct path leads from these words to one of Dostoevsky's last utterances in the *Diary of a Writer*, 1881, "Geok-Tepe. What Does Asia Mean to Us?" ("Geok-Tepe. Chto takoe dlia nas Aziia?").

6. *Literaturnoe nasledstvo*, Vol. 83, p. 254.

7. F. M. Dostoevsky, *Pis'ma II, 1867-71*, edited and annotated by A.S. Dolinin (Moscow-Leningrad: Gosizdat, 1930), p. vi.

8. Ibid.

9. Letter to A.N. Maikov from Geneva, February 18, 1868.

10. A.S. Dolinin, xiv. See note 7.

11. Letter to A.N. Maikov from Geneva, March 20, 1868.

12. A.S. Dolinin, xiv. See note 7.

13. (Lanham, New York, London: University Press of America, 1987), pp. 181-90.

14. "Vospominaniia o Fedore Mikhailoviche Dostoevskom N. N. Strakhova," *Biografiia, pis'ma i zametki iz zapisnoi knizhki, Polnoe sobranie sochinenii F. M. Dostoevskogo*, Vol. 1 (St. Peterburg, 1883), p. 290.

15. See letter to A.A. Romanov cited above.

16. The silent, burning kiss of great pity "burns in the heart of the old man" (*gorit na serdtse starika*), even though the latter "holds to his former ideas" (*ostaetsia v prezhnei idee*).

17. F.M. Dostoevsky, *Polnoe sobranie sochinenii v tridtsati tomakh* (Leningrad: Nauka), Vol. 2, pp.180 and 182.

18. Ibid., p. 302.

19. Ibid., pp. 182-83.

CHAPTER 10

Unless otherwise noted, all the translations are mine. M.W.

1. I.S. Turgenev, *Polnoe sobranie sochinenii*, Vol. 15 (Moscow-Leningrad, 1968), p. 72.

2. Ibid., p. 67.

3. See *inter alia* V.G. Belinskii, "Stat'i o Pushkine," *Polnoe sobranie sochinenii*, Vol. 7 (Moscow, 1955), pp. 347, 547.

4. N.V. Gogol', "Neskol'ko slov o Pushkine," *Sobranie sochinenii v semi tomakh*, Vol. 6 (Moscow, 1955), pp. 68-74.

5. S.L. Frank, *Etiudy o Pushkine* (Munich, 1957; reprinted Letchworth, England, 1978).

6. W. Lednicki, *Pushkin's "Bronze Horseman": The Story of a Masterpiece* (Berkeley, CA, 1955; reprinted Westport, CT, 1978), Chapter 4.

7. L. Schapiro, *Rationalism and Nationalism* . . . (New Haven, CT, 1978), pp. 45–58.

8. Quoted by Schapiro, p. 47.

9. A.S. Pushkin, *Polnoe sobranie sochinenii*, Vol. I (Moscow-Leningrad: Akademiia, 1936–38), p. 468. Further references to Pushkin's works are to this edition, cited as PSS unless otherwise specified.

10. Ibid., p. 57.

11. "Zametki po istorii XVIII veka," PSS, Vol. 5, p. 257.

12. PSS, Vol. 6, p. 66.

13. From translated text in J. Thomas Shaw, *The Letters of Alexander Pushkin* (Madison, WI and London, 1967), p. 156.

14. A.S. Pushkin, *Sobranie sochinenii v desiati tomakh*, Vol. 7 (Moscow, 1962), p. 333. Diary entry for May 21, 1834.

15. PSS, Vol. 6, p. 148.

16. Ibid., pp. 149–50.

17. See, for example, the account of the conversation given in D.D. Blagoi, *Tvorcheskii put' Pushkina, 1826–1830* (Moscow, 1967), p. 44.

18. PSS, Vol. 6, p. 126.

19. Ibid., p. 149.

20. Adam Mickiewicz, *Dzieła*, edited by J. Krzyżanowski, Vol. 10 (Warsaw, 1955), p. 359.

21. PSS, Vol. 6, p. 157.

22. PSS, Vol. 1, p. 228.

23. Ibid., p. 242.

24. Ibid., pp. 249–50.

25. Ibid., Vol. 2, p. 295.

26. Ibid., Vol. 6, p. 150.

27. S.L. Frank, *Pushkin i pol'skoe vosstanie 1830–1831 g.* (1929), p. 48.

28. PSS, Vol. 1, p. 419.

29. Philike Hetairia, or Society of Friends, an association founded in 1814 with the aim of bringing about the liberation of Greece. Cf. Hugh Seton-Watson, *The Russian Empire 1801–1917* (Oxford, 1967), p. 180.

30. PSS, Vol. 6, pp. 24–25.

31. Quoted by T. Galushko in *Literaturnaia gazeta*, No. 3 (1987).

32. PSS, Vol. 6, p. 77. Galushko argues that the intended recipient of both this and the letter cited in footnote 30 was Orlov rather than, as hitherto presumed, V.L. Davydov.

33. Ibid., pp. 74–75.

34. A. Mickiewicz, *Dzieła*, ed. S. Pigoń, Vol. 3 (Warsaw, 1958), p. 305.

35. In *Pushkinskii sbornik* (Prague, 1929), pp. 125–27.

36. *PSS*, Vol. 1, p. 384.

37. Ibid., Vol. 2, p. 11.

38. Quoted by Frantsev, p. 113.

39. *Sochineniia i pis'ma P.Ia. Chaadaeva*, edited by M. Gershenzon, Vol. 1 (Moscow, 1913), p. 166.

40. *PSS*, Vol. 6, p. 432.

41. Ibid., Vol. 3, p. 261.

42. F.M. Dostoevsky, *Polnoe sobranie sochinenii v tridsati tomakh*, Vol. 26 (Leningrad, 1984), pp. 147–48.

43. John Bayley, *Pushkin* (Cambridge, 1971), p. 17.

44. Letter of April 26, 1835, to I.I. Dmitriev, *PSS*, Vol. 6, p. 385; diary entry for January 8, 1935, in *Sobranie sochinenii v semi tomakh*, Vol. 6, p. 342.

45. *PSS*, Vol. 2, p. 78.

CHAPTER II

1. " Польское государство, построенное на подавлении, угнетении и тяжелой эксплуатации национальных меншинств, на насильственном ополячении украинского и белорусского населенииа, на беззастенчивом уничтожении всей их культурной жизни . . . подверглось при первом же сериозном испытании военному разгрому . . . Мы приветствуем любимую Красную Армиию, защитницу угнетенных, славу и гордость советского народа . . . все свободные, равноправные, счастливые народы Советского Союза сплочены вокруг правительства и Партии Ленина-Сталина." *Pravda*, September 18, 1939.

2. *Literaturnaia gazeta*, September 26, 1939.

3. Margarita Aliger, "17 сентября 1939 года"

 Пламенели листья и блестели

Улицы, умытые с утра.

Новые блестящие портфели

С важностью тащила детвора.

Ежедневно так проходят дети,

И такая осень много лет,

Только в этом солнце, в этом свете

Теплился какой-то новый свет.
И внезапно время раскололось,
И подуло свежестью иной—
Над землею прокатился голос
Теплою широкою волной.
Я не помню, сколько это длилось.
Где-то возле нас невдалеке
С миром говорила справедливость
На великом русском языке.
Наша честность подымала голос,
Наша правда начинала речь.
Все,что в нас таилось и боролось,
Мне навеки хочется сберечь.
В сердце сохранится эта дата,
Этот день, товарищ, не забудь!
В этот день советские ребята
Начинали непреложный путь.
Песня шла у них передовою,
Загораясь в сердце и в крови,
И росло у них над головою
Знамя человеческой любви.
Наше знамя, подымайся выше!
Как лучи, сверкают их штыки,
Подымают матери детишек,
Руки простирают старики.
Им навстречу, как навстречу счастью,
И как счастье, проходя вперед,
В край невзгоды входят наши части
Защищать покинутый народ.
Сильное, взволнованное знамя,
Наша верность, наша плоть и кровь,
Будь над ними словно отчий кров,
Словно небо родины над нами.

4. For a comprehensive account of what happened to Poles in the aftermath of the Soviet invasion, see J.T. Gross, *Revolution from Abroad: The Soviet Conquest of Poland's Western Ukraine and Western Belorussia* (Princeton, NJ: Princeton University Press, 1988).

5. R.F. Leslie, Antony Polonsky, Jan M. Ciechanowski, and Z.A. Pel-

czynski, *The History of Poland since 1863*, edited by R.F. Leslie (London-Cambridge: Cambridge University Press, 1987), pp. 153–54, 168–69, 175–76, 198.

6. *Pravda*, October 22, 1939.

7. "Svidetel'skie pokazania pol'skoi literatury," *Literaturnaia gazeta*, October 10, 1939.

8. *Sovetskaia iustitsiia*, No. 7 (1940), 23.

9. "Со шляхтою вы на-смерть воевали, / А нам не замутили и воды, / Ни яблока ни разу не сорвали, / Не затоптали ни однои гряды . . ." *Pravda*, November 5, 1939.

10. Gross, pp. 34–45.

CHAPTER 12

1. B. Iarustovskii, *Igor' Stravinskii* (Moscow, 1963, 1969). M.S. Druskin, *Igor' Stravinskii* (Leningrad, 1974). V. Kholopova, "O ritmicheskoi tekhnike i dinamicheskih svoistvakh ritma Stravinskogo," *Muzyka i sovremennost'* (Moscow, 1966). V.M. Blok, K.P. Portugalov, eds., *Russkaia i sovetskaia muzyka* (Moscow, 1977), pp. 80–91.

2. Druskin, "Igor' Stravinskii," *Muzykal'naia zhizn'*, Vol. 18 (1967). Quoted in *Russkaia i sovetskaia*, p. 83.

3. H. J. Drengenberg, *Die Sowjetische Politik auf dem Gebiet der Bildenden Kunst*. Forschungen zur Osteuropäischen Geschichte, Osteuropa-Institut an der Freien Universität Berlin, Historische Veröffentlichungen, Vol. 16 (Berlin, 1972), pp. 319–23. Cf. M. Owsjannikow, ed., *Marxistisch-leninistische Ästhetik* (Berlin, 1976), pp. 336–39.

4. *Bol'shaia sovetskaia entsiklopediia*, 2nd ed. (Moscow, 1954), Vol. 28, p. 514. See also Boris Schwarz, *Music and Musical Life in Soviet Russia 1917–1970* (New York: Norton, 1973), p. 110.

5. "Muzykoznanie," *Bol'shaia sovetskaia entsiklopediia*, p. 533.

6. Ibid., pp. 533–34.

7. Asaf'ev's book was reprinted forty-eight years later in Leningrad (1977).

8. Schwarz, p. 354.

9. Ibid., p. 128.

10. *Bol'shaia sovetskaia entsiklopediia* (1956), Vol. 41, pp. 57–58.

11. Druskin, "Igor' Stravinskii i Rossiia," *Muzykal'naia zhizn'*, 1972. Quoted in Blok and Portugalov, *Russkaia i sovetskaia muzyka*, p. 82.

12. Druskin,"Igor' Stravinsky . . . ," p. 82.

13. Compare Stravinsky's use of folk melodies: Richard Taruskin, "Russian Folk Melodies in *The Rite of Spring*," *Journal of the American Musicological Society*, Vol. 33, No. 3 (1980), 501–543.

14. Druskin, *Igor Stravinsky, His Life, Works and Views* (Cambridge University Press, 1983), pp. 30–31.

15. Druskin, "Igor' Stravinskii i Rossiia," *Muzykal'naia Zhizn'*, No. 12 (1972). Quoted in *Russkaia i sovetskaia muzyka*, p. 83.

16. Schwarz, pp. 272–73.

17. *Bol'shaia sovetskaia entsiklopediia*, 1956, pp. 57–58.

18. A.N. Sokhor, "Music," *Great Soviet Encyclopedia* (London, 1980), Vol. 24, pp. 263–64. Translation of the Russian edition (Moscow, 1976, 3rd ed.).

19. "Mednyi vsadnik: Peterburgskaia povest'; The Bronze Horseman: A Tale of Petersburg," Walter Arndt, *Pushkin Threefold* (New York: Dutton, 1972), p. 400.

20. Lev Raaben, "Eshche raz o neoklasitsizme," *Istoriia i sovremennost'*, edited by A.I. Klimovitskii, L.G. Kovnatskaia, and M.D. Sabinina (Leningrad, 1981), p. 201.

21. B.V. Asaf'ev, *Kniga o Stravinskom* (Leningrad, 1977), p. 250.

22. M.S. Druskin, *Igor Stravinsky, His Life, Works and Views* (Cambridge, 1983), p. 86.

23. Petrov was born in 1930 in Leningrad. His compositional work encompassed several ballet scores, symphonic music, vocal cycles, and film music. In the 1960s, Petrov was a high-ranking official of the Russian Soviet Republic. *Entsiklopedicheskii muzikal'nyi slovar'*, 2nd ed. (Moscow, 1966), p. 391.

24. Andrei Petrov, "*Muzykant, pedagog, uchenyi: vmeste predislovia,*" in *Istoriia i sovremennost'* (Leningrad, 1981), p. 4.

25. Asaf'ev; T. Levaia, O. Leont'eva, *Paul' Hindemit* (Moscow, 1974).

26. Raaben, *Eshche raz o neoklassitsizme*, pp. 197–98.

27. Ibid., pp. 198–99.

28. Schwarz, p. 354.

29. *Bol'shaia Sovetskaia Entsiklopediia*, 3rd ed. (Moscow, 1974), Vol. 17, p. 470.

30. Raaben, p. 207.

31. Ibid., pp. 209–210.

32. Ibid., p. 209.

33. Ibid., p. 199.

34. N.G. Shakhnazarova, *Problemy muzykal'noi estetiki v teoreticheskih trudakh Stravinskogo, Shenberga, Hindemita* (Moscow, 1975), pp. 233, 237.

35. Asaf'ev's *Kniga o Stravinskom* was translated into English in the late 1950s by Richard F. French. However, this translation was published only in 1982 by UMI Research Press, in the series *Russian Music Studies*, No. 5, edited by Malcolm Hamrick Brown. Iarustovskii's introduction to the second Russian edition of 1977 was not included.

Index